W9-CVZ-233

LITERATURE AND FILM

GARLAND REFERENCE LIBRARY
OF THE HUMANITIES
(VOL. 241)

LITERATURE AND FILM
An Annotated Bibliography, 1909–1977

Jeffrey Egan Welch

GARLAND PUBLISHING, INC. • NEW YORK & LONDON
1981

© 1981 Jeffrey Egan Welch
All rights reserved

Library of Congress Cataloging in Publication Data

Welch, Jeffrey Egan, 1949–
  Literature and film.

  (Garland reference library of the humanities ;
v. 241)
  Includes index.
  1. Moving pictures and literature—Bibliography.
2. Film adaptations—Bibliography. 3. Moving-
pictures and literature—Study and teaching—Bibliography. I. Title.
Z5784.M9W37 [PN1995.3]   016.79143   80-8509
ISBN 0-8240-9478-6

Printed on acid-free, 250-year-life paper
Manufactured in the United States of America

To My Mother and Father

CONTENTS

PREFACE

Literature and Film: An Annotated Bibliography, 1909–1977 lists and annotates all important books and articles published in North America and Great Britain having to do with the special relationship between films and works of literature.

For most people, the relationship between literature and film is difficult to define. For the purposes of this bibliography three general categories of works have been included. The first category consists of items touching on the process of adapting a work of literature, whether play, novel, short story or even poem, to the screen. This category includes references to films which may be loosely based on their literary source as well as the most meticulous efforts of adaptation of literary works to film. In the second category are more general discussions of the similarities and differences between film and literary genres, studies of the influences of other arts on the film, and interviews with directors, screenwriters, novelists, playwrights, actors and others who have had experience or some interest in the relationship of literature to film. The third category includes references to the teaching of the subject of literature and film in high school, college and graduate classrooms.

The items in the bibliography are listed chronologically by year and alphabetically by author's name within each year; anonymous articles are listed alphabetically by title at the beginning of each year. In order to differentiate the title of a film from the title of a novel, play, short story or poem, film titles are followed by the film's date of release in parentheses. Titles of poems are italicized. The annotations use the author's own words as far as possible in order to give the users of this bibliography both an idea of the content of the book or article and a means of judging the usefulness of the item. The original publisher is given; in cases of simultaneous publication, the American publisher is indicated.

Excluded from the bibliography are: film reviews, except where a lengthy comparison of literary source with film is undertaken; bibliographies and filmographies, except where they are directly related to the subject; screenplays; articles appearing in general-interest magazines and in newspapers; general interviews with directors, writers and actors; articles in standard reference works, such as encyclopedias; master's theses; and novels based upon screenplays.

Critical disputes are cross-referenced, and related correspondence in a single journal is gathered under one entry. A list of dissertations, organized in the same manner as the bibliography but not annotated, follows the general bibliography. In the entries in this list, the abbreviations *DA* and *DAI* signify *Dissertation Abstracts* and *Dissertation Abstracts International*, respectively.

An appendix allows the user to locate entries by the author of the work of literature on which films have been based. All films mentioned in the bibliography are listed here.

When using the index, one should be sure to examine all the title references pertaining to a work of literature and the film(s) adapted from it; this is particularly important in cases where the title of the work of literature and the film title are different.

I have consulted every available bibliography and index in my search and have checked the contents of important periodicals, but some items may have escaped me. Users of this bibliography will discover, however, that it contains several hundred useful items not included in more general film bibliographies. In cases where I have listed an item according to its year of publication but have been able to locate that item only in its reappearance in a second edition or as a reprinted article, I have cited first the original appearance but have followed it immediately in the entry with the citations for the subsequent edition or appearance, including page numbers and date. Items for which I have at least two references but which I have not been able to locate are listed and marked "not seen." Whenever I have become aware of a second printing of an important item, I have mentioned it in the entry, but I have felt no obligation to indicate every reprinting or reappearance of a book or article.

I am greatly indebted to the staff of the Graduate Library at the University of Michigan for the use of their fine collection and for their courteous and efficient help. I wish also to thank the staffs of the Doe Library at the University of California at Berkeley, of the reference library at the Pacific Film Archive at Berkeley, and of the Oberlin College Library. Many thanks are due Barbara Bergeron for her intelligent advice and meticulous editing of the manuscript. For their unflagging support in all weathers I am most deeply grateful to Professor Chester L. Shaver and Mrs. Alice Shaver of Oberlin. For his support in this and in other endeavors I am grateful to my friend Samuel Salas, Headmaster of the Cranbrook School. Professor John Olmsted must know how much I appreciate his interest and help in the long career of this enterprise and how warmly I thank him. For a grant to travel and carry out research in California during the summer of 1979 I thank the Cranbrook School, Bloomfield Hills, Michigan.

J.W.

LITERATURE AND FILM

BIBLIOGRAPHY

1909

1. Eaton, W.P. "The Canned Drama." *The American Magazine* 68: 493-500.

   "If canned dramas [motion pictures] are to retain their present extraordinary hold over the public, they can only do it, after the novelty has worn off, by being genuine dramas, well planned and well played. When they are well planned and well played it is quite possible that they can always fill a useful function, in leading the lower stratas of society up toward an appreciation of true dramatic art, which is, after all, only brought to flower on the stage of a true theater, where actual men and women speak with the voices God gave them."

1910

2. Kallen, Horace M. "The Dramatic Picture Versus the Pictorial Drama; A Study of the Influences of the Cinematograph on the Stage." *Harvard Monthly* 50 (March): 22-31.

   Not seen.

1911

3. Grau, Robert. "The 'Talking' Picture and the Drama." *Scientific American* 105: 155-56.

   Successful efforts to blend film with vaudeville offer hope that "the motion picture theater of the future will be conducted on a far more [sophisticated] basis than that of the present."

4. Hamilton, Clayton. "The Art of the Moving-Picture Play." *The Bookman* 32: 512-16.

Silent film has a greater affinity for the novel than for the stage play. The type of story best suited to film is made from material "in which the elements of action and setting are paramount and the element of character subsidiary."

1913

5. "David Copperfield on the Cinematograph." *The Dickensian* 9 (October): 267.

   Praise for a film version by Thomas Bentley.

6. "Great Plays in the 'Movies.'" *Literary Digest* 47: 172.

   Description of how a scene from *Hamlet* in which the ghost appears would be filmed.

7. "In the Interpreter's House." *The American Magazine* 76 (July): 102-05.

   Film is much like the theater in its form and appeal.

1914

8. Blackton, J. Stuart. "Literature and the Motion Picture--A Message." *The Theatre of Science.* Ed. Robert Grau. New York: Broadway Publishing, pp. xxv-xxviii. Reprinted by Benjamin Blom, New York, 1969.

   The motion picture has become another means by which the aspiring writer can see his work reach an audience.

9. Eaton, Walter Prichard. "The Theater: A New Epoch in the Movies." *The American Magazine* 78 (October): 44, 93-97.

   Charts the appearance of The Famous Players Film Company and examines the reasons why this "apparent union between the films and the stage is not nearly so close as at first it would seem to be."

10. Griffith, D.W. "A Poet Who Writes on Motion Picture Film." *The Theatre* 19 (June): 311-12, 314, 316.

    "Moving pictures can get nothing from the so-called legitimate stage because American directors have nothing to offer."

11. N., A.K. *"The Old Curiosity Shop* Cinematographed." *The
     Dickensian* 10 (April): 99-100.

     Praise for the Thomas Bentley film.

12. Phillips, Henry Albert. "Differentiation." *The Photodrama.*
     Larchmont, New York: The Stanhope-Dodge Publishing
     Company, pp. 32-38. Reprinted by Arno Press and The
     New York Times, New York, 1970.

     "The two fields--of fiction writing and photoplay
     writing--diverge into opposite directions the moment we
     discuss the narration of one and the visualization of
     the other."

13. Shaw, George Bernard. "Bernard Shaw's Unqualified Approval
     of the Cinematograph." *Current Opinion* 57: 105-06. For
     similar comments see also *Current Opinion* 58 (1915):
     411 and *The Metropolitan Magazine* 42 (May 1915): 23, 54.

     For Shaw film performs an important educative function,
     which legitimizes the film and underscores its value.

                              1915

14. "Why the Movies and the Drama Must Take Different Roads."
     Current Opinion 58: 333.

     Film and theater are distinct art forms; one should
     not attempt to encroach on the other.

15. H., F.T. *"Barnaby Rudge* on the Film." *The Dickensian* 11
     (February): 46.

     Thomas Bentley's film version, while "admirable in
     many respects," "leaves much to be desired in regard to
     dramatic interest."

16. Hitchcock, Alfred M. "Relation of the Picture Play to
     Literature." *The English Journal* (Chicago) 4: 292-98.

     "There are better ways of stocking the mind than by
     flashing before the eye a kaleidoscope jumble of unrelated
     information."

17. Kuttner, Alfred. "Drama Comes Back from the Movies."
     The New Republic 4: 51-52.

     "Moving pictures have then neither eliminated nor
     bettered the drama."

18. Lindsay, Vachel. "Thirty Differences Between the Photoplay
     and the Stage." *The Art of the Moving Picture*. New
     York: Macmillan, pp. 151-71. Revised in 1922. Reprinted
     with an Introduction by Stanley Kauffmann by Liveright,
     New York, 1970.

     Irreconcilable differences between stage and screen
     suggest that "The soundest actors, photographers, and
     producers will be those who emphasize the points wherein
     the photoplay is unique."

                              1916

19. Eaton, Walter Prichard. "Wanted--Moving Picture Authors."
     The American Magazine 81 (March): 34, 67-70, 73.

     Better scenario writers must be developed before the
     silent film can become an acceptable art form.

20. Hooker, Brian. "Shakespeare and the Movies." *Century* 93:
     298-304.

     Analyzes the "similarity of form and structure between
     the plays of Shakespeare and the modern photodrama."

21. Munsterberg, Hugo. *The Photoplay: A Psychological Study*.
     New York, London: D. Appleton and Company. Reprinted
     by Arno Press and The New York Times, New York, 1970.

     A study of the psychological and esthetic qualities of
     the motion picture that recommend it as an art form
     separate from that of the drama.

                              1917

22. Caine, Derwent Hall. "The New Old Art." *Moving Picture
     World* 33: 405.

     "Motion pictures cannot present any serious rivalry
     to the spoken drama."

23. Eaton, Walter Prichard. "The 'Art' of the Motion Picture."
     The Theatre 25 (April): 218, 248.

     "If, therefore, we find any art in the movies, it is
     not a new art, but an old one, and an art much better
     practiced on the stage of the living theatre, as every
     actor knows in his heart to be the truth."

24. Howland, Delevan. "'The Play's the Thing,'--But Not in
    Moving Pictures." *The Editor* 46 (19 September): 387-90.

    Deplores the way in which film appeals only to one sense
    and requires, unlike the stage, "no reflective effort or
    any involved mental process" for enjoyment.

25. Matthews, Brander. "Are the Movies a Menace to the Drama?"
    The North American Review 205: 447-54.

    "It is because the moving-picture has perforce to do
    without the potent appeal of the spoken word that it can
    never be really a rival of the drama."

1918

26. Belasco, David. "The Movies--My Profession's Flickering
    Bogy: A Famous Theatrical Manager Gives His Opinions on
    the Film Drama, and Tells What He Would Do If He Were
    to Direct a Motion-Picture Play." *Munsey's Magazine* 63:
    593-604.

    "Those who regard the picture play lightly because they
    cannot derive from it the artistic satisfaction which
    they find in real drama, make the mistake of demanding
    too much of it. They should remember that one cannot be
    confused with the other, for the reason that drama is
    life, while the screen is destined always to remain a
    cold picture of life."

27. Brady, William A. "Have the Movies Ideals?" *The Forum* 59:
    307-15.

    Film cannot borrow successfully from literature.

28. Nathan, George Jean. "The Motion Pictures." *The Popular
    Theatre*. New York: Alfred A. Knopf, pp. 122-45.

    Criticizes the dramaturgy of the silent screen.

29. Stannard, Eliot. "Should Dickens Be Modernized for the
    Cinema?" *The Dickensian* 14 (May): 126-28. See responses
    by J. Cuming Walters, J.W.T. Ley, T.W. Hill, Sydney
    Jeffery, Walter Dexter, Aleck Abrahams and E. Kendall
    Pearson, *The Dickensian* 14 (June): 145-52; and by
    M.H.S., *The Dickensian* 14: 193-94.

    Stannard, who wrote the scenario of a film version of
    Dombey and Son, defends his decision to adapt the novel
    into a "present-day" version. "I propose modernising

whenever I think the story will be thus more vivid, clear
and dramatic in picture form, regardless of the age, rank
or following of the original author."

1919

30. Dwan, Allan. "Filming Great Fiction: Can Literature Be
     Preserved in Motion Pictures?" *The Forum* 62: 298-305.

     The motion picture must combine action and character,
     using preferably upstanding American characters found in
     the classics of American literature. Though the motion
     picture at this time depends upon the novel and stage
     play for its material, Dwan foresees a time when the
     motion picture will have its own writers.

31. Lescarboura, Austin C. "The Present Status of the Motion
     Picture Art." *Behind the Motion-Picture Screen*. New
     York: Scientific American Publishing Company, pp. 381-
     94.

     "For a long time the motion-picture drama had been
     just a rehash of old stage plays, novels and short
     stories. To-day, however, it is finding the bulk of its
     inspiration in its own ranks."

32. London, Mrs. Jack. "Bringing Literature to the Screen."
     Theatre Magazine 30 (September): 177-78, 180.

     "With excellent filming there is no reason why, these
     days, literature cannot be brought to the screen."

1920

33. "Recent Motion Pictures Based on Current Literature."
     The Library Journal 45: 72, 400; 46: 313-14; 46: 356.

     A series of selected lists of films and their sources.

34. Atkinson, E.J. Rupert. *Key to the Adaptation of the Best
     of Shakespeare's Plays to the Stage--Cinema--Interaction
     Process for the Production of Drama*. New York: The
     Knickerbocker Press, 2 vols.

     Not seen.

35. C., A.E.B. "*Little Dorrit* on the Film." *The Dickensian*
     16 (October): 204.

Sidney Morgan's version "is probably the best Dickens film that has yet been produced."

36. Eaton, Walter Prichard. "The Latest Menace to the Movies." *The North American Review* 212: 80-87. See Jesse L. Lasky, 212: 88-92; and Otis Skinner, 212: 387-92.

    Controversy over the influence of film on the theater.

37. Hough, Emerson. "'The Soul Child': Making a Book into a Movie." *The Saturday Evening Post* 192 (27 March): 14-15, 42, 45-46.

    On-location shooting of the film adaptation of the Hough novel described.

1921

38. Beach, Rex. "The Author and the Film." *The Mentor* 9 (July): 31.

    Author and filmmaker have begun to see the need for collaboration on film projects.

39. Hughes, Rupert. "Fiction Writers and Scenarios." *The Mentor* 9 (July): 30.

    Mistreatment of an author's material by the scenario writer is becoming a thing of the past.

40. Jones, Henry Arthur. "Dramatist and the Photoplay." *The Mentor* 9 (July): 29. Reprinted in *Authors on Film*. Ed. Harry M. Geduld. Bloomington and London: Indiana University Press, 1972, pp. 161-62.

    "The film play offers to the dramatist an infinitude of opportunity compared with the spoken drama."

41. Macgowan, Kenneth. "The Movies--The Curtain Becomes the Stage." *The Theatre of Tomorrow*. New York: Boni and Liveright, pp. 178-85.

    "The screen can do everything that the realistic theatre can do; it cannot compass all the possibilities of the imaginative theatre, though it may go beyond them in certain directions."

42. Maugham, W. Somerset. "On Writing for the Films." *The North American Review* 213: 670-75. Reprinted in *Authors on Film*. Ed. Harry M. Geduld. Bloomington and London: Indiana University Press, 1972, pp. 181-87.

Writing for the screen "has not quite the freedom of
the novel, but it certainly has not the fetters of the
stage. It is a technique of its own, with its own conventions, its own limitations, and its own effects."

43. Parker, Sir Gilbert. "The Author and Motion Pictures."
    The Mentor 9 (July): 14-19.

    "I do not think the film will destroy the taste for
    the stage."

44. Patterson, Frances Taylor. "Adaptation." *Cinema Craftsman-
    ship; A Book for Playwrights*. New York: Harcourt, Brace
    and Company, pp. 64-95.

    This survey of several silent film adaptations of
    literature suggests that the screenwriter must play a
    significant role in a successful film. A lengthy quotation
    from the address "The 'Routine' of Film Adaptation," by
    Eva Unsell, is also included.

1922

45. "Pickwick on the Film." *The Dickensian* 18 (January): 28.

    Praise for the Thomas Bentley version of Charles Dickens'
    Pickwick Papers.

46. Craig, Gordon. "Cinema and Its Drama." *English Review* 34:
    119-22.

    The drama in the cinema is made "by the new school of
    the same old tyrants, to enslave *the mind* of the people."

47. Darlington, William Aubrey. "Stage and Film Technique."
    Through the Fourth Wall. London: Chapman and Hall, pp.
    110-14.

    "The badness of our worst plays is nothing like so
    bad as the badness of our worst films."

1923

48. "Screen Dealings with Dickens and Hugo." *Literary Digest*
    76 (17 February): 29-30.

    The effect of censorship on film adaptations of *Oliver
    Twist* and *The Hunchback of Notre Dame*.

49. "Shakespeare Writhing in Screen Bonds." *Literary Digest* 76 (17 March): 30-31.

    Commentary on several screen adaptations of Shakespeare's plays, particularly *Othello* (1922).

50. Ecclestone, J. "The Cinema." *The Nineteenth Century and After* 94: 634-39.

    There may be "latent" in the cinema "a new form of aesthetic expression so vital and important that children of the future will have to be taught appreciation of the great film productions as they are now taught appreciation of Shakespeare."

51. Faure, Elie. *The Art of Cineplastics*. Boston: The Four Seas Company. Reprinted in *Screen Monographs 1*. New York: Arno Press and The New York Times, 1970.

    The cinema has nothing in common with the theater except the actor.

52. Jones, Henry Arthur. "Drama *versus* Film." *Fact, Fancy and Opinion; Examples of Present Day Writing*. Ed. R.M. Gay. Boston: The Atlantic Monthly Press, pp. 109-13.

    The film offers spectacle and a greater appeal to the imagination than theater.

53. Valentino, Rudolph. "The Motion Picture Novel." *The Bookman* 56: 724-26.

    "The only friend the star has, after stardom, is the novelist."

                                1924

54. Barry, Iris. "A Comparison of Arts." *The Spectator* 132: 707.

    "Since both theatre and cinema do express farce, comedy, tragedy and melodrama, there is a common ground on which they may properly be compared, although they are different art-forms in different mediums."

55. Block, Ralph. "A Literature of the Screen?" *The Bookman* 60: 472-73.

    Looks forward to the time when the motion picture becomes independent of the conventional forms of story telling and character development found in the novel and drama.

56. Colby, Elbridge. "Literature and the Movies." *American Review* (Illinois) 2: 368-71.

"The moving pictures have actually brought to the attention of the public much excellent, and sad to say, forgotten literature."

57. Hinchman, Walter Swain. "The Human Voice Divine." *The Forum* 72: 548-51. Reprinted in *Pedestrian Papers*. Boston: Houghton Mifflin, 1928, pp. 61-67.

"The fact is movies are not dramas," because the spoken word is lacking.

58. Shaw, Bernard, and Archibald Henderson. "The Drama, the Theatre, and the Films: A Dialogue between Bernard Shaw and Archibald Henderson, His Biographer." *The Fortnightly Review* 122: 289-302. Also printed in *Harper's Magazine* 149: 425-35.

Shaw would not let his plays be filmed for the silent screen because "a play with words left out is a play spoiled."

59. Waugh, Alec. "Film and the Future." *The Fortnightly Review* 122: 524-31.

Film is an "entirely different medium" from the novel and the drama.

1925

60. Griffith, Mrs. D.W. *When the Movies Were Young*. New York: E.P. Dutton. Reprinted by Dover Publications, New York, 1970. See 963.

A personal chronicle of Griffith's rise as a movie director, written by his wife.
Chapter 17, "'Pippa Passes' Filmed," is particularly enlightening about Griffith's method of adapting literature to silent film. The film was based on the Robert Browning poem.

61. Henderson, Archibald. *Table-Talk of G.B.S.* London: Chapman & Hall, pp. 55-65.

Bernard Shaw comments on drama and the film.

1926

62. Barry, Iris. "Dolls and Dreams." *Let's Go to the Movies.*
     New York: Payson & Clark, pp. 23-33. Reprinted by Arno
     Press and The New York Times, New York, 1972.

     A comparison of film and theater, focusing on the
     effect of each on the audience. "To go to the pictures
     is to purchase a dream. To go to the theatre is to buy
     an experience, and between experience and dream there is
     a vast difference.... The theatre is a tonic, the cinema
     a sedative."

63. Block, Ralph. "Those Terrible Movies; A Medium of Art
     Expression Far Surpassing the Theatre and the Novel."
     Theatre Magazine 43 (February): 32, 52.

     "In the end the movies lack a civilized point of view
     toward their material--unequal at least to the standards
     of an intelligent world. Were a theatre to be devised for
     them and an audience created, they would have no reason
     for shame or timidity."

64. Dwan, Allan. *The Motion Picture Director* (June). [Not
     seen.] Partially reprinted in *Hollywood Directors 1914-
     1940.* Ed. Richard Koszarski. New York: Oxford Univer-
     sity Press, 1976, pp. 154-59.

     General observations on the process of adaptation are
     accompanied by a description of changes made when Rex
     Beach's novel *Padlocked* was adapted to film.

65. Eaton, Walter Prichard. "The Theatre and the Motion Pic-
     tures." *Vanity Fair* 27 (October): 73, 118.

     A summary of articles published in previous issues
     arguing that the film will not destroy the theater.

66. Huxley, Aldous. "Our Debt to Hollywood: What the Inferior
     Races Learn of White Civilization from Motion Pictures."
     Vanity Fair 26 (August): 34, 88. See also *Vanity Fair*
     3 (September): 6, 59.

     Attacks the "violent imbecilities" of Hollywood films.

67. Krows, Arthur Edwin. "Literature and the Motion Picture."
     *The Annals of the American Academy of Political and
     Social Science* 128: 70-73.

     The motion picture can "convey the worthy thoughts that
     a wide sense has attached especially to 'literature,'"

but the commercial drive of movie makers, trying to appeal
to a mass audience, prevents the making of serious, in-
tellectual films.

68. Strauss, Florence L. "A Synopsized View of Literature."
     The Bookman 64: 454-56.

     Filmmakers should not "attempt to illustrate a narrative
     written for another medium" but rather use "screen stories
     written by expert screen technicians who are actually con-
     cerned in the production of the picture."

69. Swann, R.E.C. "Art and the Cinema: A Chance for the
     British Producer." *The Nineteenth Century and After*
     100: 221-28.

     "The art of the cinema is the art of conveying sensa-
     tion by means of visual movement."

70. Woolf, Virginia. "The Cinema." *The Arts* 9: 314-16. Also
     printed in *The Nation and Athenaeum* 39: 381-83 and *The
     New Republic* 47, 4: 308-10. Reprinted in *Authors on
     Film*. Ed. Harry M. Geduld. Bloomington and London:
     Indiana University Press, 1972, pp. 86-91.

     "Yet remote as it is, intimations are not wanting that
     the emotions are accumulating, the time is coming, and
     the art of cinema is about to be brought to birth."

                                1927

71. Bennett, Arnold. "The Film 'Story.'" *Close Up* 1, 4: 27-32.

     "I have not yet seen a first-rate story told in a first-
     rate style on the screen."

72. Betts, Ernest. "The Film as Literature." *The Saturday
     Review* 144: 905-06.

     Film shares "many affinities, in conception and treat-
     ment, in substance and form, with the well-made novel,"
     but the film must continue to grow and to generate formal
     and technical innovations.

73. Block, Ralph. "Not Theatre, Not Literature, Not Painting."
     The Dial 82: 20-24. Reprinted in *Introduction to the
     Art of the Movies: An Anthology of Ideas on the Nature
     of Movie Art*. Ed. Lewis Jacobs. New York: The Noonday
     Press, 1960, pp. 101-06.

"The movie is in other words a new way in which to see life."

74. Erskine, John. "No Plot Is Needed in Moving Pictures. The Entire Technique of the Modern Film Is Wrong from the Viewpoint of One Noted Writer. Told to Sylvia B. Golden." *Theatre Magazine* 46 (December): 38, 70.

"Motion pictures will improve just as soon as producers discontinue buying novels and stage plays for their stories. Their mediums of expression are as vastly different as is the radio from pictures."

75. Glassgold, C. Adolph. "Motion Pictures." *The Arts* 12: 282-83.

Sunrise (1927), F.W. Murnau's film based on a story by Hermann Sudermann, employs too many cinematic tricks.

76. Nathan, George Jean. "Notes on the Movies." *The American Mercury* 12: 118-22.

"The moving picture will never really find itself until it divorces itself from the drama."

77. Patterson, Frances Taylor. *"The Scarlet Letter." Motion Picture Continuities: "A Kiss for Cinderella," "The Scarlet Letter," "The Last Command."* New York: Columbia University Press, pp. 91-94. Reprinted by Garland Publishing, New York, 1978.

A short introduction to the printed screenplay, based on Nathaniel Hawthorne's novel, showing that "the continuity ... cannot in the strictest sense be considered an adaptation of the novel at all."

1928

78. Bauer, Leda V. "The Movies Tackle Literature." *The American Mercury* 14: 288-94.

On the methods of developing story materials for the screen.

79. De Casseres, Benjamin. "Are the Pictures and Stage Antagonistic? Let Those of Us Who Demand Quality Seek Only the Best That Is Produced in Both Arts." *Theatre Magazine* 47 (January): 23, 68.

"Drama is not an art until the great dramatist is born.
And so with motion pictures. Like the speaking drama,
it is mostly machine-made, box-office bunk. But let an
artist handle the medium and pictures become art."

80. Disher, M. Willson. "Classics into Films." *The Fortnightly
     Review* 130: 784-92.

     "The generation that is growing up will not only be
     ignorant: it will have a very fantastic idea that what
     famous authors write is very much like what Hollywood's
     authors write--only not so good."

81. White, Eric Walter. *Parnassus to Let. An Essay about
     Rhythm in Film.* London: The Hogarth Press. Reprinted
     in *Screen Monographs 1.* New York: Arno Press and The
     New York Times, 1970.

     The rhythm of film editing is discussed in terms of
     accent in music and poetry.

                              1929

82. "H.G. Wells Predicts the Film of the Future." *Literary
     Digest* 101 (25 May): 24-25.

     "The film of the future will be a great spectacle--
     music--drama, predicts Mr. Wells."

83. Anderson, John. "Movies." *Box Office.* New York: Jonathan
     Cape and Harrison Smith, pp. 85-93.

     Contrasts the methods of presentation of the stage and
     of the screen. Movies, as they are presently made, do
     not touch the "imagination" of the audience.

84. Bishop, G.W. "The Living Talkies: An Interview with
     Bernard Shaw." *Theatre Guild Magazine* 7, 2: 32.

     "The talkies have come to stay."

85. Carter, Huntley. "The Kinema." *The New Spirit in the
     Russian Theatre 1917-28.* London: Brentano's, pp. 277-91.

     "The function of the Kinema in human life is to
     visualise hosts in action, destroying or creating. The
     function of the theatre is to illuminate the springs of
     action that set these big masses in motion."

86. Clayton, Bertram. "Shakespeare and the 'Talkies.'" *The English Review* 49: 739-48, 752.

Film adaptations of Shakespeare's plays could prove extremely effective in introducing his work to a wide audience.

87. Gerould, Katharine Fullerton. "The Lost Art of Motion-Pictures. A True Lover of the Movies Speaks in Sadness." *Century* 118 (August): 496-506.

Deplores the influence of the drama on the movies.

88. Hays, Will H. "Screen and Drama Blood-Brothers in Art: The Word 'Theatre,' of Greek Origin, Means 'To See' and Suggests the Consanguinity of the Film and Stage." *Theatre Magazine* 47 (May): 25, 47.

"In dramatic thought, stage and screen are identical. In method of expression alone is there a difference."

89. Pirandello, Luigi. "The Cinema Is Digging Its Own Grave; The Talking Film *Versus* the Theatre." *The Illustrated London News* 175 (27 July): 156, 192d.

The talking film does not threaten the theater because the introduction of sound will reduce the universality of the silent film.

90. Pudovkin, V.I. *Pudovkin on Film Technique*. London: Victor Gollancz. Reprinted in *Film Technique and Film Acting*. Trans. and ed. Ivor Montagu. New York: Grove Press, 1970, pp. 79-121.

Pudovkin draws comparisons between the theater and film in order to establish the "peculiarities" of film material.

91. Richardson, Dorothy. "Talkies, Plays and Books: Thoughts on the Approaching Battle Between the Spoken Pictures, Literature, the Stage." *Vanity Fair* 32 (August): 56.

The film will not replace books or the theater.

92. Watts, Richard, Jr. "Stage Play and Screen Play: Two Art Forms Have Been Confused Anew by the Talkies." *Theatre Guild Magazine* 6, 6: 31-33, 64.

"The stage play remains the implacable enemy of the screen and until its influence and methods have once more been beaten off, the film will continue as a mechanical carbon copy of the theatre."

93.   Wells, H.G. *The King Who Was a King: An Unconventional
      Novel.* Garden City, New York: Doubleday, Doran & Company.

      A proposed outline for a film written in the form of
      a novel.

                                1930

94.   "Galsworthy on the Talkies." *The Living Age* 338: 349-50.

      Galsworthy believes that the talking and singing film
      "should reduce the audience for the coarser and melodra-
      matic types of play, and consolidate the more fastidious
      types of playgoer." Authors, he feels, should write the
      dialogue for films adapted from their works.

95.   Blakeston, Oswell. "Our Literary Screen." *Close Up* 6:
      308-10.

      Critics often "ignore the fact that *the eye of the brain
      is very different from the physical eye.*"

96.   Carter, Huntley. *The New Spirit in the Cinema.* London:
      Harold Shaylor, pp. 374-76.

      A brief review of the cinema activities of G.B. Shaw,
      John Galsworthy, H.G. Wells, Sir James Barrie and Arnold
      Bennett.

97.   Dukes, Ashley. "The London Scene: The Theatre and the
      Talkies." *Theatre Arts Monthly* 14: 466-75.

      With talking pictures, film and theater "are coming
      closer together again, and their artistic *rapprochement*
      is much more disastrous to the immediate interest of the
      stage than was their artistic rivalry [before sound]."

98.   Klingler, Werner. "Proposed Continuity for the Ending of
      'All Quiet on the Western Front.'" *Experimental Cinema*
      1, 2: 23-27.

      This "proposed ending" to the film, adapted from
      the Remarque novel, "was considered by Universal Pictures
      Corporation but was finally not accepted."

                                1931

99.   "Dreiser on the Sins of Hollywood." *Literary Digest* 109
      (2 May): 21.

Dreiser expresses unhappiness with the 1931 screen adaptation of his novel *An American Tragedy*.

100. Marshall, Norman. "Reflections on the English Film." *The Bookman* (London) 81: 71-72.

English filmmakers have not yet found techniques suited to film as an art independent of the stage.

101. Nathan, George Jean. "The Play Is Still the Thing." *The Forum* 86: 36-39.

The film will not become a serious rival of the theater.

102. Playfair, Sir Nigel. "The Theatre and the Films." *The English Review* 52: 336-41.

Theater and film are not only compatible but complementary: "It seems clear to me that ... the success of talking films depends ... to a very large extent on the skill of actors, and the art of acting cannot conceivably be learned except before a responding audience."

103. Potamkin, H.A. "Novel into Film: A Case Study of Current Practice." *Close Up* 8: 267-79. Reprinted in *The Compound Cinema: The Film Writings of Harry Alan Potamkin*. Selected, Arranged, and Introduced by Lewis Jacobs. Studies in Culture and Communication. New York and London: Teachers College Press, 1977, pp. 186-96.

A defense of S.M. Eisenstein and G.V. Alexandrov's scenario and script of Theodore Dreiser's *An American Tragedy*. Although Dreiser supported Eisenstein, the script was rejected by Paramount.

104. Rotha, Paul. "The Revival of Naturalism: Emile Zola and the Cinema." *Celluloid: The Film To-Day*. London, New York, Toronto: Longmans, Green and Co., pp. 215-26.

"There is much in modern cinema that was foreshadowed in the Naturalistic novel of Zola. Scientific method, the theory of environment, even scenario-organization and selection of detail is common to both mediums."

105. Williams, David P. "Cinema Technique and the Theatre." *The Nineteenth Century* 110: 602-12.

The film's "greater freedom in dramatic technique" has had and will have a strong influence on the staging of plays in the theater.

106. Wolfe, Humbert. "I Look at the Theatre." *Theatre Arts Monthly* 15: 49-52.

"I conclude that the cinema has nothing to offer to the theatre except distraction and opulent irrelevance."

                                    1932

107. Beaton, Welford. "Stage Plays and Playwrights." *Know Your Movies: The Theory and Practice of Motion Picture Production*. Hollywood: Howard Hill, pp. 60-66.

Not seen.

108. Beck, Warren. "Dumb Show into Drama." *The English Journal* (Chicago) 21: 220-28.

"The talking motion picture is notable because it differs significantly from the older forms, novel and drama, in its narrative scope."

109. Carter, Huntley. "Cinema and the Theatre: The Diabolical Difference." *The English Review* 55: 313-20.

"Intimacy must always be the dividing line between the theatre and the cinema. For the cinema is a machine--a machine for seeing. A machine cannot be intimate."

110. Cousins, E.G. "The Dearth of Stories." *Filmland in Ferment*. London: Denis Archer, pp. 70-78.

Good stories are usually ruined in the process of screen adaptation because filmmakers cater to commercial interests.

111. Dark, Sidney. "The Art of the Film." *The Saturday Review* 154: 640.

Notes that "the film is escaping from the incredible magnates of Hollywood. And in such film plays as the work of René Clair there is the beginning of an art which is entirely different from the art of the theatre."

112. Fawcett, L'Estrange. *Writing for the Films*. London: Sir I. Pitman & Sons.

Not seen.

113. Klingler, Werner. "Ozep's Film, 'The Murderer Karamazov.'" *Experimental Cinema* 1, 4: 30-33.

Though this film has little connection with its source, *The Brothers Karamazov* by Feodor Dostoevsky, its cinematic qualities are exceptional.

114. Tonecki, Zygmunt. "At the Boundary of Film and Theatre." *Close Up* 9: 31-35.

Considers the experiments of dadaists and futurists in order to examine "the phase of the reciprocate reaction of the film and of the theatre."

115. Young, Stark. "Madam's Λ." *The New Republic* 72: 124-26. See also *The New Republic* 72: 259-61.

The art of the motion picture and the art of the theatre are two different things.

1933

116. Bond, Kirk. "Film as Literature." *The Bookman* (London) 84 (July): 188-89.

Film has the ability to interpret life on a plane as high as or higher than that of the novelist. In Stroheim "cinema can boast at least one rival to the novelist."

117. Eisenstein, S.M. "An American Tragedy." *Close Up* 10: 109-24. Revised and reprinted in *Sergei Eisenstein: Notes of a Film Director*. Trans. X. Danko. London: Lawrence and Wishart, 1959, pp. 98-106.

Paramount rejected Eisenstein's treatment of Dreiser's *An American Tragedy* for ideological reasons.

118. Hughes, Pennethorne. "The Historical Inception of Stage and Film." *Close Up* 10: 341-46.

Similarities between drama and film exist because "the play was, as the cinema is, essentially the entertainment of the proletariate."

119. Mann, Thomas. "On the Film." *Past Masters and Other Papers*. Trans. H.T. Lowe-Porter. New York: Alfred A. Knopf, pp. 263-66. Reprinted in *Authors on Film*. Ed. Harry M. Geduld. Bloomington and London: Indiana University Press, 1972, pp. 129-33.

Mann's reflections on the appeal of film, its relation to the drama and the lack of success filmmakers have had adapting his own work to film.

120.   Read, Herbert. "The Poet and the Film." *Cinema Quarterly*
       (Edinburgh) 1 (Summer): 197-202. Reprinted in *A Coat
       of Many Colours: Occasional Essays*. London: George
       Routledge & Sons, 1945, pp. 225-31.

       Film will not achieve the status of being a true art
       until a poet of creative or imaginative genius becomes
       a filmmaker.

121.   Richardson, Dorothy M. "Continuous Performance." *Close
       Up* 10: 130-32.

       "For Stage and Screen, falsifying the prophecies of
       those who saw in the Talkies the doom of the Theatre, have
       become a joint-stock company, to the benefit of both
       parties."

122.   Stonier, G.W. "Movie." *Gog Magog and Other Critical Essays.*
       London: Dent, pp. 177-89. Reprinted by Books for Librar-
       ies Press, Freeport, New York, 1966.

       "At one time it was interesting to watch the effect
       of other arts on the film: what is important now is the
       effect of the film on other arts."

                                   1934

123.   Ferguson, Otis. "Screen Versions." *The New Republic* 80
       (12 September): 131-32.

       Film adaptations of literature are governed predomi-
       nantly by Hollywood's perception of the audience: "the
       movies are trying to meet with, rather than mold, popular
       taste."

                                   1935

124.   Bontempelli, Massinio. "Film and Theatre." *Intercine*
       (August-September): 97.

       "There is no reason to believe, from the strictly
       aesthetic point of view, that a relation exists between
       cinema and theatre."

125.   C., A.E.B. "*David Copperfield* on the Screen." *The
       Dickensian* 31 (Summer): 223-25.

       Praise for George Cukor's film version of the Dickens
       novel.

126. C., A.E.B. "On Screen and Stage (1) *The Old Curiosity
      Shop* Film." *The Dickensian* 31 (Spring): 137-38.

      Praise for the British International Pictures version
      of the Dickens novel.

127. C., A.E.B. "The Screen Version of *Great Expectations*."
      The Dickensian 31 (Winter): 62.

      The film of the Dickens novel "sets a standard that will
      challenge and stimulate future productions."

128. C., P.T. "Drood Vanished into Nowhere." *The Dickensian*
      31 (Summer): 231-32.

      The 1935 American film adaptation of Dickens' *The
      Mystery of Edwin Drood* "makes no claim to fidelity" to
      the original.

129. Dexter, Walter. "Dickens on Screen and Stage." *The
      Dickensian* 31 (Summer): 215-18.

      Survey of critical responses to recent stage and film
      versions of Dickens' novels.

130. Ortman, Marguerite G., comp. *Fiction and the Screen*.
      Boston: Marshall Jones Company.

      Contains both a general consideration of the problems
      encountered in adapting novels and plays to film and a
      lengthy analysis of the adaptation to the screen of
      Charles Dickens' *David Copperfield* directed by George
      Cukor.

131. Spottiswoode, Raymond. "Categories of the Film: Distinc-
      tions." *A Grammar of the Film: An Analysis of Film
      Technique*. London: Faber and Faber, pp. 102-12.

      Film faces a dilemma in its development which cannot
      be solved by relying on stage techniques.

132. Watts, Richard, Jr. "Films of a Moonstruck World." *Yale
      Review* 25: 311-20. Partially reprinted in *Focus on
      Shakespearean Films*. Ed. Charles W. Eckert. Englewood
      Cliffs, New Jersey: Prentice-Hall, 1972, pp. 47-52.

      Considers the difficulties posed by a film adaptation
      of Shakespeare, and finds in *A Midsummer Night's Dream*
      (1935) a film beset by errors of judgment in casting and
      editing but one which suggests that future projects need
      not be doomed to failure.

1936

133. Barnes, Walter. "The Nature of the Photoplay" and
      "Esthetic Principles of the Photoplay." *The Photoplay
      as Literary Art.* Newark, New Jersey: Educational and
      Recreational Guides, pp. 1-3; 12-35.

      "The photoplay, for most of us, [is] a blend of stage
      play and novel, [and] we resort to the movies for some-
      thing closely similar to what we receive from the play
      and the novel."
      The film should be evaluated, judged and criticized
      according to standards applicable to the criticism of
      literature.

134. C., A.E.B. "Scrooge on the Screen." *The Dickensian* 32
      (Winter): 59-60.

      Praise for *Scrooge* (1935), a "sincere and stimulating
      version" of Dickens' *A Christmas Carol.*

135. Eisenstein, Sergei. "Through Theatre to Cinema." Trans.
      Jay Leyda. *Theatre Arts Monthly* 20: 735-47. Reprinted
      in *Film Form: Essays in Film Theory.* Ed. Jay Leyda.
      New York: Harcourt, Brace and Company, 1949, pp. 3-17.

      Eisenstein describes how he began his film career as a
      director in the theater in Moscow.

136. Herzberg, Max J. "A Preliminary Guide to the Study and
      Appreciation of the Screen Versions of Shakespeare's
      Romeo and Juliet." *"Romeo and Juliet" by William
      Shakespeare. A Motion Picture Edition.* New York: Random
      House Publishers, pp. 271-90.

      A guide to an appreciation of the film designed for
      secondary school use. It contains short discussions of
      the plot of the play, the making of the Cukor film,
      Shakespeare's language and musical effects in the film.

137. Lane, Tamar. "Story Construction." *The New Technique of
      Screen Writing: A Practical Guide to the Writing and
      Marketing of Photoplays.* New York, London: Whittlesey
      House, pp. 22-35.

      Draws comparisons among three forms of writing used
      in screen story construction: dramatic, literary and a
      blend of the dramatic and literary called "composite."

138. Margrave, Seton. "Writing for Films." *Successful Film
      Writing As Illustrated by "The Ghost Goes West."* London:
      Methuen & Co.

      The essay provides "general principles of film writing,
      aimed at gaining the approval of the largest possible
      audience."
      Included in the book is the reprinted story "Sir Tristram
      Goes West," by Eric Keown, the "first treatment" of the
      screenplay and, last, the "released script" or "finished
      scenario" of the film.

139. Mason, A. Stewart. "The Film of *A Tale of Two Cities.*"
      The Dickensian 32 (Summer): 172.

      The MGM film fails to bring out the tragic aspect of
      the Dickens story.

140. Nathan, George Jean. "The Cinema: A Dramatic Critic Looks
      at the Movies." *The Theatre of the Moment: A Journal-
      istic Commentary.* New York, London: Alfred A. Knopf,
      pp. 97–118.

      The theater is in no danger from the film.

141. Nicoll, Allardyce. *Film and Theatre.* New York: Thomas Y.
      Crowell.

      "In this book, I have sought to do merely two things--
      first, to present, in as simple and unelaborated a manner
      as possible, what appear to be the basic principles under-
      lying artistic expression in the film, and, secondly, to
      relate that form of expression to the familiar art of
      the stage."
      Contents by chapter: Shakespeare and Cinema; The Basis
      of Film Art [Movement]; The Methods of the Cinema; The
      Sound Film; Film Reality; The Cinema and the Theatre;
      Bibliography.

142. Noble, Lorraine, ed. *Four-Star Scripts: Actual Shooting
      Scripts and How They Are Written.* Garden City, New
      York: Doubleday, Doran & Company.

      Readable chapters on subjects such as "Back of the
      Scenes" and "How Scripts Are Written" are supplemented
      by printed texts of four screenplays: *Lady for a Day*
      (1933), adapted from a Damon Runyon short story; *It
      Happened One Night* (1934), based on a short story by
      Samuel Hopkins Adams; *Little Women* (1933), from the
      Louisa May Alcott novel; and *The Story of Louis Pasteur*

(1936), an original story by Sheridan Libney and Pierre Collings.

143. Pemberton, Brock. "A Theatrical Producer's Reaction to
      the Movies." *The Movies on Trial: The Views and
      Opinions of Outstanding Personalities Anent Screen
      Entertainment Past and Present*. Comp. and ed. J. Perl-
      man. New York: Macmillan, pp. 153-65.

      "I have always preached that the two mediums [stage and
      screen], instead of battling one another, should cooperate
      to the fullest degree."

144. Robertson, E. Arnot. "Intruders in the Film World." *The
      Fortnightly Review* 145: 194-98.

      An attack on Hollywood screen adaptations designed
      principally to make money.

145. Russell, Caro Mae Green. *Modern Plays and Playwrights,
      with Some Notes on the Theater and the Screen by Paul
      Green*. Chapel Hill, North Carolina: University of North
      Carolina Press.

      Not seen.

146. Seldes, Gilbert. "The Vandals of Hollywood: Why 'a Good
      Movie Cannot Be Faithful to the Original Book or Play.'"
      The Saturday Review of Literature 14 (17 October):
      3-4, 13-14.

      The central problems facing adaptation from literature
      to film have to do with motion and time.

147. Strunk, William, Jr. "Foreword to *Romeo and Juliet*."
      *"Romeo and Juliet" by William Shakespeare. A Motion
      Picture Edition*. New York: Random House Publishers,
      pp. 19-24.

      Strunk, the "literary adviser" for the 1936 Cukor film,
      discusses the differences between the play and the film.

148. Williams, W.E. "Film and Literature." *Sight and Sound*
      4, 16: 163-65.

      Max Reinhardt's adaptation of *A Midsummer Night's
      Dream* should be considered an "experiment" rather than
      an "achievement" for it does not provide an adequate
      interpretation of the play.

1937

149. Adler, Mortimer J. "Form and Matter" and "Technique."
     Art and Prudence: A Study in Practical Philosophy.
     New York, Toronto: Longmans, Green, pp. 457-512; 513-
     44.

     "Form and Matter" considers the "intrinsic or aesthetic"
     element of motion pictures, particularly what differen-
     tiates film form from other forms of art such as the
     drama, the novel and the epic. The evaluation is based
     on principles of classification established in Aristotle's
     Poetics.
     In the chapter on "Technique" the relationship between
     linguistic and pictorial syntax is explored to show "what
     makes for *style* in the use of the pictorial medium."

150. Dean, Basil. "The Future of Screen and Stage." *Footnotes
     to the Film.* Ed. Charles Davy. London: Lovat & Dickson,
     pp. 172-84.

     "The truth is that both theatre and cinema should draw
     their inspiration from humanity."

151. Greene, Graham. "Subjects and Stories." *Footnotes to the
     Film.* Ed. Charles Davy. London: Lovat & Dickson, pp.
     57-70.

     Examines the subject matter required for "a poetic yet
     commercially possible cinema."

152. Kiesling, Barrett C. "The Scenario Writer." *Talking
     Pictures: How They Are Made, How to Appreciate Them.*
     Richmond, Virginia: Johnson Publishing Company, pp.
     70-80.

     Explains the step-by-step procedure for the transforma-
     tion of a literary property into a form for filming.

153. Marion, Francis. "Adaptation." *How To Write and Sell
     Film Stories: With a Complete Shooting Script for
     "Marco Polo" by Robert E. Sherwood.* New York: Covici
     Friede, pp. 211-18.

     A general essay offering basic advice to adaptors
     of novels, stage plays, biographies and historical mate-
     rials.

154. Miller, Henry. *Scenario (A Film with Sound).* With a
     Frontispiece by Abraham Rattner. Paris: The Obelisk
     Press. Reprinted in *The Cosmological Eye.* Norfolk,

Connecticut: New Directions, 1939, pp. 75-106. See also
Henry Miller, "Scenario." *Cinemage* (Special Issue) 9
(August 1958): 39-56; and Anaïs Nin, *"The House of
Incest." Cinemage* (Special Issue) 9 (August 1958): 38-
39. [Not seen.]

A scenario by Henry Miller inspired by Anaïs Nin's
The House of Incest.

155.   Nicoll, Allardyce. "Literature and Film." *The English
       Journal* 26: 1-9.

"With the growth of the film and its incursion into the
world of literature, it is becoming increasingly necessary
that educators should explain clearly and emphasize those
things which are likely to aid in a proper appreciation
of the modern 'literary film.'"

156.   Panofsky, Erwin. "Style and Medium in the Moving Pictures."
       Transition no. 26: 121-33. Revised and printed in
       Critique 1, 3 (January-February 1947). Reprinted in
       Film: An Anthology. Ed. Daniel Talbot. New York: Simon
       and Schuster, 1959, pp. 15-32.

Film offers an experience to the viewer which cannot
be duplicated by the theater or by literature.

157.   Patterson, Frances Taylor. "The Author and Hollywood."
       The North American Review 244: 77-89.

Deplores the film's dependence on "those ventriloquists,
the stage and fiction."

                              1938

158.   Christeson, Frances Mary. *Guide to the Literature of the
       Motion Picture.* Los Angeles: The University of Southern
       California Press.

The bibliography lists and annotates 25 selected volumes
on the subject of film. Included is a list of 100 books
which trace the development of the motion picture, a list
of periodicals devoted to the motion picture and a list
of published scripts.

1939

159. Agee, James. *"Man's Fate." Films* 1, 1: 51-60. Reprinted
in *The Collected Short Prose of James Agee*. Ed. and
with a Memoir by Robert Fitzgerald. Boston: Houghton
Mifflin, 1968, pp. 205-17.

Agee's notes for a film treatment of André Malraux's
novel.

160. Brownell, Baker. "The Drama, the Novel, the Movie."
*Art Is Action: A Discussion of Nine Arts in a Modern
World*. New York: Harper & Brothers, pp. 159-70.

"It is unfortunate in some ways that the movie should
imitate the drama and the novel, compete with them and
drive them out of business. For the movie is so unique
as an instrument that it might better be the basis of
an art in its own right."

161. Gorky, Maxim. "Descent to the Lower Depths." *Films* 1, 1:
40-50.

Gorky's unfinished sketch for the scenario of his own
play.

162. Myerscough-Walker, Raymond. *Stage and Film Decor*. London:
Sir Isaac Pitman & Sons.

On the different requirements of constructing and light-
ing stage and film sets.

1940

163. Lillard, Richard. "Movies Aren't Literary." *The English
Journal* 29: 735-43.

The best sources for film should not come from literature: "No successful playwrights, no great authors, no
writers of best sellers are necessary in the studios."

164. Locke, Edwin. "Adaptation of Reality: *The Grapes of Wrath*."
Films 1, 1: 49-55.

The film's faithfulness to the Steinbeck novel is
equally matched by its faithfulness to the presentation
"of the qualities of real people."

165. Wilder, Thornton, and Sol Lesser. *"Our Town*--From Stage
to Screen." *Theatre Arts* 24: 815-24.

A correspondence between Wilder, author of *Our Town*, and Lesser, who produced the film.

1941

166. Poggioli, Renato. "Aesthetics of Stage and Screen." *The Journal of Aesthetics and Art Criticism* 1, 2-3: 63-69.

Considers questions of time and space, directorial control and technique, and acting in both stage and screen work.

1942

167. Kennedy, Margaret. "Adaptations." *The Mechanical Muse*. London: George Allen & Unwin, pp. 26-35.

Insightful remarks on the inherent problem in novel and stage play adaptation to the screen.

168. Mizener, Arthur. "The Elizabethan Art of Our Movies." *The Kenyon Review* 4: 181-94.

"The movies are an art with amazing resources and a very considerable accomplishment already to their credit, and ... they offer the critics, who have been looking so hard in other places for such a thing, the makings of a great popular art."

169. Nichols, Dudley. "Film Writing." *Theatre Arts* 26: 770-74.

"It is no easy thing to translate a good novel or play into terms of film: it is certainly as difficult as a good literary translation, in my own opinion more so, and the perfect literary translation calls for a talent not inferior to that of the original creator."

1943

170. Eisenstein, Sergei M. "Word and Image." *The Film Sense*. Trans. and ed. Jay Leyda. London: Faber and Faber, pp. 3-65.

Eisenstein finds a similarity between the way poets structure effects in poetry and the way the filmmaker structures his effects through the use of montage.

171. Gassner, John. "The Screenplay as Literature." *Twenty Best
      Film Plays*. Ed. John Gassner and Dudley Nichols. 2 vols.
      New York: Crown Publishers, I, vii-xxx. Reprinted in
      *Great Film Plays: Being Volume I of a New Edition of
      "Twenty Best Film Plays."* Ed. John Gassner and Dudley
      Nichols. New York: Crown Publishers, 1959.

      The screenplay is a new form of literary art.

172. Nichols, Dudley. "The Writer and the Film." *Twenty Best
      Film Plays*. Ed. John Gassner and Dudley Nichols. 2 vols.
      New York: Crown Publishers, I, xxxi-xl. Partially
      reprinted in *Theatre Arts* 28: 591-602. Fully reprinted
      in *A Casebook on Film*. Ed. Charles Samuels. New York:
      Van Nostrand Reinhold Company, 1970, pp. 71-77.

      On the subject of the writer's contribution to film-
      making.

                                1944

173. Dozier, William. "Sold to the Movies." *The Saturday
      Evening Post* 216 (3 June): 24-25, 101.

      Traces "the career of a novel on its way to your neigh-
      borhood movie."

174. Hutton, C. Clayton. *The Making of "Henry V."* London: E.J.
      Day.

      Account of the making of the Olivier film.

175. Nathan, George Jean. "Movies Versus the Stage." *The
      American Mercury* 58: 682-86.

      Rouben Mamoulian discusses differences between stage
      and screen.

176. Vale, Eugene. *The Technique of Screenplay Writing: A Book
      About the Dramatic Structure of Motion Pictures*. With
      a Foreword by Marc Connelly. New York: Crown Publishers.

      Draws numerous parallels between the structure of the
      screenplay and the structure of other literary genres,
      particularly the drama.

                                    1945

177. Chandler, Raymond. "Writers in Hollywood." *The Atlantic Monthly* 176 (November): 50-54.

      "In spite of all I have said, the writers of Hollywood *are* winning their battle for prestige."

178. Croydon, John. "Film Prospecting Among the Yorkshire Schools." *The Dickensian* 41 (Summer): 121-25.

      The associate producer of a film version of *Nicholas Nickleby* describes the search for the original of Dotheboys Hall.

179. Nichols, Dudley. "Writer, Director and Film." *Best Film Plays of 1943-1944.* Ed. John Gassner and Dudley Nichols. New York: Crown Publishers, pp. xxi-xxx. Reprinted by Garland Publishing, New York, 1977.

      "Film is not limited to the dramatic and narrative forms but can also find its counterpart in all the poetic forms."

                                    1946

180. Deans, Marjorie. *Meeting at the Sphinx: Gabriel Pascal's Production of Bernard Shaw's "Caesar and Cleopatra."* London: Macdonald.

      Not seen.

181. Manvell, Roger. "The Poetry of the Film." *New Road: Directions in European Art and Letters. Number 4.* Ed. Fred Marnau. London: Grey Walls Press, pp. 152-64. Reprinted in *The Penguin Film Review* 6 (1948): 111-24 and in *The Penguin Film Review 1946-1949.* Ed. Roger Manvell. 2 vols. London: The Scolar Press, II, 111-24.

      "The medium of cinema, like that of poetry, derives its strength from the comparison of images, the swift relation of ideas through the juxtaposition of human actions."

182. Nathan, Robert. "A Novelist Looks at Hollywood." *Hollywood Quarterly* 1: 146-47.

      A "picture is not at all like a play; ... on the contrary, it is like a novel, but a novel to be seen, instead of told."

183. Nichols, Dudley. "The Machine from the God." *Best Film Plays--1945.* Ed. John Gassner and Dudley Nichols. New York: Crown Publishers, pp. xxiii-xxxvii. Reprinted by Garland Publishing, New York, 1977.

The writer's challenge in Hollywood.

184. Phillips, James E. "Adapted from a Play by W. Shakespeare." *Hollywood Quarterly* 2: 82-87.

In his adaptation of Shakespeare's *Henry V*, "Mr. Olivier has given us ... a twentieth-century conception of a sixteenth-century conception of a historical fifteenth-century king."

185. Shelley, Frank. *Stage and Screen.* London: Pendulum Publications.

Not seen.

1947

186. Ball, Robert Hamilton. "If We Shadows Have Offended." *The Pacific Spectator* (Winter): 97-104.

Not seen.

187. S., L.C. "*Great Expectations* Realised." *The Dickensian* 43 (Spring): 79-81.

Praise for "both a good film and a worthy transcription of a great book."

188. S., L.C. "*Nicholas Nickleby* as a Film." *The Dickensian* 43 (Summer): 131-33.

The film is "as near perfection as any reasonable Dickensian could expect."

189. Salemson, Harold J. "The Camera as Narrator--Technique or Toy." *Screen Writing* 2 (March): 38-41.

Not seen.

1948

190. Bentley, Eric. "*Monsieur Verdoux* as 'Theater.'" *The Kenyon Review* 10: 705-16.

Chaplin's performance in his film draws much of its inspiration from the comic stage.

191. Cross, Brenda, ed. *The Film "Hamlet": A Record of Its Production*. London: The Saturn Press.

On the making of the Laurence Olivier film.

192. Dent, Alan, ed. *"Hamlet": The Film and the Play*. London: World Film Publications.

Not seen.

193. Hunt, Peter. "Research for Films for Dickens." *The Dickensian* 44 (Winter): 94-97.

Recounts anecdotes about problems encountered while researching the background for David Lean's adaptation of *Oliver Twist*.

194. Leech, Clifford. "Dialogue for Stage and Screen." *The Penguin Film Review* 6: 97-103. Reprinted in *The Penguin Film Review 1946-1949*. Ed. Roger Manvell. 2 vols. London: The Scolar Press, 1977, II, 97-103.

"Only in the cinema is 'real life' dialogue possible."

195. Lindgren, Ernest. "The Anatomy of the Fiction Film." *The Art of the Film*. New York: The Macmillan Company, 2nd ed., 1963, pp. 45-54.

General survey of kinds of fictional representation open to the novelist, playwright and script writer.

196. S., L.C. "David Lean's *Oliver Twist*." *The Dickensian* 44 (Autumn): 203-05.

"David Lean's attempt to tell the story by means of a camera to which everything is subservient is, in my view, brilliantly successful."

197. Schmidt, Georg; Werner Schmalenbach; and Peter Bälchin. *The Film: Its Economic, Social, and Artistic Problems*. London: The Falcon Press.

Use of pictorial displays and diagrams to summarize and reinforce the special qualities film possesses as opposed to the other arts.

198. Shakespeare, William, and Laurence Olivier. "*Hamlet*: The Play and the Screenplay." *Hollywood Quarterly* 3: 293-300.

Excerpts from Shakespeare's *Hamlet* and from Olivier's screenplay printed in parallel columns for the sake of comparison.

1949

199. Ashworth, John. "Olivier, Freud, and Hamlet." *Atlantic Monthly* 183 (May): 30-33.

Criticizes Olivier for acting in and directing "a *Hamlet* with a simplified Freudian interpretation."

200. Barbarow, George. "Hamlet Through a Telescope." *The Hudson Review* 2: 98-104.

The Olivier film is marred by confusing camera work, a drastically shortened text, and imperfectly conceived dramatic moments.

201. Eisenstein, Sergei. "Dickens, Griffith, and the Film Today." *Film Form: Essays in Film Theory*. Trans. and ed. Jay Leyda. New York: Harcourt, Brace and Company, pp. 195-255. Reprinted in *Film and the Liberal Arts*. Ed. T.J. Ross. New York: Holt, Rinehart and Winston, 1970, pp. 103-10.

This classic study traces Dickens' influence upon D.W. Griffith and the American film esthetic. Technical elements in Griffith's films, examined in light of Dickens' method, style, viewpoint and exposition, reveal that he inspired innovative technical achievements in Griffith's work. For Eisenstein the most important innovation was the use of parallel montage.

202. Lawson, John Howard. *Theory and Technique of Playwrighting and Screenwriting*. New York: G.P. Putnam's Sons. A revised edition of the author's *Theory and Technique of Playwrighting*, 1936, with a new section on screenwriting.

Not seen.

203. McManaway, James G. "The Laurence Olivier *Hamlet*." *Shakespeare Association Bulletin* 24 (January): 3-11.

Not seen.

204. Manvell, Roger. "The Film of 'Hamlet.'" *The Penguin Film Review* 8: 16-24. Reprinted in *The Penguin Film Review 1946-1949*. Ed. Roger Manvell. 2 vols. London: The Scolar Press, 1977, II, 16-24.

In *Hamlet*, Laurence Olivier has come nearest to the successful solution or "artistic compromise" required in "bringing verbal poetry into a pictorial art."

205. Tyler, Parker. "*Hamlet* and Documentary." *The Kenyon Review* 11: 527-32. See M.D. Heckscher, *The Kenyon Review* 11: 673-74.

"By accepting the two most obvious 'interpretations' of Hamlet's character, Olivier utterly relieved himself of the obligation of a personal interpretation; thus, he has operated more as director than actor and composed a 'filmic essay' on Everybody's 'Hamlet' (i.e., one in 'black and white')."

206. Vardac, Nicholas. *Stage and Screen: Theatrical Method from Garrick to Griffith*. New York: Benjamin Blom.

Demonstrates how thoroughly almost every technical device employed by the silent film had its equivalent in nineteenth-century stage techniques.

207. Wilson, Richard. "'Macbeth' on Film." *Theatre Arts* 33, 5: 53-55.

On the preparation for and filming of Orson Welles' version of *Macbeth*.

1950

208. Asheim, Lester. "From Book to Film." *Reader in Public Opinion and Communication*. Ed. Bernard Berelson and Morris Janowitz. Glencoe, Illinois: The Free Press, pp. 299-306.

Excerpt from Asheim's dissertation indicating his method of analysis for determining the probable pattern of change likely to occur in the adaptation of novels to film.

209. Babcock, R.W. "George Lyman Kittredge, Olivier, and the Historical Hamlet." *College English* 11: 256-65.

Compares Kittredge's interpretation of an "active" Hamlet with Olivier's "amazingly similar" interpretation of Hamlet in the film.

210. Balchin, Nigel. "Writing in Pictures." *Diversion: Twenty-two Authors on the Lively Arts*. Ed. John Sutro. London: Max Parrish & Co., pp. 146-55.

   "My problems have not been the normal ones that most novelists seem to strike in writing for the film industry, but the duller technical ones arising from trying to translate a story from one medium to another."

211. Cocteau, Jean. *Diary of a Film ("La Belle et la Bête")*. Trans. Ronald Duncan. New York: Roy Publishers. Reprinted as *Beauty and the Beast: Diary of a Film*. Dover Publications, New York, 1972.

   The diary was kept while Cocteau was making *Beauty and the Beast*, a film inspired by Mme. Leprince de Beaumont's eighteenth-century fairy tale. While the diary does not contain a consistent record of the adaptation, it does record Cocteau's varied experiences making the film.

212. Koch, Howard. "A Playwright Looks at the Filmwright." *Sight and Sound* 19, 5: 210-14. See Thorold Dickinson, *Sight and Sound* 19, 1: 20-25.

   The role of the writer cannot be dismissed when one discusses any feature or story film.

213. MacMullan, Hugh. "Translating 'The Glass Menagerie' to Film." *Hollywood Quarterly* 5: 14-32.

   "The translation of background and symbol" from Tennessee Williams' play to screen was not "too difficult" but "continuity and performance were another matter."

214. Manvell, Roger; Thorold Dickinson; and Michael Bell. "A Symposium on 'The Queen of Spades.'" *The Cinema 1950*. Ed. Roger Manvell. Harmondsworth, Middlesex: Penguin Books, pp. 46-77.

   The film of Pushkin's story "The Queen of Spades" is used as a basis for argument about the problems of film adaptations of literature. Here printed is an essay by Manvell which comments on the story and the film, followed by director Dickinson's essay responding to Manvell, and finally Bell's essay commenting on the two previous essays and on the art of film in general.

215. Rattigan, Terence. "A Magnificent Pity for Camels." *Diversion: Twenty-two Authors on the Lively Arts*. Ed. John Sutro. London: Max Parrish & Co., pp. 85-96.

The screenwriter is not accorded the same respect as the playwright, nor will the disparity be eliminated until proper attention is paid to the screenwriter as opposed to the director.

216. Schary, Dore. *Case History of a Movie*. By Dore Schary as told to Charles Palmer. New York: Random House. Reprinted by Garland Publishing, New York, 1978.

      Account of the writing and making of the film *The Next Voice You Hear*, which was inspired by George Sumner Albee's short story.

1951

217. Asheim, Lester. "From Book to Film: Mass Appeals." *Hollywood Quarterly* 5: 334-49.

      Discusses three methods often used to simplify and make more appealing film adaptation of novels: solving universal problems through personal solutions, individualizing evil and emphasizing sensationalism.

218. Asheim, Lester. "From Book to Film: The Note of Affirmation." *The Quarterly of Film, Radio, and Television* 6: 54-68.

      Discusses the use of mass-appeal formulas--the "love story" and the "happy ending"--in the adaptation of novels to film.

219. Asheim, Lester. "From Book to Film: Simplification." *Hollywood Quarterly* 5: 289-304.

      "No matter how demanding the novel may be, the film is generally so reorganized as to state its major points in terms that are reasonably unmistakable even to him who only passively receives the film's communication."

220. Debrix, Jean R. "The Movies and Poetry: Fundamentally and Potentially Their Missions Are the Same." *Films in Review* 2 (October): 17-22.

      "Movies are able, in the highest degree, to make reality poetical, and to make the poetical appear real."

221. Dickinson, Thorold. *"The Mayor of Casterbridge." Sight and Sound* 19: 363-71.

Excerpts from the screenplay by Dickinson and Wolfgang Wilhelm, illustrations for designs and notes by Thorold Dickinson, all for the adaptation of Hardy's novel to film. The film was not made.

222. Dickinson, Thorold, and Roger Manvell. "A Film Is Made." *The Cinema 1951.* Ed. Roger Manvell and R.K. Neilson Baxter. Harmondsworth, Middlesex: Penguin Books, pp. 9-56.

Pretending that Turgenev's short novel *The Torrents of Spring* is to be made into a film, John Sutro, Dickinson and Manvell take the parts of Producer, Director and Visitor, respectively, in order to show what must be done to adapt a work of literature to the film.

223. Dowling, Alan. "Scenarios Are an Art Form: The Best Writers Should Use It." *Films in Review* 2 (March): 9-10.

Since "a great novel is not necessarily the best material for a great movie," the scenario ought to be consciously developed into an art form.

224. Hinsdale, Harriet. "Writing for Stage and Screen: The Means, and the Ends, Are the Same." *Films in Review* 2 (January): 25-28.

"In writing for both stage and screen, technique is secondary and content, or, if you like, character and idea, are paramount."

225. Hutchins, Patricia. "James Joyce and the Cinema." *Sight and Sound* 21: 9-12.

Joyce was interested in the cinema and collaborated on a film project with Stuart Gilbert. Includes "Sketch of a Scenario of 'Anna Livia Plurabelle'" by Stuart Gilbert.

226. Maugham, Somerset. *Encore.* London: Heinemann.

Contains three original stories by Maugham, "The Ant and the Grasshopper," "Winter Cruise" and "Gigolo and Gigolette," together with the screenplays written by T.E.B. Clarke, Arthur Macrae and Eric Ambler.

227. Phillips, James. "By William Shakespeare—with Additional Dialogue." *Hollywood Quarterly* 5: 224-36.

Laurence Olivier's adaptations of Shakespeare, *Henry V* and *Hamlet*, and Orson Welles' *Macbeth* suggest that the

film directors had no faith in Shakespeare's dramatic or
theatrical sense whatsoever.

228.   Stern, Seymour. "Griffith and Poe: One of America's
       Greatest Authors Influenced America's Greatest Director."
       Films in Review 2 (September): 23-28.

       "Griffith used Poe's material with due respect for its
       essential quality, but with a free rein to his own
       spirited originality, imagination and touch."

229.   Thorp, Margaret. "The Motion Picture and the Novel."
       American Quarterly 3: 195-203.

       Points out the lack of attention paid by filmmakers to
       point of view. "The expert director, to be sure, shoots
       almost always from a defined point of view but he seems
       to select it by instinct rather than design."

230.   Weeks, Ruth Mary. "Use Films--Yes, But Keep It English."
       The English Journal 40: 139-43.

       Comments on the use in the classroom of films adapted
       from classic works of literature.

                                1952

231.   Asheim, Lester. "From Book to Film: Summary." *The Quarterly
       of Film, Radio, and Television* 6: 258-73.

       In this study of twenty-four novels and their film
       adaptations, it is shown that "the simplification imposed
       on adaptations ... is clearly a result of assumed audience
       intelligence more than it is of the needs of the medium."

232.   Balázs, Béla. "Dialogue," "The Script" and "Art Form and
       Material." *Theory of the Film (Character and Growth of
       a New Art)*. London: Dennis Dobson, pp. 221-31; 246-57;
       258-65.

       The development of the sound film at first encouraged
       filmmakers to resort to filmed theater, but dialogue in
       film, as filmmakers have learned, must be used differently
       from stage dialogue.
       The film script must be recognized as a distinct art
       form conditioned by the materials of the art of film.
       The art form need not be dictated by the nature of the
       material being used by the artist; therefore, an adapta-
       tion of material from one art form to another need not
       be thought "inartistic" on principle.

233. Ball, Robert Hamilton. "The Shakespeare Film as Record: Sir Herbert Beerbohm Tree." *Shakespeare Survey* 3: 227-36.

Early films of Shakespeare's plays show us "something of the history and nature of performance."

234. Barbarow, George. "Dreiser's Place on the Screen." *The Hudson Review* 5: 290-94.

"*A Place in the Sun* is a pathetic misreading of the novel, whether deliberate or not, pathetic because Stevens seems to be sincere in his effort to 'base' his picture on Dreiser, and because the director's methods lack the scope to encompass the subject."

235. Benedek, Laslo. "Directing *Death of a Salesman* for the Screen." *Theatre Arts* 36, 1: 36-37, 87.

Every effort was made to bring the Arthur Miller play to the screen "with complete honesty and integrity."

236. Benedek, Laslo. "Play into Picture." *Sight and Sound* 22: 82-84, 96.

On the film adaptation of *Death of a Salesman*.

237. Brooks, Richard. "A Novel Isn't a Movie: And to Become One It Should--and Must--Be Changed." *Films in Review* 3: 55-59.

A movie must be "a good movie *first*" and "a good adaptation of a novel, story, play or whatnot, *second*."

238. Broughton, James. "Some Notes on Poetry and Film." *Sight and Sound* 21: 126-27.

Draws comparisons between film and poetry.

239. Eliot, T.S. "Preface." *The Film of "Murder in the Cathedral."* London: Faber and Faber, pp. 7-10. Reprinted in *Authors on Film*. Ed. Harry M. Geduld. Bloomington and London: Indiana University Press, 1972, pp. 190-95. See 241.

"In some respects--notably in the choral passages--this film version makes the meaning clearer and in that way is nearer to what the play would have been, had it been written for the London theatre and by a dramatist of greater experience."

240. Fawcett, F. Dubrez. "Dickens on the Screen." *Dickens the*
      Dramatist on Stage, Screen and Radio. London: W.H. Allen,
      pp. 193-208. See "Appendix A: Plays and Adaptations of
      the Works of Charles Dickens for Stage, Screen and
      Television," pp. 232-54.

      Brief commentary on silent and sound film adaptations
      of Dickens' works.

241. Hoellering, George. "Preface." *The Film of "Murder in*
      the Cathedral." London: Faber and Faber, pp. 11-14.
      See also "The Film of *Murder in the Cathedral.*" *Film*
      no. 7 (January-February 1956): 6-9. [Not seen.] See 239.

      "I should like *Murder in the Cathedral* [(1952)] to be -
      garded as an experiment in a new type of film, where
      dialogue is at last given an equal place to picture, and
      where the audience is called upon to listen and to look."

242. Huston, John. *"The African Queen." Theatre Arts* 36, 2:
      48-49, 92.

      Huston and James Agee collaborated on the script for
      the adaptation of C.S. Forester's novel.

243. Kazan, Elia. "Elia Kazan on 'Zapata.'" *The Saturday Review*
      35 (5 April): 22. See Hollis Alpert, 35 (9 February):
      25-26; Carleton Beals, 35 (24 May): 25-27; and Elia
      Kazan, 35 (24 May): 28.

      A response to a review defending the Kazan-Steinbeck
      interpretation in the film.

244. Lean, David. "Extract from the Post-Production Script
      of *Great Expectations*: Pip Steals the Food." *The Cinema*
      1952. Ed. Roger Manvell and R.K. Neilson Baxter. Har-
      mondsworth, Middlesex: Penguin Books, pp. 19-29.

      "What we wanted to create all the time was the world
      as it seemed to Pip when his imagination was distorted
      with fear. That, after all, was what Dickens himself
      did."

245. MacLiammóir, Mícheál. *Put Money in Thy Purse: The Film*
      of "Othello." With a Preface by Orson Welles. London:
      Methuen and Co.

      An account of the genesis and filming of Welles' version
      of *Othello.*

246. Mendilow, A.A. "Fiction and the Other Arts." *Time and the Novel*. London, New York: P. Nevill. Reprinted by Humanities Press, New York, 1972, pp. 53-59.

    A brief examination of ways in which novelists have borrowed and applied the techniques of both music and film.

247. Pichel, Irving. "Revivals, Reissues, Remakes and 'A Place in the Sun.'" *The Quarterly of Film, Radio, and Television* 6: 388-93.

    George Stevens' adaptation of Theodore Dreiser's *An American Tragedy* "may not be the story Dreiser wrote, but it is what remains today of the novel."

248. Raynor, Henry. "Shakespeare Filmed." *Sight and Sound* 22: 10-15.

    Comments on Olivier's *Hamlet* (1948) and *Henry V* (1944) and Welles' *Macbeth* (1948). "A Shakespeare play has not yet been successfully transplanted to the screen."

249. Reisz, Karel. "Substance into Shadow." *The Cinema 1952*. Ed. Roger Manvell and R.K. Neilson Baxter. Harmondsworth, Middlesex: Penguin Books, pp. 188-205.

    An examination of "what is gained and what is lost in the film adaptations of four ... novels, Hammett's *The Maltese Falcon*, Hemingway's *To Have and Have Not*, Faulkner's *Intruder in the Dust*, and Henry Brown's *A Walk in the Sun*, and the nature of style in authorship and film-making."

250. Ross, Lillian. "Onward and Upward with the Arts." *The New Yorker* 28 (24 May): 32-36+; 28 (31 May): 29-32+; 28 (7 June): 32-34+; 28 (14 June): 39-40; 28 (21 June): 31-32+. Reprinted as *Picture*. New York, Toronto: Rinehart & Company, 1952.

    Anecdotes and experiences acquired during the making of John Huston's *The Red Badge of Courage* (1951).

251. Williams, Tennessee. "In the Script: *A Streetcar Named Desire*." *Sight and Sound* 22: 173-75.

    Printed here are "two slightly different versions" of the ending of the screenplay of *A Streetcar Named Desire*, "the first being a revision (about two months later) of the second. In addition, a final note attached to the script indicates the various possibilities seen by Elia

Kazan and Tennessee Williams." For the sake of comparison, the original ending of the play is included as well.

252. Young, Vernon. "Dickens Without Holly: David Lean's *Oliver Twist*." *New Mexico Quarterly* 22: 425-30.

Lean has successfully adapted Dickens' *Oliver Twist* to the film medium.

1953

253. Ball, Robert Hamilton. "Shakespeare in One Reel." *The Quarterly of Film, Radio, and Television* 8: 139-49.

Traces the history of Shakespeare films of a thousand feet or less and contained in one reel.

254. Fabun, Don. "Science Fiction in Motion Pictures, Radio and Television." *Modern Science Fiction*. Ed. Reginald Bretnor. New York: Coward-McCann, pp. 43-70.

A survey of a number of science fiction films adapted from literature.

255. Fulton, A.R. "'It's Exactly Like the Play.'" *Theatre Arts* 37, 2: 78-83.

A survey of a number of films adapted from novels and plays. "The more literally good plays are filmed, the better the theatre is served. But not the motion pictures."

256. Griffin, Alice Venezky. "Shakespeare Through the Camera's Eye--*Julius Caesar* in Motion Pictures; *Hamlet* and *Othello* on Television." *Shakespeare Quarterly* 4: 331-36.

Joseph L. Mankiewicz's *Julius Caesar* is "the best Shakespeare film Hollywood has ever made."

257. Griggs, Earl Leslie. "II. The Film Seen and Heard." *The Quarterly of Film, Radio, and Television* 8: 93-99. See 269.

The effect of the combination on film of recited poetry (S.T. Coleridge's "The Rime of the Ancient Mariner") and Gustave Doré's illustrations upon a viewer is "extra-ordinary."

258. Houseman, John. "Filming *Julius Caesar*." *Sight and Sound* 23: 24-27.

On the challenges of filming the Mankiewicz adaptation of *Julius Caesar* (1953).

259. Houseman, John. "*Julius Caesar*: Mr. Mankiewicz's Shooting Script." *The Quarterly of Film, Radio, and Television* 8: 109-24.

Two fragments of the screenplay are presented "as a practical example of one way in which a classic stage piece may be adapted" to film.

260. Houseman, John. "On Filming 'Julius Caesar.' The Problem Was to Present Shakespeare's Words in a Medium Primarily Visual." *Films in Review* 4: 184-88.

Special solutions were required to preserve Shakespearean dialogue in the film.

261. Houseman, John. "This Our Lofty Scene." *Theatre Arts* 37, 5: 26-28.

On the problems inherent in "translating Shakespeare's bloody and turbulent melodrama into a medium where both mass effects and personal conflicts can be closely observed and more fully developed than under the constant and unchanging focus of a playhouse stage."

262. Jones, Dorothy B. "William Faulkner: Novel into Film." *The Quarterly of Film, Radio, and Television* 8: 51-71.

"The motion picture *Intruder in the Dust* is fundamentally a faithful screen adaptation of the Faulkner story."

263. Kaplan, Abraham. "Realism in the Film: A Philosopher's Viewpoint." *The Quarterly of Film, Radio, and Television* 7: 370-84.

The Long Voyage Home (1940) is discussed in the context of definitions of realism appropriate to traditions in Western literature.

264. Langer, Susanne K. "Appendix: A Note on the Film." *Feeling and Form: A Theory of Art Developed from "Philosophy in a New Key."* New York: Charles Scribner's Sons, pp. 411-15.

The structure of the motion picture lies closer to that of the drama than the novel. The artistic potential of film "became evident only when the moving camera was introduced."

265. Pasinetti, P.M. "*Julius Caesar*: The Role of the Technical
      Advisor." *The Quarterly of Film, Radio, and Television*
      8: 131-38.

      The technical advisor explains his role in adapting
      Shakespeare's play for the film.

266. Phillips, James E. "*Julius Caesar*: Shakespeare as a
      Screen Writer." *The Quarterly of Film, Radio, and Tele-
      vision* 8: 125-30.

      Julius Caesar (1953) reveals "a fidelity to Shakespeare's
      original in adaptation and filming that would have satis-
      fied even the hypercritical Hamlet."

267. Reinhardt, Gottfried. "Sound Track Narration: Its Use
      Is Not Always a Resort of the Lazy and Incompetent."
      Films in Review 4: 459-60.

      Effectiveness of sound track narration in John Huston's
      The Red Badge of Courage (1951).

268. S., L.C. "*Pickwick* on the Screen." *The Dickensian* 49
      (March): 75-76.

      The film version is "frequently delightful, sometimes
      exasperating."

269. Shull, William M. "I. Translating with Film." *The
      Quarterly of Film, Radio, and Television* 8: 88-92. See
      257.

      Gustave Doré's illustrations are used as part of a
      filmed recording of S.T. Coleridge's "The Rime of the
      Ancient Mariner."

270. Smith, John Harrington. "Oscar Wilde's *Earnest* in Film."
      The Quarterly of Film, Radio, and Television 8: 72-79.

      The film adaptation "is a respectable production, in
      some ways a delightful one, on which much care has been
      expended."

271. Walker, Roy. "Look Upon Caesar." *The Twentieth Century*
      154: 469-74.

      Though the Houseman-Mankiewicz adaptation of Shakespeare's
      Julius Caesar is marred by their political bias, it is
      "the best Shakespeare film to date."

1954

272. Cocteau, Jean. *Cocteau on the Film.* A conversation re-
      corded by André Fraigneau, trans. Vera Traill. New
      York: Roy Publishers. Reprinted by Dover, New York,
      1972.

      An interview with Cocteau in which scattered, thoughtful
      remarks touch upon the relationship between film and
      literature.

273. Davidson, James F. "Memory of Defeat in Japan: A Reap-
      praisal of 'Rashomon.'" *The Antioch Review* 14: 492-501.
      Reprinted in *Focus on "Rashomon."* Ed. Donald Richie.
      Englewood Cliffs, New Jersey: Prentice-Hall, 1972,
      pp. 119-28.

      A comparison of the Akutagawa stories with the film
      is used to suggest that the film reflects in its overtones
      and in many details emotions felt by a people recently
      defeated in war.

274. Dehn, Paul. "The Filming of Shakespeare." *Talking of
      Shakespeare.* Ed. John Garrett. London: Hodder & Stoughton,
      pp. 49-72.

      A survey of the merits and faults of a number of films
      of Shakespeare's plays, with advice as to which would
      be most accessible to young students of Shakespeare.
      Generous attention is paid to Olivier's *Henry V* (1944)
      and *Hamlet* (1948), Mankiewicz's *Julius Caesar* (1953)
      and Welles' *Othello* (1951).

275. Goodman, Paul. "Special Problems of Unity." *The Structure
      of Literature.* Chicago: The University of Chicago Press,
      pp. 235-45.

      René Clair's adaptation of Labiche's play *Un Chapeau
      de Paille d'Italie* is compared with the original in this
      consideration of the film adaptation of the drama.

276. Knight, Arthur. "Three Problems in Film Adaptation."
      The Saturday Review 37 (18 December): 26-28.

      Examines Renato Castellani's *Romeo and Juliet* (1954),
      George Seaton's adaptation of Clifford Odets' *The Country
      Girl* and the animated cartoon version of George Orwell's
      Animal Farm.

277. Mason, James. "Back to the Stage: A Distinguished British
      Actor Begins Appraising the Two Facets of His Career."
      Films in Review 5: 327-32.

      Weighs the merits and disadvantages of working in both
      arts.

278. Orrom, Michael. "Film and Its Dramatic Techniques." *Preface
      to Film.* By Raymond Williams and Michael Orrom. London:
      Film Drama Limited, pp. 57-117.

      Provides a "reappraisal of film's technical and dramatic
      conventions" by way of encouraging experimentation in
      new forms and themes in filmmaking.

279. Schary, Dore. "Literature and the Screen." *The English
      Journal* 43: 135-41.

      A consideration of "problems that face the motion-pic-
      ture writer and director and producer when they translate
      literature from one form to another."

280. Wald, Jerry. "Screen Adaptation: It Is More of an Art
      Than the Cognoscenti Admit and More Effective Than
      Audiences Realize." *Films in Review* 5, 2: 62-67.

      "The screenwriter who adapts a well known play or novel
      lives in a special kind of Purgatory, for he can never
      entirely please the original author, and *everyone* who
      has read the original work has positive and definite ideas
      and illusions about plot, characterization, background
      and motivation which a mere screen writer, and a mere
      producer, and a few mere stars, and a couple of mere
      million dollars, can never equal."

281. Walker, Roy. "In Fair Verona." *The Twentieth Century*
      156: 464-71. Partially reprinted in *Focus on Shakespearean
      Films.* Ed. Charles W. Eckert. Englewood Cliffs, New
      Jersey: Prentice-Hall, 1972, pp. 115-21.

      Castellani's adaptation of *Romeo and Juliet* captures
      the spectacle and beauty of the city of Verona but lacks
      the passion and coherence in Shakespeare's play.

282. Williams, Raymond. "Film and the Dramatic Tradition."
      Preface to Film. By Raymond Williams and Michael Orrom.
      London: Film Drama Limited, pp. 1-55.

      "I shall discuss in this essay: first, the general
      nature of drama; second, the nature of dramatic conven-

tions; third, the conventions, and the habits, of the
drama and film of our own time; and fourth, the concept
of *total performance*, which is the film's particular
opportunity."

1955

283. Alpert, Hollis. "Movies Are Better Than the Stage." *The
Saturday Review* 38 (23 July): 5-6, 31-32. See Robert
Carroll, Robert Downing, Stanley J. Geller, Constance
S. Lapham and Dore Schary, *The Saturday Review* 38 (13
August): 19.

Laments the decline of the theater in America.

284. Fulton, A.R. "Stroheim's 'Greed.'" *Films in Review* 6:
263-68.

"*Greed* [(1923)] is a more nearly literal transcription
of a novel than is any other film."

285. Greg, W.W. "Shakespeare Through the Camera's Eye."
Shakespeare Quarterly 6: 63-66.

Not seen.

286. Jorgensen, Paul A. "Castellani's *Romeo and Juliet*:
Intention and Response." *The Quarterly of Film, Radio,
and Television* 10: 1-10. Reprinted in *Focus on
Shakespearean Films*. Ed. Charles W. Eckert. Englewood
Cliffs, New Jersey: Prentice-Hall, 1972, pp. 108-15.

The film was a remarkable experiment and deserved better
than the lackluster critical response it received.

287. Kozelka, Paul. "A Guide to the Screen Version of Shakespeare's *Othello*." *Audio-Visual Guide* 22, 8: 31-40.

Not seen.

288. Macgowan, Kenneth. "The Story Comes to the Screen--1896-
1906." *The Quarterly of Film, Radio, and Television*
10: 64-88.

Through the discovery of editing techniques, early
filmmakers were able to develop the narrative fiction
film.

289. Manvell, Roger. "'Poetic Realism.'" *The Film and the
Public*. Baltimore: Penguin Books, pp. 90-95.

"The imagery of the sound film is the foundation of its
poetry."

290. Weinberg, Herman G. *"Greed." Film Culture* 1, 1: 45-48.
     [Not seen.] Reprinted in *Saint Cinema: Selected Writings
     1929-1970.* New York: DBS Publications, 1970, pp. 128-36,
     and in *"Greed": A Film by Erich von Stroheim.* Ed. Joel
     W. Finler. London: Lorrimer Publishing, 1972, pp. 14-21.

     Outlines the genesis of Stroheim's adaptation of Frank
     Norris' *McTeague* and provides a description of the
     principal scenes in the book that are missing from the
     film.

                                  1956

291. "A Quiz for Kazan." *Theatre Arts* 40, 11: 30-32.

     Kazan talks about Tennessee Williams and the film
     Baby Doll (1956).

292. Bluestone, George. "Word to Image: The Problem of the
     Filmed Novel." *The Quarterly of Film, Radio, and Tele-
     vision* 11: 171-80.

     In the process of adaptation, the film abandons
     language for the visual image, an alteration usually
     fatal to the success of the adaptation.

293. Debrix, Jean. "Cinema and Poetry." *Yale French Studies*
     17: 86-104.

     "Cinema, *essentially*, is magic--is poetry."
     "Thus the film maker conscious of his art will proceed
     as does the poet, not the prose writer. Where the last-
     named seeks the greatest possible clarity, precision,
     and intellectual efficacy, the film maker aims at the
     greatest emotional intensity and psychic resonance."

294. Giesler, Rodney. "Shakespeare on the Screen." *Films and
     Filming* 2 (July): 6-7.

     Not seen.

295. Gray, Martin. "New Testament for the Old Testament."
     Films and Filming 2 (January): 8.

     Not seen.

296. Griffin, Alice. "Shakespeare Through the Camera's Eye: III." *Shakespeare Quarterly* 7: 235-40.

Among film adaptations of Shakespeare recently released—Welles' *Othello* (1951), Castellani's *Romeo and Juliet* (1954) and Olivier's *Richard III* (1955)—"only the last-named can be considered an artistic success."

297. Houston, Penelope. "The Private Eye." *Sight and Sound* 26: 22-23, 55.

On film adaptations of Raymond Chandler's and Dashiell Hammett's private detective fiction.

298. Kallich, Martin, and Malcolm M. Marsden. "Teaching Film Drama as Literature." *The Quarterly of Film, Radio, and Television* 11: 39-48. See the response by Gerald Weales, "Teaching Film Drama as Film Drama." *The Quarterly of Film, Radio, and Television* 11 (1957): 394-98.

Outline and reading selections for a course on film and theater.

299. Kozelka, Paul. "A Guide to the Screen Versions of Shakespeare's *Richard III*." *Audio-Visual Guide* 23, 8: 51-57.

Not seen.

300. Lillich, Meredith. "Shakespeare on the Screen: A Survey of How His Plays Have Been Made into Movies." *Films in Review* 7: 247-60. See 517.

In the early days it was thought that the only difficulty in filming Shakespeare plays was lack of sound; with sound, however, it became clear that "the real problem was to show visually what the Elizabethans had been called upon to imagine."

301. Oxenhandler, Neal. "Poetry in Three Films by Jean Cocteau." *Yale French Studies* 17: 14-20.

In *La Belle et la Bête*, *Le Sang d'un Poète* and *Orphée*, "Cocteau has attempted ... to convey through the cinematic medium, the conception of poetry which exists in his purely literary works."

302. Phillips, James E. "*Richard III*: Two Views I. Some Glories and Some Discontents." *The Quarterly of Film, Radio, and Television* 10: 399-407. See 305.

The praise given Olivier's adaptation of Shakespeare's *Richard III* is not wholly deserved.

303. Reisman, Leon. "The Oral Tradition, the Written Word, and the Screen Image." *Film Culture* 2: 1-5.

     Not seen.

304. Rivette, Jacques, and François Truffaut. "Howard Hawks: One of Our Most Versatile Directors Believes the Story Is More Important Than Anything Else." *Films in Review* 7: 443-52.

     Hawks discusses a number of his films, several of which were adapted from literature.

305. Schein, Harry. "*Richard III.* Two Views II. A Magnificent Fiasco?" *The Quarterly of Film, Radio, and Television* 10: 407-15. See 302.

     Although Olivier's interpretation of Richard III has simplified the character's complexity, the film remains a remarkable achievement.

306. Seaton, George. "A Comparison of the Playwright and the Screen Writer." *The Quarterly of Film, Radio, and Television* 10: 217-26.

     A screenwriter adapting a stage play must consider camera movement, the structural needs of screen continuity, differences in acting styles, audience expectations of technical sophistication, the audience's need to understand all references in the dialogue and the inevitable need to simplify.

307. Silbajoris, Frank R. "*War and Peace* on the Screen." *College English* 18: 41-45.

     "The film whets the appetite for the book. This is its achievement. In most other respects it fails."

308. Stern, Milton R. "The Whale and the Minnow: *Moby Dick* and the Movies." *College English* 17: 470-73.

     "Destroying symbolic unity in an attempt to meet the demands of the film medium, scriptwriter Ray Bradbury has lifted most of the book's scenes of pure action out of their meaningful context, and has regrouped them in order to create a fast-paced narrative."

309. Walker, Roy. "Bottled Spider." *The Twentieth Century* 159: 58-68.

Despite the director's "tampering with the text," Olivier's adaptation of Shakespeare's *Richard III* is a "triumph."

310. West, Jessamyn. *To See the Dream.* New York: Harcourt, Brace and Company.

A delightful record in diary form of Jessamyn West's involvement with the adaptation of her novel *The Friendly Persuasion* into the film *Friendly Persuasion* (1956).

                                    1957

311. Arnheim, Rudolf. "Epic and Dramatic Film." *Film Culture* 3: 9-10.

The use of the terms dramatic and epic are appropriate for the criticism of film as well as literature. Like the stage play, the dramatic film focuses on a specific "problem" and follows that problem to its resolution. The epic film is not bound by a narrow unravelling of internal conflicts but rather deals with timeless questions of man's relation to his world.

312. Atkins, John. "The Curse of the Film." *Graham Greene.* London: John Calder, pp. 78-87. Reprinted in *Graham Greene: Some Critical Considerations.* Ed. Robert O. Evans. Lexington, Kentucky: University of Kentucky Press, pp. 207-18.

Greene's increasing animosity toward American films revealed in this analysis of his film criticism in *The Spectator* and in *Night and Day* brought finally the law action of libel against him in 1937-1938.

313. Bluestone, George. *Novels into Film.* Baltimore: The Johns Hopkins Press.

"I have assumed, and attempted to demonstrate, that the two media are marked by such essentially different traits that they belong to separate artistic genera." Contents: Ch. 1, "The Limits of the Novel and the Limits of the Film," remains a classic discussion of the subject; in the remaining chapters, film adaptations of *The Informer* (1935), *Wuthering Heights* (1939), *Pride and Prejudice* (1940), *The Grapes of Wrath* (1940), *The Ox-Bow*

Incident (1943) and *Madame Bovary* (1949) are compared
with their sources.

314. Costello, Donald P. "G.B.S. The Movie Critic." *The
     Quarterly of Film, Radio, and Television* 11: 256-75.

     "Shaw was completely enthusiastic about the cinema,
     because it eliminated so many of the restrictions of the
     stage."

315. Diether, Jack. "*Richard III*. The Preservation of a Film."
     The Quarterly of Film, Radio, and Television 11: 280-93.

     "In the case of *Richard III*, 'practical' commercialism
     is definitely winning out over artistic considerations."

316. Funke, Lewis. "'Uncle Vanya' ... From Fourth Street to
     Film." *Theatre Arts* 41, 10: 28-29.

     Very minor changes were made in the theater performance
     of the Chekhov play before it was filmed by David Ross.

317. Hillway, Tyrus. "Hollywood Hunts the White Whale." *The
     Colorado Quarterly* 5: 298-305.

     A Melville scholar recounts his experiences as an ad-
     visor during the John Huston film adaptation of *Moby
     Dick*.

318. Kazan, Elia. "Writers and Motion Pictures." *The Atlantic
     Monthly* 199 (April): 67-70.

     "For as the theatre once freed itself from stale
     routines, so now pictures are beginning to make room for
     the best that a writer can bring to them. It follows
     that for the first time American writers are turning
     seriously to pictures."

319. Kirschner, Paul. "Conrad and the Film." *The Quarterly
     of Film, Radio, and Television* 11: 343-53.

     Examines the "affinity between the way Conrad imagined
     scenes and the way a film director would have to imagine
     them."

320. Riesman, Evelyn T. "Film and Fiction." *The Antioch
     Review* 17: 353-63.

     Examines film and fiction in order to show "how they
     overlap each other and where they exert pressures on one
     another, as well as differ from each other."

321. Roud, Richard. "The Empty Streets." *Sight and Sound* 26: 191-95.

    "*Member of the Wedding* is far from being a perfect film," largely because it contains "most of the short-comings that may attend the translation of [the Carson McCullers] stage play to the screen."

322. Schulberg, Budd. *A Face in the Crowd: A Play for the Screen.* Introduction by Elia Kazan. New York: Bantam Books.

    Not seen.

1958

323. Arnheim, Rudolf. "1938. A New Laocoön: Artistic Composites and the Talking Film." *Film as Art.* London: Faber and Faber, pp. 164-89. Reprinted Berkeley and Los Angeles: University of California Press, 1960, pp. 199-230.

    Investigates the ways in which words and images can be used successfully, as in the theater, and the reasons why they clash and remain irreconcilable in the "talking" film.

324. Arnheim, Rudolf. "Who Is the Author of a Film?" *Film Culture* 4: 11-13.

    "Certain films resemble animals and plants in that they have only one father. Others have a more intricate genealogy--which may be deplored by devotees of tidy setups and welcomed by anybody who enjoys the natural splendor of manifold creation."

325. Brooks, Richard. "On Filming 'Karamazov': The Problems Were All Related to the Need to Make Dostoievski Enter- taining." *Films in Review* 9: 49-52.

    "We think what [Dostoevsky] intended is in the film."

326. Clarke, T.E.B. "Every Word in Its Place." *Films and Filming* 4, 5: 10+.

    Not seen.

327. Finlay, Ian F. "Dickens in the Cinema." *The Dickensian* 54 (May): 106-09. See *The Dickensian* 54 (September): 192.

Includes general commentary and a chronological list
of films adapted from Dickens' work between 1902 and
1958.

328.   Greene, Graham. "The Novelist and the Cinema--A Personal
       Experience." *International Film Annual No. 2.* Ed.
       William Whitebait. Garden City, New York: Doubleday
       & Company, pp. 54-61.

       "It isn't the way books are made. We have to learn
       our craft more painfully, more meticulously, than these
       actors, directors and cameramen who are paid, and paid
       handsomely, whatever the result. They can always put the
       blame for a disaster elsewhere which no novelist can do."

329.   Macgowan, Kenneth. "O'Neill and a Mature Hollywood Outlook."
       Theatre Arts 42, 4: 79-81.

       Irwin Shaw's script for Delbert Mann's film *Desire
       Under the Elms* "condenses" O'Neill's play "without elimi-
       nating too much, and it expands on the past."

330.   Parker, Cecil. "Success to Dickens on the Screen." *The
       Dickensian* 54 (Spring): 73-76. See reply by Athene
       Scyler, *The Dickensian* 54 (Spring): 76-78.

       An actor's views on film versions of Dickens' novels.

331.   Richie, Donald, and Joseph L. Andrews. "Traditional
       Theater and the Film in Japan." *Film Quarterly* 12, 1:
       2-9.

       "The truth is that the traditional theater in Japan
       has given almost nothing to the film."

332.   Roman, Robert C. "Dickens' 'A Christmas Carol': The
       Screen Versions Have Been Surprisingly Few and Never
       Really Adequate." *Films in Review* 10: 572-74.

       Survey of film adaptations of Dickens' story.

333.   Roman, Robert C. "O'Neill on the Screen: His Sense of
       Fate and His Disintegrating Themes Have Rarely Been
       Profitable." *Films in Review* 9: 296-305.

       A brief survey of eight film adaptations of the works
       of Eugene O'Neill.

334.   Rudman, Harry W. "Shaw's *St. Joan* and Motion Picture
       Censorship." *The Shaw Bulletin* 2, 6: 1-14.

Although scripted by Graham Greene, the film version
of Shaw's *St. Joan* was a "critical fiasco." It failed
because "it is the kind of eviscerated version which in
1936 Shaw refused to allow to be made."

335. S., L.C. "The New Film Version of *A Tale of Two Cities*."
     The Dickensian 54: 119-20.

     Despite some "eccentricities" in the script, this ver-
     sion "gives ample evidence of a sincere desire to keep
     as closely to the ... novel as the exigencies of film-
     making permit."

336. Scott, Kenneth W. "Hawk-Eye in Hollywood: A James Fenimore
     Cooper Hero Still Awaits a Truly Appreciative Producer."
     Films in Review 9, 10: 575-79.

     Cooper's Leatherstocking Tales have not fared well in
     the many Hollywood adaptations made to date.

337. Thorp, Margaret Farrand. "Shakespeare and the Movies."
     Shakespeare Quarterly 9: 357-66.

     An adaptation of Shakespeare's plays to film must not
     fail to retain the scene proportion, the rhythm and a
     substantial amount of the poetry of the original. Olivier's
     Hamlet (1948) and *Richard III* (1955) have observed these
     requirements more successfully than Welles has done in
     Macbeth (1948) and *Othello* (1951) or Castellani in *Romeo
     and Juliet* (1954).

                              1959

338. Bluestone, George. *"The Informer." Film: An Anthology*.
     Comp. and ed. Daniel Talbot. New York: Simon and
     Schuster, pp. 221-43. Reprint of the chapter in 313.

     John Ford's adaptation of the Liam O'Flaherty novel
     respects the original but "the cumulative changes are
     so great that the result is a new species."

339. Ginna, Robert Emmett. *"Our Man in Havana." Horizon* 2
     (November): 27-31, 122-26.

     Sir Carol Reed discusses his methods of adapting
     Graham Greene's novel to film.

340. Glenville, Peter. "Roll Call for 'Rashomon.'" *Theatre
     Arts* 43, 2: 12-65.

The director of the stage version, written by Fay and
Michael Kanin after the film was made, discusses the play
and the film.

341. Hodgens, Richard. "A Brief, Tragical History of the Science
      Fiction Film." *Film Quarterly* 13, 2: 30-39.

      Despite the vitality of much science fiction, film
      adaptations have not been satisfactory.

342. Lillich, Richard B. "Hemingway on the Screen: His Univer-
      sal Themes Fared Better Than His Topical Ones." *Films
      in Review* 10: 208-18.

      A survey of thirteen film adaptations of Hemingway's
      work. "Hollywood's attempts to put Hemingway on the
      screen have succeeded when they stuck closest to Heming-
      way, and failed when they did not."

343. Robinson, David. *"Look Back in Anger." Sight and Sound*
      28, 3-4: 122-24, 179.

      The film adaptation of John Osborne's play "could not
      have the breathtaking impact of the play's first appear-
      ance; but it has still contemporaneity, exhilaration,
      excitement. And it owes them not just to Osborne's rich
      and eruptive dialogue, but to its own inherent merits."

344. Ryf, Robert S. "Joyce's Visual Imagination." *Texas
      Studies in Literature and Language* 1: 30-43.

      Demonstrates how Joyce's technique in his novels, *A
      Portrait of the Artist as a Young Man*, *Ulysses* and
      Finnegans Wake, "closely parallels, in several respects,
      that of the motion picture."

345. Tupper, Lucy. "Dickens on the Screen: His Books Have
      Been Used for Some All-time Best Pictures." *Films in
      Review* 10: 142-52.

      Silent and sound film adaptations of Dickens' work
      surveyed.

346. Wald, Jerry. "Faulkner & Hollywood: He Has Worked There
      But Never on His Own Books." *Films in Review* 10: 129-33.

      "Though Faulkner has worked on screenplays, he has
      preferred to let others adapt his books to the screen."

1960

347. Ball, Robert Hamilton. "Pioners and All: The Beginnings of Shakespeare Film." *Theatre Survey* 1: 18-42. Reprinted as a chapter in 470.

   Some uses of Shakespearean material by early filmmakers.

348. Bergman, Ingmar. "Introduction: Bergman Discusses Film-making." *Four Screenplays of Ingmar Bergman*. Trans. Lars Malmstrom and David Kushner. New York: Simon and Schuster, pp. xiii-xxii. Excerpts reprinted in "Film Has Nothing to Do with Literature." *Film: A Montage of Theories*. Ed. Richard Dyer MacCann. New York: E.P. Dutton, 1966, pp. 142-46.

   Bergman cautions against the adaptation of literary works to film, for "the character and substance of the two art forms are usually in conflict."

349. Bluestone, George. "The Changing Cowboy: From Dime Novel to Dollar Film." *Western Humanities Review* 14: 331-37.

   The changing treatment of the figure of the cowboy in literature and film.

350. Connor, Edward. "The 4 'Ellery Queens': Were No Great Shakes as Interpreters and Neither Were the Films." *Films in Review* 11: 338-42.

   "Why has Ellery Queen gotten such shoddy treatment in Hollywood?"

351. Hill, Derek. "A Writers' Wave?" *Sight and Sound* 29: 56-60.

   Commentary by a variety of British novelists and play-wrights on the obligations of screenwriting.

352. Hutton, Clayton. *"Macbeth": The Making of the Film*. London: Max Parrish, pp. 42-46.

   The story behind the making of *Macbeth* (1960), with some discussion of problems of adaptation.

353. Johnson, Albert. *"Studs Lonigan* and *Elmer Gantry."* *Sight and Sound* 29: 173-75.

   Irving Lerner, director of *Studs Lonigan* (1960), and Richard Brooks, director of *Elmer Gantry* (1960), discuss their film adaptations of the novels.

354. Kracauer, Siegfried. "The Theatrical Story" and "Interlude:
      Film and Novel." *Theory of Film: The Redemption of
      Physical Reality.* New York: Oxford University Press,
      pp. 215-31; 232-44.

      Among story types found in the cinema the prototype of
      the "theatrical story" is the theatrical play. The use
      of the "theatrical story" in the cinema, especially if
      it is adapted from a play, usually presents problems to
      the filmmaker. "The theatrical story stems from formative
      aspirations which conflict irrevocably with the realistic
      tendency. Consequently, all attempts to adjust it to the
      cinema by extending its range into regions where the
      camera is at home result at best in some compromise of
      some sort."

      "Novel and film also differ from each other: their formal
      properties are anything but identical. And the worlds
      to which they reach out do not coincide either." The
      world of the film must depend upon the use of material
      phenomena to express what is not visible and material.
      Almost all novels, however, "lean toward internal develop-
      ments or states of being. The world of the novel is
      primarily a mental continuum. Now this continuum often
      includes components which elude the grasp of the cinema
      because they have no physical correspondences to speak
      of."

355. Lambert, Gavin. "Lawrence: The Script." *Films and Filming*
      6 (May): 9.

      Not seen.

356. Malraux, André. "The Novel and the Film." *The Creative
      Vision: Modern European Writers on Their Art.* Ed.
      Haskell M. Block and Herman Salinger. New York: Grove
      Press, pp. 162-64.

      "The novel seems to retain one advantage over the film:
      the possibility of moving to the *inside* of its charac-
      ters."

357. Tyler, Parker. "The Dream-Amerika of Kafka and Chaplin."
      The Three Faces of Film: The Art, the Dream, the Cult.
      New York, London: Thomas Yoseloff, pp. 94-100.

      A comparison of Kafka's "Karl" and Chaplin's "Charlie"
      which shows that each character is a hero in "the iden-
      tical international myth: the great adventure of the
      young foreigner coming head-on to the United States to

start a new life and hoping to rise to a level beyond any available to him in his native land."

358. Young, Colin. "Tony Richardson: An Interview in Los Angeles." *Film Quarterly* 13, 4: 10-15.

Though Richardson directed both *Look Back in Anger* and *The Entertainer* for the stage before he adapted them to film, he vows never again to make a film of a play he has staged.

1961

359. Bluestone, George. "Adaptation or Evasion: 'Elmer Gantry.'" *Film Quarterly* 14, 3: 15-19.

"Because Sinclair Lewis was telling the truth, reading him, even today, is almost unbearable. Richard Brooks, locked in the evasions of a difficult set of conventions, has rendered the vision harmless."

360. Bluestone, George. "Time in Film and Fiction." *The Journal of Aesthetics and Art Criticism* 19: 311-15.

"Both novel and film are time arts, but whereas the formative principle in the novel is time, the formative principle in the film is space."

361. Connor, Edward. "Sherlock Holmes on the Screen: Has Never Been Exactly the Man Conan Doyle's Readers Imagined." *Films in Review* 12: 409-18.

Survey of silent and sound film adaptations of Doyle's Sherlock Holmes stories.

362. Croce, Arlene. *"The Misfits." Sight and Sound* 30: 142-43.

The film adaptation of Arthur Miller's short story fails because the screenplay itself is uninspired.

363. Marcus, Mordecai. *"A Farewell to Arms:* Novel into Film." *Journal of the Central Mississippi Valley American Studies Association* 2: 69-71.

Not seen.

364. Morsberger, Robert E. "Shakespeare and Science Fiction." *Shakespeare Quarterly* 12: 161.

The main situation of the film *Forbidden Planet* is
almost identical with that of Shakespeare's *The Tempest*.

365. Noxon, Gerald. "The Anatomy of the Close-Up: Some Literary
     Origins in the Works of Flaubert, Huysmans, and Proust."
     Journal of the Society of Cinematologists 6: 1-24.

     Not seen.

366. Roman, Robert C. "Mark Twain on the Screen: The Movies
     Have Made Indifferent Use of His Prime Literary Mate-
     rial." *Films in Review* 12: 20-33.

     "Only twenty odd films have been based on his writings,
     and only two or three of them were good pictures cine-
     matically."

367. Roman, Robert C. "Poe on the Screen: Has Largely Been
     a Matter of Cheap Horror Pictures." *Films in Review*
     12: 462-73.

     Silent and sound film adaptations of Poe's works sur-
     veyed.

                              1962

368. Alpert, Hollis. "Film and Theater." *The Dreams and the
     Dreamers*. New York: The Macmillan Company, pp. 233-51.

     "The love for film, I would submit, is actually love
     for the theater."

369. Chandler, Raymond. "Chandler on the Film World and
     Television." *Raymond Chandler Speaking*. Ed. Dorothy
     Gardiner and Kathrine Sorley Walker. Boston: Houghton
     Mifflin, pp. 113-44. Reprinted by Books for Libraries
     Press, Plainview, New York, 1971.

     Excerpts from letters in which Chandler comments on
     his scriptwriting work in Hollywood.

370. Gessner, Robert. "The Faces of Time: A New Aesthetic
     for Cinema." *Theatre Arts* 46, 7: 13-17.

     Examines differences between film and theater.

371. Niebuhr, Reinhold. *"Lolita." Show* 2 (August): 63-69.

     "Kubrick has done better than most directors. He has
     made very few changes in the novel."

372. Nizhny, Vladimir. "Mise-en-shot." *Lessons with Eisenstein.* Ed. Ivor Montagu and Jay Leyda. New York: Hill and Wang, pp. 95-139.

Originally made as part of a "lesson" in creating the *mise-en-scène* and the *mise-en-shot*, Eisenstein's notes on a scene from Dostoevsky's *Crime and Punishment* are here printed.

373. Pasolini, Pier Paolo. "Cinematic and Literary Stylistic Figures." *Film Culture* 24: 42-43. Reprinted in *Interviews with Film Directors.* Ed. Andrew Sarris. Indianapolis, Kansas City, New York: The Bobbs-Merrill Company, 1967, pp. 309-12.

An exploration of the similarity in the way the writer and the filmmaker, employing words and images respectively, achieve meaning.

374. Richie, Donald. "Dostoevsky with a Japanese Camera." *Horizon* 4 (Spring): 42-47.

Kurosawa's great affection for Dostoevsky is apparent in all his films.

375. Roud, Richard. "Novel Novel: Fable Fable." *Sight and Sound* 31: 84-88. See reply by Eric Rhode, *Sight and Sound* 31: 154-55.

"Recent developments in the cinema can best be understood by considering what course the novel has taken since Joyce (or was it Henry James?) killed it."

376. Tucker, Nicholas. "Shakespeare and Film Technique." *The Use of English* 14: 98-104.

Comparisons between Shakespeare's artistic conventions and those of the cinema.

1963

377. Chiaromonte, Nicola. "Priests of the Highbrow Cinema: On Word and Image." *Encounter* 20 (January): 40-45. Reprinted in *The Movies as Medium.* Ed. Lewis Jacobs. New York: Farrar, Straus & Giroux, 1970, pp. 37-60.

Filmmakers like Resnais, Antonioni and Bergman have failed in their experiments in trying to make cinematic images in their films function like words in a text. "The

reason is that, never being able to signify anything
other than itself, impervious and indifferent to verbal
meanings, the cinematic image can support interpretations
that are absolutely contradictory."

378. Deren, Maya; Parker Tyler; Dylan Thomas; Arthur Miller;
     and William Maas. "Poetry in the Film: Symposium."
     Film Culture 29: 55-70. Reprinted in *Film Culture
     Reader*. Ed. P. Adams Sitney. New York, Washington:
     Praeger Publishers, 1970, pp. 171-86.

     Excerpts from a lively symposium held in 1953 and
     published here for the first time.

379. Durgnat, Raymond. "*Orphée.*" *Films and Filming* 10, 1:
     45-48. Revised and reprinted in *Films and Feeling*.
     Cambridge, Massachusetts: The M.I.T. Press, pp. 239-50.

     On the dangers of subjecting a film to a too-close
     critical scrutiny for "meaning."

380. Freedman, Florence B. "A Motion Picture 'First' for
     Whitman: O'Connor's 'The Carpenter.'" *Walt Whitman
     Review* 9: 31-33.

     William Douglas O'Connor's short story "The Carpenter,"
     published in 1868, in which the hero resembled Walt
     Whitman and which is known to be the first treatment of
     Whitman in fiction, was made into a film--now lost--by
     Vitagraph in 1913.

381. Goode, James. *The Story of "The Misfits."* Indianapolis,
     New York: The Bobbs-Merrill Company.

     On the making of the film *The Misfits* based on a short
     story by Arthur Miller.

382. Kelman, Ken. "Film as Poetry." *Film Culture* 29: 22-27.

     Film can communicate like the lyric poem; each shares
     the "common goal of direct communication of sensibilities
     and visions."

383. Laurie, Edith. "Film, the Rival of Theater." *Film Comment*
     1, 6: 51-53.

     Minutes of a discussion of the merits of theater vs.
     film that took place at the International Drama Conference
     in Edinburgh in 1963.

384. Luchting, Wolfgang A. "'Hiroshima, Mon Amour,' Time, and Proust." *The Journal of Aesthetics and Art Criticism* 21: 299-313.

A discussion of "the difference between Proust and Resnais in relation to their common subject, time."

1964

385. "Shakespeare on the Screen." *World Theatre* 13: 132-34.

A selective international list of twentieth-century Shakespeare films.

386. Brecht, Bertolt. "The Film, the Novel, and Epic Theatre." *Brecht on Theatre.* Ed. John Willett. New York: Hill and Wang.

Not seen.

387. Butcher, Maryvonne. "Look First Upon This Picture: Books and Films." *The Wiseman Review* 238 (Spring): 55-64.

The film and its literary source are distinct works and each must be judged on its own merits, for "to confuse the two is to be fair to neither."

388. Durgnat, Raymond. "This Damned Eternal Triangle." *Films and Filming* 11, 3: 14-18; 11, 4 (1965): 44-48; 11, 5: 46-50; 11, 6: 19-22.

"The cinema is really a pot-pourri of art-forms, sharing elements in common with each, but weaving them into a pattern of its own."

389. Gillet, John, and David Robinson. "Conversation with George Cukor." *Sight and Sound* 33: 188-93.

Cukor discusses several of his films adapted from literature.

390. Johnson, Ian. "Merely Players: The Impact of Shakespeare on International Cinema." *Films and Filming* 10, 7: 41-48. Reprinted in *Focus on Shakespearean Films.* Ed. Charles W. Eckert. Englewood Cliffs, New Jersey: Prentice-Hall, 1972, pp. 7-26.

Survey of principal sound film adaptations of Shakespeare's plays.

391. Kitchin, Laurence. "Shakespeare on the Screen." *The Listener* 71 (14 May): 788-90. See Arthur Calder-Marshall, *The Listener* 71 (7 May): 772; and Kitchin, *The Listener* 71 (14 May): 801.

Comments on Olivier's three film adaptations of Shakespeare: *Henry V* (1944), *Hamlet* (1948) and *Richard III* (1955).

392. Klein, Michael. "The Literary Sophistication of François Truffaut." *Film Comment* 3, 3: 24-29. Reprinted in *The Emergence of Film Art*. Ed. Lewis Jacobs. New York: Hopkinson and Blake, 1969, pp. 303-12.

"Truffaut's literary sophistication is a matter of technique and sensibility."

393. Lawson, John Howard. "Film and Novel." *Film: The Creative Process. The Search for an Audio-Visual Language and Structure*. New York: Hill and Wang. Second edition, published by Hill and Wang, 1967, pp. 205-18.

"We shall find that the most distinguished adaptations of novels show marked differences from their fictional prototypes." Includes commentary on David Lean's *Great Expectations* (1946), Erich von Stroheim's *Greed* (1923) and John Ford's *The Informer* (1935) and *The Grapes of Wrath* (1940).

394. Merritt, Russell L. "The Internal Monologue in Books and Films." *Tri-Quarterly* 6, 3: 25-29.

A defense of the use of internal monologue, inspired by such writers as Joyce and Faulkner, in film.

395. Morris, Peter. *Shakespeare on Film*. Ottawa: Canadian Film Institute. Revised 1972.

A survey of film and television sound versions of Shakespeare's plays.

396. Nolan, Jack Edmund. "Graham Greene's Movies: Most of Them Have Teetered on the Edge of Significance." *Films in Review* 15: 23-25. Reprinted as "Graham Greene's Films." *Literature/Film Quarterly* 2 (1973): 302-09.

A survey of film adaptations of Greene's work and of films for which he wrote screenplays.

397. Overstreet, William. "Interview with George Cukor."
      Film Culture 34: 1-16. Reprinted in *Interviews with
      Film Directors*. Ed. Andrew Sarris. Indianapolis, Kansas
      City, New York: The Bobbs-Merrill Company, 1967, pp.
      69-96.

      A wide-ranging discussion of Cukor's many film adapta-
      tions of literary works.

398. Taylor, John Russell. "Shakespeare in Film, Radio, and
      Television." *Shakespeare: A Celebration 1564-1964.*
      Ed. T.J.B. Spencer. Harmondsworth, Middlesex: Penguin
      Books, pp. 97-113.

      Briefly surveys eight film adaptations of Shakespeare
      worth taking seriously, and finds only in Welles' *Othello*
      (1951) a film which offers "a sort of cinematic equivalent
      to the Shakespearean experience, using all the resources
      of the modern cinema to do so."

1965

399. Albert, Richard N. "An Annotated Guide to Audio-Visual
      Materials for Teaching Shakespeare." *The English Journal*
      54: 704-15.

      Lists films, film strips and recordings.

400. Bachmann, Gideon. "How I Make Films: An Interview with
      John Huston." *Film Quarterly* 19, 1: 3-13. Reprinted in
      Interviews with Film Directors. Ed. Andrew Sarris.
      Indianapolis, Kansas City, New York: The Bobbs-Merrill
      Company, 1967, pp. 209-25.

      Huston discusses a number of film adaptations he has
      made of literary works.

401. Blumenthal, J. "*Macbeth* into *Throne of Blood*." *Sight and
      Sound* 34: 190-95. See 711.

      Kurosawa's film adaptation is the "only work ... that
      has ever completely succeeded in transforming a play of
      Shakespeare's into a film."

402. Bolt, Robert. "Author's Note." *Doctor Zhivago: The
      Screenplay. Based on the Novel by Boris Pasternak.*
      New York: Random House, pp. ix-xv.

      "For a writer to produce a screenplay and then hand it
      over to a director whose intention is quite different is

a waste of time and effort for the writer--and for
the director an exasperation. The sensible thing is for
them to work together. This is what David Lean and I
did on this film."

403. Brooks, Richard. "Richard Brooks." *Movie* 12: 2-9.

Brooks comments on a number of his films made from
literary works.

404. Costello, Donald P. *The Serpent's Eye: Shaw and the Cinema.*
Notre Dame & London: University of Notre Dame Press.

A close study of George Bernard Shaw's cinema theories
and cinema practice.

405. Fadiman, William. "But Compared to the Original." *Films
and Filming* 11, 5: 21-23.

To judge a film on its merits alone, not on how well
or ill it might have resembled its literary source, ought
to be the primary interest of the critic.

406. Field, Sydney. *"Outrage." Film Quarterly* 18, 3: 13-39.

On the making of the film *The Outrage*, adapted from the
play by Fay and Michael Kanin, which was itself inspired
by the film *Rashomon*. Includes Michael Kanin discussing
his adaptation from play to screen.

407. Kitchin, Laurence. "Shakespeare on the Screen." *Shakespeare Survey* 18: 70-74.

The film treatments of Shakespeare may have the value
of recording great performances for posterity but,
overall, the influence of film on the presentation of
Shakespeare in the theater and on the public perception
of Shakespeare is pernicious.

408. Nolan, Jack Edmund. "Simenon on the Screen: Has Not Been
So Successful as He Has Been in Print." *Films in
Review* 16: 419-37.

Survey of films adapted from the work of Georges Simenon.

409. Noxon, Gerald F. "Some Observations on the Anatomy of
the Long Shot: An Extract from Some Literary Origins
of Cinema Narrative Being the First of a Series--Three
Studies in Cinema." *The Journal of the Society of
Cinematologists* 5: 70-80.

Examines the area of distinction between the "informa-
tional and psychological" functions of the "long-shot"
in terms of some literary origins in Balzac, Stendhal,
Flaubert and Zola.

410. Reeves, Geoffrey. "Shakespeare on Three Screens: Peter
Brook Interviewed." *Sight and Sound* 34: 66–70. Printed,
in a shortened form, as "Finding Shakespeare on Film,"
Tulane Drama Review 11 (1966): 117–21.

Discussion of problems faced by adaptors of Shakespeare's
plays.

411. Richie, Donald. *The Films of Akira Kurosawa*. Berkeley and
Los Angeles: University of California Press.

Discussion of Kurosawa's films, including his adaptations of *The Idiot*, *Macbeth* and Gorky's *The Lower Depths*.

412. Sheridan, Marion C.; Harold H. Owen, Jr.; Ken Macrorie;
and Fred Marcus, eds. *The Motion Picture and the Teaching of English*. New York: Appleton-Century-Crofts.

This handbook discusses the relationship between literature and film, relating film techniques to the standard
language of literary analysis and providing a discussion
of the use of film in teaching English. Includes an
analysis of *The Grapes of Wrath* (1940).

413. Silverstein, Norman. "Movie-Going for Lovers of *The
Wasteland* and *Ulysses*." *Salmagundi* 1, 1: 37–55.

Antonioni and Godard each in his own way creates in
film a complexity of experience as rich as that arising
from reading modern works of literature.

414. Stern, Seymour. "Research," in "Griffith: I--*The Birth
of a Nation*: Part I." *Film Culture* 36: 34–37.

Listing of books D.W. Griffith consulted as resources
for making *The Birth of a Nation*. The primary source was
Dixon's *The Clansman*.

415. Stern, Seymour. "The Screen-Stage Conflict Up to 1965,"
in "Griffith: I--*The Birth of a Nation*: Part I." *Film
Culture* 36: 148–49.

History of the controversy over whether the film has
replaced the stage, particularly as the controversy is
related to the phenomenal success of Griffith's film.

1966

416. Alpert, Hollis. "The Film Is Modern Theatre." *Film: A Montage of Theories*. Ed. Richard Dyer MacCann. New York: E.P. Dutton & Co., pp. 108-12.

      The film has outperformed the theater.

417. Battestin, Martin C. "Osborne's 'Tom Jones': Adapting a Classic." *Virginia Quarterly Review* 42: 378-93.

      On the adaptation of the Fielding classic. "One of the most successful cinematic adaptations of a novel ever made, and, what is more, one of the most imaginative of comic films, a classic in its own right."

418. Bergman, Ingmar. "Each Film Is My Last." *Tulane Drama Review* 11: 94-101.

      "There are many reasons why we ought to avoid filming existing literature, but the most important is that the irrational dimension, which is the heart of a literary work, is often untranslatable and that in its turn it kills the special dimension of the film."

419. Blossom, Roberts. "On Filmstage." *Tulane Drama Review* 11: 68-72.

      Ways in which film can be adapted for use in the theater.

420. Callenbach, Ernest. "The Natural Exchange: From an Interview with Vito Pandolfi." *Tulane Drama Review* 11: 137-40.

      A stage director explains why he turned to film directing.

421. Cobos, Juan, and Miguel Rubio. "Welles and Falstaff." *Sight and Sound* 35: 158-63.

      Welles discusses *Chimes at Midnight* (1966).

422. Cobos, Juan; Miguel Rubio; and J.A. Pruneda. "A Trip to Quixoteland: Conversations with Orson Welles." *Cahiers du Cinema in English* 5: 35-47. Reprinted in *Focus on "Citizen Kane."* Ed. Ronald Gottesman. Englewood Cliffs, New Jersey: Prentice-Hall, 1971, pp. 7-24.

      Welles on his adaptation of *The Trial* (1962), his film of *Don Quixote*, his Shakespeare adaptation, *Chimes at*

Midnight (Falstaff) (1966) and on the subject of directing for theater vs. directing for film.

423. de Pomerai, Odile. "A Novelist Turns to Films: Jean Giono
and the Cinema." *Twentieth Century Literature* 12: 59-65.

French novelist Jean Giono successfully adapted his
novel *Un Roi sans Divertissement* to the screen.

424. Gauteur, Claude. "A Frenzy of Images: An Interview with
Roger Planchon." *Tulane Drama Review* 11: 133-36.

"Directing should aim to approach the ideal image into
which the ideal of the play or film script melts."

425. Godfrey, Lionel. "The Private World of William Inge."
Films and Filming 13, 1: 19-24.

Films based on Inge's plays *Come Back, Little Sheba*,
Picnic and *Bus Stop*, and Inge's own involvement in the
process of adapting them to film, are discussed.

426. Gray, Paul. "Cinema Verité: An Interview with Barbet
Schroeder." *Tulane Drama Review* 11: 130-32.

Discussion of the relationship between French theater
and film.

427. Gray, Paul. "Class Theatre, Class Film: An Interview with
Lindsay Anderson." *Tulane Drama Review* 11: 122-29.

"My tendency is towards a very controlled and rhythmic
form. I am not sure if that makes my theatre work 'cinematic,' or my films 'theatrical.'"

428. Griffin, Alice. "Shakespeare Through the Camera's Eye:
IV." *Shakespeare Quarterly* 17: 383-87.

Comparison of Olivier's acting styles in the films
Othello (1965), *Henry V* (1944) and *Richard III* (1955).

429. Hamilton, Harlan. "Using Literary Criticism to Understand
Film." *Exercise Exchange* 14: 16-17.

Not seen.

430. Huss, Roy, and Norman Silverstein. "Film Study: Shot
Orientation for the Literary Minded." *College English*
27: 566-68.

To view films properly one must not be simply "literary-
conscious"--looking for the "story" only--but rather
"shot-conscious"--aware of the technical devices, like
the shot, used by the filmmaker to create responses in
the viewer.

431. Kirby, Michael. "The Uses of Film in the New Theater."
      Tulane Drama Review 11: 49-61. Reprinted in *The Art of
      Time: Essays on the Avant-Garde*. New York: E.P. Dutton
      & Co., 1969, pp. 117-31.

      Describes recent performances of plays "which, by using
      film in new ways, have shown formal alternatives to both
      traditional movies and traditional theatre."

432. Kozintsev, Grigori. *Shakespeare: Time and Conscience*.
      New York: Hill and Wang.

      Reflections by a director of plays and of films on the
      concerns and questions raised by the production for stage
      and screen of a number of Shakespeare plays, among them
      Hamlet, King Lear, Richard III and *Henry V*. Comments on
      British and American film versions of Shakespeare abound.
      The appendix, "Ten Years with Hamlet," records
      Kozintsev's diary entries over a period during which he
      directed *Hamlet* for the stage and then for the screen.

433. Leonard, Neil. "Theodore Dreiser and the Film." *Film
      Heritage* 2, 1: 7-16.

      On the film adaptations of Dreiser's *An American
      Tragedy*.

434. Nelson, Harland S. *"Othello." Film Heritage* 2, 1: 18-22.

      "Olivier's *Othello* [(1965)] on film works. It derives
      from the stage, but some of its effects come from the
      camera and are unobtainable without it."

435. Pasolini, Pier Paolo. "The Cinema of Poetry." *Cahiers
      du Cinema in English* 6: 35-43.

      The "cinema of poetry" is a step in the evolution of
      film which has had a considerable influence on Italian
      literature in the postwar years and part of the 1950's.

436. Reeves, George. "Finding Shakespeare on Film: From an
      Interview with Peter Brook." *Tulane Drama Review* 11:
      117-21. Reprinted in *Focus on Shakespearean Films*.
      Ed. Charles W. Eckert. Englewood Cliffs, New Jersey:
      Prentice-Hall, 1972, pp. 37-41.

The major problem with filming Shakespeare is finding a means "to reflect the mobility of thought that blank verse demands."

437. Richardson, Robert D., Jr. "Visual Literacy: Literature and the Film." *Denver Quarterly* 1, 2: 24-36.

Vachel Lindsay's perception that the actual process of film is a literary process deserves to be reexplored, for "it now seems arguable that the film has served principally to provide another realm for the literary spirit or imagination."

438. Sontag, Susan. "Film and Theatre." *Tulane Drama Review* 11: 24-37. Reprinted in *Styles of Radical Will*. New York: Farrar, Straus, 1969, pp. 99-122.

A series of insightful notes on the differences and similarities between film and theater which concludes that the cinema is the successor, the rival and the revivifier of the theater.

439. Sontag, Susan. "A Note on Novels and Films." *Against Interpretation and Other Essays*. New York: The Noonday Press, pp. 242-45.

"There are useful analogies which may be drawn between the cinema and the novel--far more, it seems to me, than between the cinema and the theater."

440. Steele, Robert. "The Two Faces of Drama." *Cinema Journal* 6: 16-32.

"Film and theatre, to climb to their highest pinnacles, must both, from time to time, depend upon verbalization, but the verbal language has to be handled differently in films and plays if maximum artistic effectiveness is to be attained."

441. Truffaut, François. "The Journal of 'Fahrenheit 451.'" *Cahiers du Cinema in English* 5: 11-23; 6: 11-23; 7 (1967): 9-19.

A record in diary-entry form of the director's thoughts while shooting his adaptation of Ray Bradbury's *Fahrenheit 451*.

442. Virmaux, Alain. "Artaud and Film." *Tulane Drama Review* 11: 154-65.

"His stage production should not overshadow the importance of his contribution to film."

443. Worth, Sol. "Film as a Non-Art: An Approach to the Study
      of Film." *The American Scholar* 35: 322-34.

      "My concern is not whether film is art or not, but
      whether the process by which we get meaning from film
      can be understood and clarified."

                                1967

444. Altshuler, Thelma, and Richard Paul Janaro. *Responses
      to Drama: An Introduction to Plays and Movies*. Boston:
      Houghton Mifflin Company.

      An introduction to the viewing and critical assessment
      of drama and film.

445. Bazin, André. "In Defense of Mixed Cinema," "Theater and
      Cinema--Part I," and "Theater and Cinema--Part II."
      What Is Cinema? Trans. and ed. Hugh Gray. 2 vols.
      Berkeley and Los Angeles: University of California
      Press, I, 53-75; 76-94; 95-124.

      "The success of filmed theater helps the theater just
      as the adaptation of the novel serves the purpose of
      literature.... The truth is there is here no competition
      or substitution, rather the adding of a new dimension
      that the arts had gradually lost from the time of the
      Reformation on: namely the public."
      The latter two essays provide an enlightening discussion
      of differences between the theater and cinema, and of
      the problems inherent in adaptation of drama to film.

446. Becker, Jacques; Jacques Rivette; and François Truffaut.
      "Howard Hawks." *Interviews with Film Directors*. Ed.
      Andrew Sarris. Indianapolis, Kansas City, New York:
      The Bobbs-Merrill Company, pp. 187-205.

      Hawks discusses a number of his film adaptations of
      literary works.

447. Bontemps, Jacques, and Richard Overstreet. "Measure for
      Measure: Interview with Joseph L. Mankiewicz." *Cahiers
      du Cinema in English* 8: 31-41.

      Mankiewicz comments on several films he adapted from
      literature.

448. Brown, Constance A. "Olivier's *Richard III*: A Re-evalua-
tion." *Film Quarterly* 20, 4: 23-32. Partially reprinted
in *Focus on Shakespearean Films*. Ed. Charles W. Eckert.
Englewood Cliffs, New Jersey: Prentice-Hall, 1972, pp.
131-45.

Despite a considerable number of alterations from play
to film, Olivier has been successful in his adaptation
of Shakespeare's play.

449. Delahaye, Michel. "A Natural Phenomenon: Interview with
Elia Kazan." *Cahiers du Cinema in English* 9: 13-35.

Kazan comments on a variety of films adapted from
literature, including *Baby Doll* (1956), *A Streetcar
Named Desire* (1951) and *East of Eden* (1955).

450. Downer, Alan S. "The Monitor Image." *Man and the Movies*.
Ed. W.R. Robinson. Baton Rouge: Louisiana State University Press, pp. 13-30.

Shrewd comments on John Huston as a director of films
adapted from literature.

451. Durgnat, Raymond. "The Angel of Poetry Hovering." *Films
and Feeling*. Cambridge, Massachusetts: The M.I.T. Press.

An exploration of the relationship between film and
poetry. Not only do film techniques and images express
or enhance ideas and emotions just as do association of
images, similes and metaphors in poetry, but also the
film has the same power as poetry to appeal to the unconscious mind.

452. Earle, William. "Some Notes on the New Film." *Tri-Quarterly* 8 (Winter): 157-64.

The "new film" or "poetic film" should break from the
conventional form of the narrative feature film.

453. French, Philip. "All the Better Books." *Sight and Sound*
36: 38-41.

Hollywood's attitude toward and use of books.

454. Geduld, Harry M., ed. *Film Makers on Film Making: Statements on Their Art by Thirty Directors*. Bloomington
and London: Indiana University Press.

A collection of statements by film directors on their
art. A number of directors discuss their attitudes towards
the adaptation of literature to film.

455. Godfrey, Lionel. "It Wasn't Like That in the Book." *Films
      and Filming* 13, 7: 12-16; "It Wasn't Like That in the
      Play." *Films and Filming* 13, 11: 4-8.

      "It would be naive ... not to expect changes to occur
      during such translations, for what may work admirably
      between the covers of a novel may have no chance at all
      of success within the context of a film."
      "As the makers of the early talkies soon found out,
      you translate literally from the theatre to the cinema
      at your peril: an aesthetic claustrophobia sets in, so
      different are the dimensions and values of the two media."

456. Jensen, Paul. "H.G. Wells on the Screen: His Science
      Fiction Has Filmed Better Than His Fabianism." *Films
      in Review* 18: 521-27.

      A brief survey of twenty-one silent and sound films
      adapted from Wells' fiction. "The films so far made from
      [his works] point to a sociologically significant fact:
      the least 'ephemeral' of Wells' novels are those in which
      science fiction predominates."

457. MacCaffrey, Donald W. "Adaptation Problems in the Two
      Unique Media: The Novel and the Film." *Dickinson Review*
      1 (Spring): 11-17.

      Not seen.

458. Macdonald, Dwight. "Agee & the Movies." *Film Heritage*
      3, 1: 3-11.

      A tribute to the film critic, poet and novelist.

459. Madden, David. "James M. Cain and the Movies of the
      Thirties and Forties." *Film Heritage* 2, 4: 9-25.

      On Cain's experiences as a screenwriter in Hollywood,
      the fate of his novels adapted to the screen and the in-
      fluence of film on his writing techniques.

460. Madden, Robert. "'The Blue Hotel': An Examination of
      Story and Film Script." *Film Heritage* 3, 1: 20-34.

      Agee's film script of Stephen Crane's story, though
      never made into a film, is a "perceptive treatment of
      the original story."

461. Mayersberg, Paul. "The Great Rewrite." *Sight and Sound*
      36: 72-77. Part of Chapter 6 in *Hollywood, the Haunted
      House*. London: Allen Lane, The Penguin Press, pp. 111-30.

Surveys the troubles writers face when they work in
Hollywood.

462. Roll-Hansen, Diderik. "Shaw's 'Pygmalion': The Two Versions
of 1916 and 1941." *A Review of English Literature* 8:
81-90.

A comparison of the original published text (1916) of
Pygmalion with that of the printed text of the film
version of the play (1941) shows that all modern percep-
tions of Shaw's original intentions as a playwright and
of his stagecraft must be based only on the earlier
publication.

463. Rossen, Robert, and Jean-Louis Noames. "Lessons Learned
in Combat." *Cahiers du Cinema in English* 7: 21-28.

Rossen's comments on a variety of film adaptations from
literature.

464. Sarris, Andrew, ed. *Interviews with Film Directors.*
Indianapolis, Kansas City, New York: The Bobbs-Merrill
Company.

Interviews with forty-one directors of film, many of
whom discuss the subject of adaptation of literature to
film.

465. Sterne, Richard L. *John Gielgud Directs Richard Burton
in "Hamlet": A Journal of Rehearsals.* New York: Random
House.

Not seen.

466. Sullivan, Sister Bede, O.S.B. "The Language Distinguishes
Among Art Forms." *Movies: Universal Language.* Notre
Dame, Indiana: Fides Publishing, pp. 41-55.

An elementary examination of the relation of film to
other art forms.

467. Welles, Orson; Juan Cobos; and Miguel Rubio. "Welles on
Falstaff: Interview with Orson Welles." *Cahiers du
Cinema in English* 11: 5-14.

Welles talks about his research for, direction of and
performance in the film *Chimes at Midnight (Falstaff)*
(1966).

468. Widmer, Eleanor. "The Lost Girls of U.S.A.: Dos Passos'
30s Movie." *The Thirties: Fiction, Poetry, Drama.*

Ed. Warren French. Deland, Florida: Everett/Edwards.
Second edition, revised, 1976, pp. 11-19.

"The sordid patterns of defeat and the harsh cadences
of the style, with their hypervisuality of place, poetic-
ize the U.S.A., providing us with an America as recog-
nizable and painfully endearing as an old movie. The
experience of reading *U.S.A.* represents just this poetic
and cinematic image of America, and in this Dos Passos
does not fail."

469. Wilbur, Richard. "A Poet and the Movies." *Man and the
Movies*. Ed. W.R. Robinson. Baton Rouge: Louisiana
State University Press, pp. 223-26.

Wilbur acknowledges that much in his poetry "may owe
as much to the camera as to the sharp noticing of poets
like Hopkins and Ponge."

1968

470. Ball, Robert Hamilton. *Shakespeare on Silent Film: A
Strange Eventful History*. New York: Theatre Arts Books.

Designed to appeal both to general readers and to
specialists alike, this book provides a "straightforward
narrative" which treats in chronological fashion what
was done with Shakespeare on the silent screen, and in
addition includes a section called "Explanations and
Acknowledgements" in which each film treated in the text
is given more particular treatment and elucidation.

471. Budgen, Suzanne. "Some Notes on the Sources of *La Règle
du Jeu*." *Take One* 1, 12: 10-12.

Traces inspiration for the film to a number of plays
with elements similar to those in the film.

472. Cocteau, Jean. "Preface (1946)." *Two Screenplays: "The
Blood of the Poet," "The Testament of Orpheus."*
Trans. Carol Martin-Sperry. New York: The Orion
Press, pp. 3-6.

"Above all, what really marks *The Blood of the Poet*
is, I think, a complete indifference to what the world
finds 'poetic,' the care taken, on the contrary, to
create a vehicle for poetry--whether it is used as such
or not."

473. Corbett, Thomas. "The Film and the Book: A Case Study of *The Collector.*" *The English Journal* 57: 328-33.

Compares the film adaptation's use of metaphors in the Fowles novel and the differing characterizations of Miranda.

474. Crump, G.B. "*The Fox* on Film." *The D.H. Lawrence Review* 1: 238-44.

"Given the considerable difficulties of mounting a production of Lawrence's story at all, this is no mean accomplishment."

475. Dart, Peter. "Figurative Expression in the Film." *Speech Monographs* 35: 170-74.

Since the photograph has about it an almost intractable literal significance, the filmmaker must introduce some kind of tension between shots in order to generate a figurative significance from images.

476. Denson, Alan. *Franco Zeffirelli's Production of William Shakespeare's "Romeo and Juliet."* Kendal: Low Fellside.

Not seen.

477. Farber, Stephen. "The Writer in American Films." *Film Quarterly* 21, 4: 2-13.

John Boorman explains how he adapted Richard Stark's novel *The Hunter* into the film *Point Blank.*

478. Fernandez, Henry. "*Blow Up*; From Cortázar to Antonioni: Study of an Adaptation." *Film Heritage* 4, 2: 26-30.

"The tension between photography and written narrative in Cortázar becomes a tension between photography and cinematography in Antonioni."

479. Finler, Joel W. *Stroheim.* Berkeley: University of California Press.

Generous attention is given Stroheim's adaptation of Norris' *McTeague.*

480. Fuller, Stanley. "Melville on the Screen: Only 'Moby Dick' and 'Billy Budd' Have Been Fittingly Filmed." *Films in Review* 19: 358-63.

A brief analysis of the four "major" films adapted from Melville's fiction: *The Sea Beast* (1926), *Moby Dick* (1930 and 1956) and *Billy Budd* (1962).

481. Geduld, Harry M. "Return to Méliès: Reflections on the
      Science-Fiction Film." *The Humanist* 28, 6: 23-24, 28.
      Partially reprinted in *Focus on the Science Fiction
      Film*. Ed. William Johnson. Englewood Cliffs, New Jersey:
      Prentice-Hall, 1972, pp. 142-47.

      Includes an analysis of the differences between A.C.
      Clarke's story "The Sentinel" and the Stanley Kubrick film
      2001: A Space Odyssey (1968), which was based on Clarke's
      story.

482. Gessner, Robert. *The Moving Image: A Guide to Cinematic
      Literacy*. New York: E.P. Dutton & Co.

      "The aim of this book is to discover the unique patterns
      and structures that, through the visualization of ideas
      and emotions, make cinema an art."
      This purpose is accomplished by the printing of a
      variety of excerpts from film scripts, most of which have
      been adapted from literary works, with accompanying
      comments and references both to the film and to the orig-
      inal work of literature. Excerpts are taken from film
      scripts of *Pygmalion* (1941) and *The Informer* (1935).

483. Huss, Roy, and Norman Silverstein. "Imagery," "Tone and
      Point of View," and "Theme." *The Film Experience: Ele-
      ments of Motion Picture Art*. New York, Evanston, and
      London: Harper & Row, pp. 81-104; 105-26; 127-44.

      "Film images may be empty or cliché-ridden, but they
      may also, like a great image of poetry, organize diverse
      elements of a chaotic world so that for a moment a spec-
      tator has the sensations of harmony and plenitude as
      principles of life."
      A discussion of tone and point of view in cinema based
      upon a variety of references to the literature of fiction
      and illustrated by analyses of films adapted from litera-
      ture.
      "Toward the effective presentation of his theme all
      matters of rhythm, imagery, and tone are techniques, but,
      as in poetry, what one says is intimately tied up with
      the way one says it. As the tone of voice may qualify
      the literal meaning of a sentence, a film maker's tempo,
      his images, and his point of view will modify the theme."

484. Kauffmann, Stanley. "A Year with *Blow-Up*. Some Notes."
      Salmagundi 7: 67-74.

      Not seen.

485. Kozloff, Max. *"In Cold Blood." Sight and Sound* 37: 148-49.

A comparison between *In Cold Blood* (1967), Richard Brooks' adaptation of the Capote novel, and *The Outsider* (1967), Visconti's adaptation of the Camus novel.

486. Kuhns, William, and Robert Stanley. *Teaching Program: Exploring the Film.* Dayton, Ohio: Geo. A. Pflaum.

Contains discussions of "filmic drama" and the "fiction film."

487. Marder, Louis. "Sex in Shakespeare." *The Shakespeare Newsletter* 18: 10-11.

Zeffirelli distorts the role of sex in both *Romeo and Juliet* (1968) and *The Taming of the Shrew* (1966).

488. Milne, Tom. "The Difference of George Axelrod." *Sight and Sound* 37: 165-69.

The playwright-scriptwriter-director discusses his work.

489. Petrie, Graham. "The Films of Sidney Lumet: Adaptation as Art." *Film Quarterly* 21, 2: 9-18.

"At his best, his films show clearly that adaptation need not be inferior to 'pure cinema' as long as the director is able to create a cinematic style which respects and corresponds to the intention and subject-matter of his source."

490. Sarris, Andrew. "Film: The Illusion of Naturalism." *The Drama Review* 13, 2: 108-12.

"Naturalism in the cinema ... has never meant exactly the same thing as Naturalism in the theatre." In a number of ways film has been and remains more prone to theatricality than the theater.

491. Sweeney, Patricia Runk. "Mr. House, Mr. Thackeray & Mr. Pirrip: The Question of Snobbery in *Great Expectations*." *The Dickensian* 64: 55-63.

Decries the introduction of the false "overt moral," that Pip is a "snob," into the film.

492. Wald, Malvin. "Who Is the Film Author?" *Cineaste* 2, 3: 11-12.

"It is my contention that the first requisite of a
good filmmaker is a thorough course in screen writing,
preferably taken from a professional screenwriter. A
background in literature, the novel, drama, the short
story, and a history of film are other vital requirements."

493. Ward, John. "Alain Robbe-Grillet: the Novelist as Director."
      Sight and Sound 37: 86-90.

      "*Trans-Europ* [sic] *Express* [(1966)] indicates that Robbe-
      Grillet has begun successfully to make the transition from
      a literary to a film style."

                                1969

494. Camp, Gerald M. "Shakespeare on Film." *The Journal of
      Aesthetic Education* 3: 107-20.

      "Olivier's *Henry V* (1944), does a better job of realiz-
      ing the full meaning of the play than any stage production
      could ever accomplish."

495. Capote, Truman; Eleanor Perry; and Frank Perry. *Trilogy:
      An Experiment in Media.* New York: The Macmillan Company.

      A case study of the process by which the Capote short
      stories "Miriam," "Among the Paths of Eden" and "A Christ-
      mas Memory" were first adapted for television and later
      reedited to 110 minutes for distribution as the feature-
      length film entitled *Truman Capote's Trilogy* (1969).

496. Cirillo, Albert R. "The Art of Franco Zeffirelli and
      Shakespeare's *Romeo and Juliet*." *TriQuarterly* 16 (Fall):
      69-92.

      Zeffirelli "understands and makes part of his design
      precisely the kind of effect which can be achieved by a
      perfect synthesis of color and sound, of visual and aural
      techniques."

497. Deane, Paul. "Motion Picture Technique in James Joyce's
      'The Dead.'" *James Joyce Quarterly* 6: 231-36.

      "All major film techniques are present in 'The Dead.'
      Whether Joyce was consciously influenced by the movies
      or not, the story is virtually a scenario and could be
      filmed almost exactly as it is."

498. Eisenstein, S.M.; G.V. Alexandrov; and Ivor Montagu.
     "An American Tragedy: Scenario. Based upon the Novel
     by Theodore Dreiser." *With Eisenstein in Hollywood:
     A Chapter of Autobiography.* Ed. Ivor Montagu. New York:
     International Publishers, pp. 209-341.

     The "characterization is worked out," but "the paragraph-
     ing, though it represents carefully and in detail the
     succession of the *action,* does not yet so clearly or
     precisely prescribe the exact eventual image-succession"
     that one would expect in a final script of a film.

499. Feyen, Sharon. "The Stage Play Adapted." *Screen Experience:
     An Approach to Film.* Ed. Sharon Feyen and Donald Wigal.
     Dayton, Ohio: Geo. A. Pflaum, pp. 33-39.

     Brief discussion designed for classroom use.

500. Field, Edward. "The Movies as American Mythology." *Con-
     cerning Poetry* 2, 1: 27-31.

     Hollywood's use of the Frankenstein legend suggests
     that "Our great myth maker has been the movie, and all the
     other arts are beginning to be aware of this."

501. Gollin, Richard M. "Film as Dramatic Literature." *College
     English* 30: 424-29. Reprinted in *The Compleat Guide to
     Film Study.* Ed. G. Howard Poteet. Urbana, Illinois:
     National Council of Teachers of English, 1972, pp. 55-62.

     It is the responsibility of literature departments to
     teach film as dramatic literature: "For all their tech-
     nological and conventional differences from stage dramas,
     films remain unquestionably a mode of dramatic literature,
     no more a mutation from the common stock of drama than
     was the masque from its several origins, or renaissance
     drama from earlier pageant plays, or drama itself from
     earlier religious rituals."

502. Gow, Gordon. "In Search of a Revolution: Peter Hall Talks
     about His Work in the Cinema and the Theatre." *Films
     and Filming* 15, 12: 40-44.

     On Hall's treatment of Shakespeare's *A Midsummer Night's
     Dream.*

503. Hurtgen, Charles. "The Operatic Character of Background
     Music in Film Adaptations of Shakespeare." *Shakespeare
     Quarterly* 20 (Winter): 53-64.

"As in the differences in structure of Shakespeare's
scenes and film continuity, formalistic and naturalistic
settings, theatrical and camera distance and angles, the
additional music has more frequently proved a hindrance
than a help in conveying the dramatic poetry."

504. James, Clive. "*2001*: Kubrick vs. Clarke." *Cinema*
     (Cambridge) 2 (March): 62-79. [Not seen.] Reprinted in
     Film Society Review 5, 5 (1970): 27-34.

     Kubrick seems to have "frozen out" Clarke when making
     the film: "It seems to be a case of Kubrick's idea of
     consistency being different from Clarke's: scientific
     extrapolation, the SF art of creating a credible future,
     is simply not Kubrick's main concern."

505. Koch, Stephen. "The Art That Matters, Fiction and Film:
     A Search for New Sources." *Saturday Review* 52 (27
     December): 12-14, 38.

     "Literature has a great deal to learn from its big,
     brash, rich brother [the film]."

506. Koningsberger, Hans. "From Book to Film--Via John Huston."
     Film Quarterly 22, 3: 2-4.

     The author of the novel *A Walk with Love and Death*
     discusses his experiences working with Huston on the film
     adaptation.

507. Kwapy, William. "Literary Adaptations." *Screen Experience:
     An Approach to Film*. Ed. Sharon Feyen and Donald Wigal.
     Dayton, Ohio: Geo. A. Pflaum, pp. 25-32.

     Brief discussion designed for classroom use.

508. McBride, Joseph. "Welles' *Chimes at Midnight*." *Film
     Quarterly* 23, 1: 11-20.

     "*Chimes at Midnight* [(1966)] is Welles' masterpiece."

509. McKee, Mel. "*2001*: Out of the Silent Planet." *Sight and
     Sound* 38: 204-07.

     "In Kubrick and Clarke's work, with its analogies in
     Lewis' trilogy [C.S. Lewis' Ransom trilogy] and the
     Christian myth, man can't get to God; God gets to man."

510. Mench, Fred. "Film Sense in *The Aeneid*." *Arion* 8: 380-97.

Virgil can be seen "to employ the techniques of a
film director" when one looks at *The Aeneid* as if it
were the scenario for a film.

511. Nolan, William F. *Dashiell Hammett: A Casebook.* Santa
Barbara: McNally & Loftin, pp. 102-05.

Brief analysis of John Huston's adaptation of *The
Maltese Falcon.*

512. Phillips, Gene D. "Graham Greene: On the Screen." *The
Catholic World* 209 (August): 218-21. Reprinted in
Graham Greene: A Collection of Critical Essays. Ed.
Samuel Hynes. Englewood Cliffs, New Jersey: Prentice-
Hall, 1973, pp. 168-75. See also Robert Murray Davis,
"More Graham Greene on Film: Uncollected Reviews and
Fragments of Reviews." *Literature/Film Quarterly* 2
(1973): 384-85.

An interview in which Greene discusses his own screenplays and the screen adaptations of several of his works.
Includes a listing of bibliographical materials.

513. Plotkin, Frederick. "*Othello* and Welles: A Fantastic
Marriage." *Film Heritage* 4, 4: 9-15.

"From the perspective of fifteen years, the word for
Welles' *Othello* [1951] is decadent."

514. Richardson, Robert. *Literature and Film.* Bloomington and
London: Indiana University Press.

"The plan of this book is ... as simple as its double
subject and double interest will permit. After a sketch
of the subject, there are two chapters which look for
literary backgrounds and influences in the film during
its rise. Chapters four and five take up some of the
important ways in which literature and film are actually
alike, and chapter six tries to suggest something of the
impact of the film upon modern literature. The final
three chapters are concerned largely with poetry and film
and with the argument that these two forms have, between
them, high significance for us."

515. Schneider, Alan. "On Directing *Film.*" "*Film*" *by Samuel
Beckett. Complete Scenario/ Illustrations/ Production
Shots.* New York: Grove Press, pp. 63-94.

Genesis and execution of Beckett's film project.

516. Schreivogel, Paul A. *"An Occurrence at Owl Creek Bridge":*
      Film by Robert Enrico; Story by Ambrose Bierce; A Visual
      Study. Dayton, Ohio: Geo. A. Pflaum.

      Not seen.

517. Sewell, John B. "Shakespeare on the Screen: II. An Updating
      of Our Lillich Article of Twelve Years Ago." *Films in*
      Review 20: 419-26. See 300.

      Survey of film adaptations of Shakespeare plays from
      1955, including mention of some films omitted from the
      Lillich article.

518. Sobchack, Thomas. *"The Fox*: The Film and the Novel."
      Western Humanities Review 23: 73-78.

      The film "fails to capture the essential quality of
      the novel: Lawrence's evocation of the ambiguous and
      enigmatic nature of the relationships between men and
      women."

1970

519. Agel, Jerome, ed. *The Making of Kubrick's "2001."*
      New York: New American Library.

      Provides an account of the planning and production of
      the film and includes reviews, interviews and related
      documents.

520. Bancroft, David. "Alain Resnais: Towards a New Concept
      of Cinema." *Meanjin Quarterly* 29: 215-25.

      "To talk about Resnais is to talk not merely of the
      New Wave, but of the whole function of cinema, of the
      nature of film as an art, of the relationship between
      film and literature, of the parallels between film and
      musical structure."

521. Benair, Jonathan. *"They Shoot Horses, Don't They?" Film*
      Society Review 5, 9: 32-37.

      The Horace McCoy novel "was eviscerated, misconstrued
      and turned finally from what could have been straight
      uncluttered B-movie precision into its dreaded nemesis,
      Hollywood glossy."

522. Budgen, Suzanne. *"La Règle du Jeu." Screen* 11, 1: 3-13.

Compares Alfred de Musset's *Les Caprices de Marianne*, the source of *La Règle du Jeu*, with Renoir's film.

523. Buscombe, Edward. "Dickens and Hitchcock." *Screen* 11: (August-September): 97-114.

Not seen.

524. Casty, Alan. "The New Style in Film and Drama." *The Midwest Quarterly* 11 (Winter): 209-27.

Contemporary film and drama are following esthetic movements having similar aims, and each is benefitting from developments in the other. The effort of modern practitioners in each art is to subvert the "authority of conventional realism," long established in the tradition of each art, by means of techniques and devices--a number of which are analyzed--that force the viewer to assume a more objective attitude toward what he is seeing and hearing.

525. Cohen, Larry. "The Making of 'Little Murders.'" *Saturday Review* 53 (8 August): 19-21.

An analysis of Alan Arkin's film adaptation of Jules Feiffer's play.

526. Delpino, Louis. "Transliteration: Joseph Strick's *Tropic of Cancer*." *Film Heritage* 6: 27-29.

"Strick has captured a surprising amount of the book's essence."

527. Dempsey, Michael. "They Shaft Writers, Don't They? James Poe Interviewed." *Film Comment* 6, 4: 65-73.

An interview with James Poe, who contributed substantially to the screenplay for the film adaptation of Horace McCoy's novel *They Shoot Horses, Don't They?*

528. Eisenstein, Sergei. "Lessons from Literature." *Film Essays and a Lecture*. New York and Washington: Praeger, pp. 77-84.

A short essay written in 1939 in which the visual effectiveness of Zola's style is compared with Balzac's. For Eisenstein, Zola's superiority at visualizing can provide much for a student of film to learn.

529. Fell, John L. "Dissolves by Gaslight: Antecedents to the
      Motion Picture in Nineteenth-Century Melodrama." *Film
      Quarterly* 23, 3: 22-34.

      "There appears to be ample evidence of striking simi-
      larities between theatrical and filmed melodrama in terms
      of structure, techniques, and the aesthetic implicit to
      both."

530. Folson, James K. "*Shane* and *Hud*: Two Stories in Search of
      a Medium." *Western Humanities Review* 24: 359-72.

      "*Shane* [by Jack Schaefer] and *Horseman, Pass By* [by
      Larry McMurtry] lend themselves to film adaptation if
      only because they are short and fairly simple books, both
      with straightforward plot lines and relatively few charac-
      ters."

531. Gerard, Lillian N. "Of Lawrence and Love." *Film Library
      Quarterly* 3, 4: 6-12.

      The Ken Russell adaptation of D.H. Lawrence's novel
      Women in Love could have been better: "Sharper editing
      would have made for greater dramatic impact and the values
      of Lawrence would not then be diluted by the self-con-
      sciousness of a director who has talent but no control."

532. Haller, Robert. "The Writer and Hollywood: An Interview
      with Lawrence Durrell." *Film Heritage* 6, 1: 25-26.

      Durrell talks about the writer's place in Hollywood.

533. Hammond, Robert M., ed. *"Beauty and the Beast": Scenario
      and Dialogs by Jean Cocteau*. New York: New York Univer-
      sity Press.

      The definitive annotated edition of Cocteau's script
      for the film.

534. Hanhardt, George. "George Axelrod and *The Manchurian
      Candidate*." *Film Comment* 6, 4: 9-13.

      Axelrod "skillfully transposed" Richard Condon's novel
      to the screen.

535. Higham, Charles. *The Films of Orson Welles*. Berkeley,
      Los Angeles, London: University of California Press.

      This book "concentrates wholly on Welles' films them-
      selves and is intended as a descriptive and critical

study of these works, breaking with the format only to
provide information about the circumstances of their
production."

Besides discussion of the films, included in the study
are: a description of David Smith's 1924 version of Booth
Tarkington's *The Magnificent Ambersons* and an account of
the cuts and changes made in Welles' *The Magnificent
Ambersons* "after Welles had finished his rough cut."

536. Hitchens, Gordon. "'A Breathless Eagerness in the Audi-
      ence ...': Historical Notes on Dr. Frankenstein and His
      Monster." *Film Comment* 6, 1: 49-51.

      Account of adaptations for stage and screen of the
      Frankenstein story.

537. Isaacs, Neil D. "Fiction into Film." *Fiction into Film:
      "A Walk in the Spring Rain."* Ed. Rachel Maddux, Stirling
      Silliphant and Neil D. Isaacs. Knoxville: The University
      of Tennessee Press, pp. 135-227.

      Describes the genesis and the experience of making the
      film *A Walk in the Spring Rain* (1969), adapted from the
      Rachel Maddux novel.

538. Linden, George W. "The Staged World" and "The Storied
      World." *Reflections on the Screen*. Belmont, California:
      Wadsworth Publishing Company, pp. 1-29; 32-59.

      "The Staged World" deals with the influence of drama
      on the early film and with the differences between the
      theater and the film.
      "The Storied World" examines the differences between
      the novel and the film, and includes analyses of *Hud*
      (1963), *Lord of the Flies* (1963), adapted from the Golding
      novel, and *Tom Jones* (1963).

539. McConnell, Frank. "A Rough Beast Slouching: A Note on
      Horror Movies." *The Kenyon Review* 32: 109-20.

      An insightful survey of the development of the horror
      film and its origins in imaginative literature and art.

540. McGlynn, Paul D. "Rhetoric in Fiction and Film: Notes
      Toward a Cultural Symbiosis." *English Record* 21, 2:
      15-22.

      "Literature and the film each employ a rhetoric analogous
      to the other."

541. Morgan, Gwen, and Donald Skoller. "Dreyer in Double
      Reflection. An Annotated Translation of Carl Dreyer's
      1946 Essay 'A Little on Film Style.'" *Cinema* 6, 2: 8-15.

      Dreyer's essay was written after he had completed *Day
      of Wrath* (1943), a film based on a stage play. In the
      essay, Dreyer considers the differences between film and
      drama.

542. Nulf, Frank. "Luigi Pirandello and the Cinema." *Film
      Quarterly* 24, 2: 40-48.

      "What he was after was innovation in filmic form which
      would make use of all the elements available in the other
      arts in a synthesized, uniquely cinematic structure."

543. Phillips, Gene D. "An Interview with Ken Russell."
      Film Comment 6, 3: 10-17.

      Russell discusses his film adaptation of D.H. Lawrence's
      novel *Women in Love*.

544. Powell, Dilys. "Postscript: Dickens on Film." *The
      Dickensian* (Centenary Number) 66: 183-85. See 831.

      A comparison of Cukor's *David Copperfield* (1935) and
      Delbert Mann's 1970 version shows that "It is easier to
      film Shakespeare than to film Dickens" because the back-
      ground of lesser but essential characters which gives
      depth to the central characters cannot be captured on
      the screen.

545. Rhode, Eric. "Dostoevsky and Bresson." *Sight and Sound*
      39: 82-83.

      Bresson's *A Gentle Creature* (1969) alters and deepens
      the Dostoevsky short story.

546. Roman, Robert C. "G.B.S. on the Screen: Shaw's Plays
      Became Successful Movies Only When He Adapted Them."
      Films in Review 11: 406-18.

      Survey of film adaptations of a number of Shaw's plays.

547. Rosen, Robert. "Enslaved by the Queen of the Night: The
      Relationship of Ingmar Bergman to E.T.A. Hoffmann."
      Film Comment 6, 1: 27-30.

      The "inspiration" for Bergman's film *Hour of the Wolf*
      (1966) "derives to a significant extent from E.T.A.
      Hoffmann."

548. Ross, Theodore J., comp. *Film and the Liberal Arts.* New York: Holt, Rinehart and Winston.

Not seen.

549. Rule, Philip C., S.J. "Teaching the Film as Literature." *Soundings* 53: 77-87.

"The long-range survival of the English department in an undergraduate curriculum may very well depend upon the incorporation of film study into the program."

550. Silverstein, Norman. "Film Semiology." *Salmagundi* 13 (Summer): 73-80.

An examination of the origin and purpose of semiology, the study of signs, as it relates to the study of film, literature and painting.

551. Sragow, Michael. *"Becket* and *The Lion in Winter." Film Society Review* 5, 4: 36-43.

Discussion of Anouilh's *Becket* and its film adaptation by Peter Glenville, and of James Goldman's play and screenplay *The Lion in Winter.*

552. Sragow, Michael. *"End of the Road." Film Society Review* 5, 6: 36-39.

John Barth's novel *End of the Road* has been completely reworked for the film version.

553. Sragow, Michael. *"A Man for All Seasons/Anne of a Thousand Days." Film Society Review* 6, 1: 41-46.

Robert Bolt's screenplay for his *A Man for All Seasons* keeps intact the play's intentions. By contrast, the Hal Wallis production of the Maxwell Anderson play *Anne of a Thousand Days* "fails to provoke interest on any level."

554. Tarratt, Margaret. "An Obscene Undertaking." *Films and Filming* 17, 2: 26-30.

None of the adaptations of D.H. Lawrence's work "have been satisfactorily able to carry the weight of Lawrence's symbolism because they have avoided the intricate nuances of perception and have ignored the often unpalatable psychological insight which gives Lawrence's work much of its power."

555. Thegze, Chuck. "'I See Everything Twice': An Examination
      of *Catch-22*." *Film Quarterly* 24, 1: 7-17.

      The film is "an artistic reflection of the Catch-22
      state of affairs of the modern world."

556. Thomaier, William. "Conrad on the Screen: Poses Cinematic
      Difficulties Which Haven't Yet Been Overcome." *Films
      in Review* 21: 611-21.

      A survey of film adaptations of Conrad's novels and
      short stories.
      Though Conrad's visual sense makes his works likely
      material for film adaptation, "the depths of his charac-
      terizations and his subjective preoccupations with
      moral and philosophical issues, make successful cinema-
      tion of his work difficult."

557. Tiessen, Paul G. "Malcolm Lowry and the Cinema." *Canadian
      Literature* 44 (Spring): 38-49. Reprinted in *Malcolm
      Lowry: The Man and His Work*. Ed. George Woodcock.
      Vancouver: University of British Columbia Press, 1971,
      pp. 133-43.

      Lowry's interest in the film and his work as a screen-
      writer encouraged in his writing a cinematic style and
      technique most comprehensively apparent in *Under the
      Volcano*.

558. Tyler, Parker. "The Play Is Not the Thing." *The Hollywood
      Hallucination*. New York: Simon and Schuster, pp. 3-21.

      "Whereas the tradition of the legitimate theater con-
      ceives presentation as a sort of centripetal operation,
      all forces tending toward the center of a single artistic
      inspiration and directly deriving their character from
      contact with it, the genius of Hollywood has progressively
      opposed such a conception and tended centrifugally to
      regard the story as but a jumping-off place for a complex
      series of superimposed and often highly irrelevant opera-
      tions."

559. Wegner, Hart. "The Literate Cinema." *Western Humanities
      Review* 24: 279-82.

      "The application of scholarly methods to film studies
      will not destroy the poetry of image and word, but will
      heighten the appreciation of the inherent values of [the]
      medium."

560. Weightman, John. "Trifling with the Dead." *Encounter* 34: 50-53.

Ken Russell's adaptation of D.H. Lawrence's novel *Women in Love* communicates the wrong conception of the book.

561. Welles, Orson. "Orson Welles on *The Trial*." *"The Trial": A Film by Orson Welles*. English translation and description of action by Nicholas Fry. London: Lorrimer Publishing, pp. 9-11.

Welles on his film adaptation of the Kafka novel.

562. Youngblood, Gene. "Intermedia Theatre." *Expanded Cinema*. New York: E.P. Dutton & Co., pp. 365-86.

An introduction to a number of experiments in "intermedia theatre" which combine in various ways traditional elements of theater and cinema.

1971

563. Adams, Robert H. "Pictures and the Survival of Literature." *Western Humanities Review* 25: 79-85.

"Film is not ... in combat with literature. Where it is replacing certain literary forms it is doing so because the artist can, in films, say what he cannot in other ways--he can reveal again the holiness, beyond complaint, in the surface of life."

564. Bazin, André. "An Aesthetic of Reality: Neorealism." *What Is Cinema? Vol. II*. Ed. and trans. Hugh Gray. Berkeley, Los Angeles, London: University of California Press, pp. 16-40.

Comparison is drawn between the techniques of neo-realist filmmakers and modern novelists and short story writers. "The aesthetic of the Italian cinema, at least in its most elaborate manifestations and in the work of a director as conscious of his medium as Rossellini, is simply the equivalent on film of the American novel."

565. Birdsall, Eric R., and Fred H. Marcus. "Schlesinger's *Midnight Cowboy*: Creating a Classic." *Film and Literature: Contrasts in Media*. Ed. Fred H. Marcus. Scranton, London, Toronto: Chandler Publishing, pp. 178-89.

In John Schlesinger's adaptation of James Leo Herlihy's
novel *Midnight Cowboy*, the main characters, Ratso and
Joe, are made more sympathetic, and Herlihy's view of
New York City as a force "acting upon Joe and debilitating
him" is not reflected by Schlesinger in the film, in
which the city becomes simply "an evil and destructive
force."

566. Brody, Alan. "Jules and Catherine and Jim and Hedda."
     The Journal of Aesthetic Education 5, 2: 91-101.

     In its "treatment of the themes of freedom, power and
     identity, in its delineation of the enigmatic heroine
     and her relationship to the men who surround her, in the
     very actions she performs and the images Truffaut uses
     to suggest the implications of those actions, there is
     a remarkable similarity between the film, *Jules and Jim*
     [(1961)], and the play, *Hedda Gabler*."

567. Brown, John Russell, ed. *Drama and the Theatre: With Radio,
     Film and Television: An Outline for the Student*. London:
     Routledge & Kegan Paul.

     Not seen.

568. Byron, Stuart, and Martin L. Rubin. "Elia Kazan Inter-
     view." *Movie* 19: 1-13. See Joseph Hillier, *Movie* 19:
     38-40.

     Kazan comments on his work as theater and film director.

569. Camper, Fred. "The Tarnished Angels." *Screen* 12 (Summer):
     68-92.

     Not seen.

570. Clancy, Jack. "The Film and the Book: D.H. Lawrence and
     Joseph Heller on the Screen." *Meanjin Quarterly* 30:
     96-97, 99-101.

     "My objection to Ken Russell's *Women in Love* [(1969)]
     is not that it is not faithful to Lawrence, but that in
     trying so earnestly to be faithful it falls on its face."
     "*The Virgin and the Gypsy* [(1970)] is not a great film
     but it is a worthwhile minor one."
     The film adaptation of *Catch-22* (1970) lacks coherence.

571. Comito, Terry. "*Touch of Evil*." *Film Comment* 7, 2: 51-53.
     Reprinted in *Focus on Orson Welles*. Ed. Ronald Gottesman.
     Englewood Cliffs, New Jersey: Prentice-Hall, 1976, pp.
     157-63.

Welles' changing the scene in Whit Masterson's novel
from San Diego to a Mexican-American border town provides
a perfect setting for a complicated narrative about the
ambiguity of borders in an individual's perception of
reality.

572. Conrad, Randall. "Diaries of Two Chambermaids." *Film
      Quarterly* 24: 48-51.

      Discussion of Renoir's and Bunuel's adaptations of
      Mirbeau's novel *Diary of a Chambermaid*.

573. Crump, G.B. "Gopher Prairie or Papplewick?: *The Virgin
      and the Gypsy* as Film." *The D.H. Lawrence Review* 4:
      142-53.

      The director, Christopher Miles, "does not have so
      complete an understanding of Lawrence as we might desire."

574. Crump, G.B. "*Women in Love*: Novel and Film." *The D.H.
      Lawrence Review* 4: 28-41.

      "Although the movie ... is only a partial success,
      director Russell and screenwriter Kramer remain remark-
      ably faithful to what is Lawrence's most difficult,
      representative, and ambitious work--both to its story
      and its deeper conception of man and civilization."

575. Enser, A.G.S. *Filmed Books and Plays: A List of Books
      and Plays from Which Films Have Been Made, 1928-1967*.
      Revised and with a supplementary list from 1968 and
      1969. London: Andre Deutsch.

576. Farber, Stephen. "*The Magnificent Ambersons*." *Film
      Comment* 7, 2: 49-50. Reprinted in *Focus on Orson Welles*.
      Ed. Ronald Gottesman. Englewood Cliffs, New Jersey:
      Prentice-Hall, 1976, pp. 123-28.

      In its "study of the claustrophobic intensity of family
      life" Welles' film follows the Tarkington novel closely.

577. Ford, John, and Dudley Nichols. *Stagecoach, a Film by
      John Ford and Dudley Nichols*. New York: Simon and
      Schuster.

      Includes Ernest Haycox's short story "Stage to Lords-
      burg," Dudley Nichols' original screenplay for the film
      and footnotes detailing differences between the original
      script and the finished film.

578. French, Warren. "Film and the Undergraduate Literature
      Program." *The Bulletin of the Midwest Modern Language
      Association* 4, 1: 17-19.

      "Departments concerned primarily with literature also
      have a special role to play in film study."

579. Gerard, Lillian N. "*The Virgin and the Gypsy* and 'D.H.
      Lawrence in Taos.'" *Film Library Quarterly* 4, 1: 36-42.

      A comparison of D.H. Lawrence's novel with the film:
      "In many ways the book is superior to the film."
      Attached is a description of the short biographical
      film "D.H. Lawrence in Taos," about his stay in Taos,
      New Mexico.

580. Goldman, Frederick, and Linda R. Burnett. *Need Johnny
      Read? Practical Methods to Enrich Humanities Courses
      Using Film and Film Study.* Dayton, Ohio: Pflaum/Standard.

      The book argues the need for courses in visual literacy
      at the high school and college levels, and also documents
      why media and film should be studied.

581. Gomez, Joseph A. "The Theme of the Double in *The Third
      Man.*" *Film Heritage* 6, 4: 7-12, 24.

      Outlines the genesis of the film and analyzes its
      structure.

582. Graham, John. "'Damn Your A Priori Principles--Look!'
      W.R. Robinson Discusses Movies as Narrative Art." *The
      Film Journal* 1 (Summer): 49-53.

      W.R. Robinson discusses the relation of his interest
      in philosophy and literature to film study.

583. Graham, John. "Fiction and Film: An Interview with George
      Garrett." *The Film Journal* 1, 2: 22-25.

      Garrett discusses his experience adapting Julian
      Halevy's novel *The Young Lovers* to film.

584. Hardy, Barbara. "The New Dickens Musical." *The Dickensian*
      67 (January): 41-42.

      Despite careful research, the film *Oliver!* seriously
      distorts the Dickens novel.

585. Houston, Penelope. "Kubrick Country." *Saturday Review* 54
      (25 December): 42-44.

Kubrick discusses his adaptation of the Anthony Burgess novel *A Clockwork Orange*.

586. Jinks, William. "Ch. 5: Figurative Language." *The Celluloid Literature: Film in the Humanities*. Beverly Hills, California: The Glencoe Press, Macmillan, pp. 110-27.

    A discussion of the use of metaphor in film and literature.

587. Kline, Herbert. "On John Steinbeck." *Steinbeck Quarterly* 4: 80-88.

    Anecdotal account of the making of *The Forgotten Village* (1941), a film scripted by and made in consultation with Steinbeck.

588. Knoll, Robert F. *"Women in Love."* *Film Heritage* 6, 4: 1-6.

    "Much attention is paid to the letter and spirit of the original, yet the film accentuates the novel's weaknesses and doesn't suggest many of its (admittedly linear) riches and strengths."

589. Linden, George W. "Ten Questions about Film Form." *The Journal of Aesthetic Education* 5, 2: 61-73.

    Seeks to establish an aesthetic of film using three approaches: the genetic, the intuitive and the structural.

590. Long, Robert Emmet. "Adaptations of Henry James's Fiction for Drama, Opera, and Films; With a Checklist of New York Theatre Critics' Reviews." *American Literary Realism, 1870-1910* 4: 268-78.

    Listing of four films adapted from James's works giving credits and the names of some members of the cast: *Berkeley Square* (1933), *The Lost Moment* (1947), *The Heiress* (1949) and *The Innocents* (1962).

591. Luciano, Dale. *"Long Day's Journey into Night*: An Interview with Sidney Lumet." *Film Quarterly* 25, 1: 20-29.

    Lumet discusses the technical achievements in his adaptation of Eugene O'Neill's play.

592. MacCann, Richard Dyer. "Teaching the Film Teacher." *The Bulletin of the Midwest Modern Language Association* 4, 1: 19-22.

A consideration of the responsibilities assumed by the
teacher of film, whether he has "moved over" to film
teaching from another discipline or he has been trained
in a graduate film program.

593. McCarty, Clifford. *Published Screenplays: A Checklist*.
Kent, Ohio: The Kent State University Press.

Lists published screenplays in complete and in excerpted
form.

594. Mailer, Norman. "A Course in Filmmaking." *"Maidstone"*:
A Mystery. New York: The New American Library, Signet,
pp. 137-80.

Mailer discusses the theory behind the making of his
"existentialist" film, *Maidstone*.

595. Manvell, Roger. *Shakespeare and the Film*. New York,
Washington: Praeger Publishers.

A study of "the principal sound films which have been
adapted from Shakespeare's plays, using either the original
text or some form of close translation." The interest
of analysis is "to show how the plays have been presented
to make them effective as films, and how the technique
of the film itself has to be modified considerably to
make it effective as a medium for Shakespeare, more espe-
cially if Shakespeare's verse is to become living, dramatic
speech for film audiences."

Considers twenty-five films: Sam Taylor's *The Taming
of the Shrew* (1929); Reinhardt's *A Midsummer Night's
Dream* (1935); Cukor's *Romeo and Juliet* (1936); Czinner's
As You Like It (1936); Olivier's *Henry V* (1944), *Hamlet*
(1948) and *Richard III* (1955); Welles' *Macbeth* (1948),
Othello (1951) and *Chimes at Midnight* (1966); Yutkevitch's
Othello (1955); Kozintsev's *Hamlet* (1964) and *King Lear*
(1970); Mankiewicz's and Burge's *Julius Caesar* (1953 and
1969); Castellani's and Zeffirelli's *Romeo and Juliet*
(1954 and 1968); Zeffirelli's *The Taming of the Shrew*
(1966); Kurosawa's *Macbeth, The Castle of the Spider's
Web* (1957); Schaefer's *Macbeth* (1960); Dunlop's *The Winter's
Tale* (1966); Burge's *Othello* (1965); Peter Hall's *A Midsummer Night's Dream* (1969); Richardson's *Hamlet* (1969);
and Peter Brook's *King Lear* (1970).

596. Marcus, Fred H. "Film and Fiction: *An Occurrence at Owl
Creek Bridge*." *Film and Fiction: Contrasts in Media*.
Scranton, London, Toronto: Chandler Publishing, pp.

260-71. Also printed in the *California English Journal*
7 (February 1971): 14-23. [Not seen.]

Robert Enrico's film adaptation of the Ambrose Bierce
short story succeeds in rendering the mental and emotional
texture of the protagonist in the story.

597. Marcus, Fred H., and Paul Zall. *"Catch-22*: Is Film Fidelity
      an Asset?" *Film and Literature: Contrasts in Media.*
      Ed. Fred H. Marcus. Scranton, London, Toronto: Chandler
      Publishing, pp. 127-36.

An analysis of Mike Nichols' adaptation of Joseph
Heller's novel *Catch-22*, in which the film is found to be
"intelligent, technically excellent, filled with memor-
able sequences, verbally articulate, faithful to a difficult novel, daring in conception, and reasonably successful in execution."

598. Margolies, Alan. "F. Scott Fitzgerald's Work in the Film
      Studios." *Princeton University Library Chronicle* 32:
      81-110.

Fitzgerald, though "not an exceptional scriptwriter,"
did "work seriously at his craft" in 1937, employing
not only technical skills he had learned during previous
stints as a screenwriter in Hollywood in 1927 and 1931
but also skills drawn from his work as a writer of fiction.

599. Mellen, Joan. *"Death in Venice." Film Quarterly* 25: 41-47.
      Reprinted in *Women and Their Sexuality in the New Film.*
      New York: Horizon Press, 1973, pp. 203-15.

Luchino Visconti's adaptation of Thomas Mann's story
is "confused and painfully callow."

600. Metzger, Charles R. "The Film Version of Steinbeck's
      'The Pearl.'" *Steinbeck Quarterly* 4: 88-92.

The film was made at a time, 1947-48, when "the
standard of realistic portrayal and fidelity to original
texts" was not particularly high.

601. Mitry, Jean. "Remarks on the Problem of Cinematic Adapta-
      tion." *The Bulletin of the Midwest Modern Language
      Association* 4, 1: 1-9.

"We talk as if adaptation were a matter of translation,
like passing from one language to another, when in fact
it is a matter of passing from one *form* to another, a
matter of transposition, of reconstruction."

602. Morton, James. "From the Book of the Same Name." *Contem-
       porary Review* 219: 100-04.

       A consideration of five films that remain "more or less
       faithful to their books": Luchino Visconti's adaptation
       of Thomas Mann's *Death in Venice*; Jean-Gabriel Albicocco's
       The Wanderer (1969), made from the novel by Alain-Fournier;
       Thomas Berger's *Little Big Man*, adapted by Arthur Penn;
       Mike Hodges' film *Get Carter*, adapted from Ted Lewis'
       Jack's Return Home; and the adaptation by Ossie Davis
       of Chester Himes' novel *Cotton Comes to Harlem*.

603. Nichols, Bill. *"Walkabout." Cinema* 7, 1: 8-12.

       An analysis of the film and the book, *Walkabout* by
       James Marshall, on which it was based.

604. O'Grady, Gerald. "The Dance of *The Misfits*: A Movie
       Mobile." *The Journal of Aesthetic Education* 5, 2: 75-89.

       "The description of the film as [Arthur] Miller con-
       ceived it as a sort of mobile, as having the structure
       of a puzzle, the pieces of which again and again just
       miss fitting together, as placing its characters like
       a group of dancers in a ballet, sometimes linking arms,
       sometimes performing solo, but always in motion, is an
       important perception," which can be confirmed by comparing
       the short story and the cinema-novel version of the film.

605. O'Grady, Gerald. "Teaching the Film." *Filmmakers News-
       letter* 4, 12: 23-30.

       "We must be prepared to examine how a technology re-
       gardless of its content, interacts with our conscious-
       ness and thus transforms our cultures."

606. Roud, Richard. "Going Between." *Sight and Sound* 40:
       158-59.

       L.P. Hartley's novel *The Go-Between* has been success-
       fully adapted to the screen by Harold Pinter and Joseph
       Losey.

607. Samuels, Charles Thomas. "Talking with Truffaut." *The
       American Scholar* 40: 482-86.

       For Truffaut, the adaptation of a work of literature
       to film poses dangers to the filmmaker not "cinematically
       armed" for the job.

608. Sarris, Andrew. "Literature and Film." *The Bulletin of the Midwest Modern Language Association* 4, 1: 10-15.

"The problem that we face in talking about film and literature is that instead of mediating between them (much less bringing them together in marriage) we merely invent an aesthetic sub-stratum common to them both, and then talk about that."

609. Schultheiss, John. "The 'Eastern' Writer in Hollywood." *Cinema Journal* 11, 1: 13-45.

The experiences in Hollywood of writers who obtained a previous literary reputation in the East.

610. Scobie, Stephen. "Concerning Horses: Concerning Apes." *Riverside Quarterly* 4: 258-62.

The satire in *Planet of the Apes* (1968) and *Beneath the Planet of the Apes* (1970) is compared to the satire in Swift's *Gulliver's Travels*.

611. Silverstein, Norman. "Film and Language, Film and Literature." *Journal of Modern Literature* 2: 154-60.

"Although structuralist film criticism is one interesting kind, literary critics have methodologies, along with a vocabulary drawn from rhetoric, that can draw essences from film."

612. Simon, John. "Adaptations." *Movies into Film: Film Criticism 1967-1970.* New York: Dial Press, pp. 25-65.

An extended discussion of various film adaptations of works of literature.

613. Smith, John M. "Elia Kazan's *The Arrangement.*" *Movie* 18: 14-17.

"The film is a dense, rich and full work--partly the result no doubt of being worked and re-worked, first as a novel, then through the scripting, production and directing of the film."

614. Stewart, Lawrence D. "Fitzgerald's Film Scripts of 'Babylon Revisited.'" *Fitzgerald/Hemingway Annual 1971.* Ed. Matthew J. Bruccoli and C.E. Frazer Clark, Jr. Washington: NCR/Microcard Editions, pp. 81-104.

Through analysis of Fitzgerald's several efforts to write a screenplay for his story, it is shown "what went wrong" with them.

615. Vronskaya, Jeanne. "Polanski's 'Macbeth' and Its Antece-
      dents." *Film* (Great Britain) 62: 23.

      A listing of film versions of Shakespeare's *Macbeth*.

616. Yutkevitch, Sergei. "The Conscience of the King: Kozintsev's
      King Lear." *Sight and Sound* 40: 193-96.

      Commentary on Grigori Kozintsev's film adaptation of
      Shakespeare's *King Lear*.

                              1972

617. "Further Comment." *Focus on the Science Fiction Film*.
      Ed. William Johnson. Englewood Cliffs, New Jersey:
      Prentice-Hall, pp. 148-70.

      Some writers of science fiction and several filmmakers
      give their views on science fiction films.

618. Barrett, Gerald R., and Thomas L. Erskine. *From Fiction
      to Film: Conrad Aiken's "Silent Snow, Secret Snow."*
      Encino, California: Dickenson Publishers.

      Not seen.

619. Beylie, Claude. "*Macbeth*, or the Magical Depths." *Focus
      on Shakespearean Films*. Ed. Charles W. Eckert. Engle-
      wood Cliffs, New Jersey: Prentice-Hall, pp. 72-75.

      Orson Welles' *Macbeth* (1948) praised.

620. Carey, Gary. *More About "All About Eve": A Colloquy by
      Gary Carey with Joseph L. Mankiewicz Together with His
      Screenplay "All About Eve."* New York: Random House.

      Discussion of the stages of development in the adapta-
      tion of Mary Orr's story "The Wisdom of Eve" to the screen.

621. Clair, René. "Theater and Cinema." *Cinema Yesterday and
      Today*. Ed. R.C. Dale. Trans. Stanley Appelbaum. New
      York: Dover Publications, pp. 159-69.

      Comments Clair originally wrote on this subject in a
      newspaper article in 1932 are excerpted and compared
      with his revised view of 1950; both of these views then
      become the object of a second revision and commentary
      in 1970.

622. Clarke, Arthur C. *The Lost Worlds of "2001."* New York: New American Library.

This diary-like account of Clarke's engagement with the making of *2001: A Space Odyssey* (1968) includes the different versions of the scenario as they evolved before the film was made.

623. Cohen, Hubert. *"The Heart of Darkness* in *Citizen Kane."* *Cinema Journal* 12, 1: 11-25.

"There is evidence that Conrad's character, Kurtz, was a partial source of the film's Charles Foster Kane, that other characters in the Conrad story suggested either wholly or in part characters in the film, and that there are similarities between the film and the novel in structure, points of view, and details of action and style."

624. Erickson, James. "Teaching Literature and Film: Some Useful Examples." *Kansas Quarterly* 4, 2: 21-29.

Description of a course on narrative in literature and film.

625. Froug, William. *A Screenwriter Looks at the Screenwriter.* New York: The Macmillan Company.

A collection of enlightening interviews with twelve screenwriters.

626. Fuegi, John. "Explorations in No Man's Land: Shakespeare's Poetry as Theatrical Film." *Shakespeare Quarterly* 23: 37-49.

Criticism of the Shakespearean film requires a willingness to cut through to "the primary problem, the aesthetic relationship of a text to its mode of production." Commentary on thirteen films: Cukor's *Romeo and Juliet* (1936); Welles' *Macbeth* (1948) and *Othello* (1951); Olivier's *Hamlet* (1948), *Henry V* (1944) and *Richard III* (1955); Castellani's *Romeo and Juliet* (1954); Mankiewicz's *Julius Caesar* (1953); Yutkevitch's *Othello* (1955); Schaefer's *Macbeth* (1960); Kozintsev's *Hamlet* (1964); Zeffirelli's *Romeo and Juliet* (1968); and Fried's *Twelfth Night* (1955).

627. Fuegi, John. "Feuchtwanger, Brecht and the 'Epic' Media: The Novel and the Film." *Lion Feuchtwanger: The Man, His Ideas, His Work. A Collection of Critical Essays.* Ed. John M. Spalek. Los Angeles: Hennessey & Ingalls, pp. 307-22.

Compares and contrasts these two writers and illustrates
"differences in Weltanshauung, in urbanity, and in political and aesthetic balance revealed by their decades of
work in the major epic [Brecht's "episches Theater," the
novel and the film] modes of the twentieth century."

628. Geduld, Harry M., ed. *Authors on Film*. Bloomington and
      London: Indiana University Press.

      A miscellany designed to reveal the many aspects of
      writers' attitudes toward film.
      "The first part of the book contains articles, essays
      and reviews pertaining to the silent cinema and the
      transition to sound. The second section provides a selec-
      tion of general statements on the film medium or film-
      makers and their messages."

629. Giannetti, Louis D. "Cinematic Metaphors." *The Journal
      of Aesthetic Education* 6, 4: 49-61.

      "This brief survey is an adequate demonstration that
      metaphors thrive in film, despite the denials that have
      been made by both literary critics and some film directors
      (mostly realists and neorealists, who tend to avoid
      figurative techniques)."

630. Giannetti, Louis D. "Drama" and "Literature." *Understand-
      ing Movies*. Englewood Cliffs, New Jersey: Prentice-Hall,
      pp. 266-310; 311-76.

      A survey of the similarities and differences between
      film and drama considered in light of several categories:
      "Time, Space, and Language," "The Director," "The Actor"
      and "Costumes, Makeup, and Settings."
      The relationship between film and the novel and the
      short story is examined from the point of view of "The
      Writer," "The Script," "Motifs, Symbols, Metaphors,
      and Allusions" and "Point-of-View and Literary Adapta-
      tions."

631. Gottesman, Ronald, and Harry M. Geduld. "Adaptation."
      Guidebook to Film: An Eleven-in-One Reference. New
      York: Holt, Rinehart and Winston, pp. 30-35.

      Not seen.

632. Grossvogel, David I. "When the Stain Won't Wash: Polanski's
      Macbeth." *Diacritics: A Review of Contemporary Criti-
      cism* 2, 2: 46-51.

      Not seen.

633. Gumenik, Arthur. "*A Clockwork Orange*: Novel into Film."
     Film Heritage 7, 4: 7-18, 28.

     "In adapting Burgess' novel to film, Kubrick greatly
     increases the importance of the libido."

634. Guzzetti, Alfred. "The Role of Theory in Films and Novels."
     New Literary History 3: 547-58.

     Demonstrates by means of a comparison of Godard's
     film *Contempt* with the film's source, Alberto Moravia's
     Il Disprezzo, that the foundations of theoretical approaches
     to novels and films are and must be different. "For its
     intelligibility ... the novel depends more directly and
     fundamentally on language, whose organization and powers
     of narrative reference are assured by circumstances which
     are not, and cannot be, the responsibility of the indi-
     vidual writer. In film, no comparable guarantee exists
     for the form of the image or the sound."

635. Halliday, Jon. *Sirk on Sirk: Interviews with Jon Halliday*.
     New York: Viking.

     Discussion of problems of adaptation and of the connec-
     tion of *The Tarnished Angels* (1957) with William Faulkner's
     Pylon.

636. Henderson, Robert M. *D.W. Griffith: His Life and Work*.
     New York: Oxford University Press.

     "The book is an attempt to sort out the reality of
     Griffith from the legend."
     The first chapter, "From Playwright to Screen Writer,"
     is especially interesting.

637. Katz, John Stuart; Curt Oliver; and Forbes Aird. "The
     Film-Literature Study Project." *A Curriculum in Film*.
     Toronto: The Ontario Institute for Studies in Educa-
     tion, pp. 6-18.

     Description of a program of study designed to develop
     in students an increased sensitivity to film and litera-
     ture.

638. Kauffmann, Stanley. "Notes on Theater-and-Film."
     Performance 1, 4: 104-09. Reprinted in *Living Images:
     Film Comment and Criticism*. New York, Evanston, San
     Francisco, London: Harper & Row, 1975, pp. 353-62.

     A reexamination of some "received ideas" on the sub-
     ject of theater and film in note form.

639. Kawin, Bruce F. *Telling It Again and Again: Repetition in
      Literature and Film*. Ithaca and London: Cornell Univer-
      sity Press.

      On the use of repetition in literature and film.

640. Kermode, Frank. "Shakespeare in the Movies." *The New York
      Review of Books* (4 May): 19-21.

      Analyses of Charlton Heston's *Antony and Cleopatra*
      (1972), Roman Polanski's *Macbeth* (1971) and Peter Brook's
      King Lear (1970).

641. Kestner, Joseph A., III. "Stevenson and Artaud: *The Master
      of Ballantrae*." *Film Heritage* 7, 4: 19-28.

      "It is in Robert Louis Stevenson's *The Master of
      Ballantrae* that Artaud discovered the moral complexity
      which he felt would enhance the new art of the cinema."

642. Kozintsev, Grigori. "'Hamlet' and 'King Lear': Stage and
      Film." *Shakespeare 1971*. Proceedings of the World
      Shakespeare Congress, Vancouver, August 1971. Ed.
      Clifford Leech and J.M.R. Margeson. Toronto and Buffalo:
      University of Toronto Press, pp. 190-99.

      "In making a Shakespeare film it is important not to
      fall between the two stools of theatre and cinema. The
      result is likely to be either a bad production, on the
      one hand, or a lifeless film on the other."

643. Lemaitre, Henri. "Shakespeare, the Imaginary Cinema and
      the Pre-cinema." *Focus on Shakespearean Films*. Ed.
      Charles W. Eckert. Englewood Cliffs, New Jersey:
      Prentice-Hall, pp. 27-36.

      An "inquiry into the exact nature of those secret
      rapports between the worlds of Shakespeare ... and the
      world of cinema."

644. Lenning, Arthur. "D.W. Griffith and the Making of an
      Unconventional Masterpiece." *The Film Journal* 1, 3-4:
      2-15.

      Adapted from Thomas Burke's story "The Chink and the
      Child," D.W. Griffith's film *Broken Blossoms* (1919) cap-
      tured its "general tone and spirit."

645. McConnell, Frank D. "Film and Writing: The Political
      Dimension." *The Massachusetts Review* 13: 543-62.

Argues that the "complementarity" of "literary" and "filmic" ideas must be admitted into any serious discussion of "the possibility of a truly political cinema."

"What I wish to suggest is simply this: that 'politics,' if it makes sense at all as a term we can use, must signify its most general meaning, 'life in time.' And that *no* sign-system, either language or the succession of images which is cinema, can escape from the fundamental contradiction of all sign-systems which try to deal with 'politics' in our sense: the contradiction being that they are attempting to signify precisely what no system can signify, the higher system which is its cause."

646.   Magny, Claude-Edmonde. *The Age of the American Novel: The Film Aesthetic of Fiction Between Two Wars.* New York: Frederick Ungar Publishing.

A study of the influence of techniques of filmmakers on the development of the French and, principally, the American novel up to the end of World War II.

After discussions of methods of narration, the use of ellipsis and cutting in film and the novel, specific chapters deal with Dos Passos: "Dos Passos's *U.S.A.*, or the Impersonal Novel" and "Time in Dos Passos"; Hemingway: "Hemingway, or the Exaltation of the Moment"; Steinbeck: "Steinbeck, or the Limits of the Impersonal Novel"; and Faulkner: "Faulkner, or Theological Inversion."

647.   Merritt, Russell. "Dixon, Griffith, and the Southern Legend." *Cinema Journal* 12, 1: 26-45.

An investigation of the sources, the dynamics and the impact of Griffith's *The Birth of a Nation* (1915).

648.   Munden, Kenneth W. "Sinclair Lewis and the Movies." *Cinema Journal* 12, 1: 46-56.

References to movies in Lewis' novels are surveyed. "Whether Lewis saw film art as good or bad, he was not ... indifferent to it."

649.   Murray, Edward. *The Cinematic Imagination: Writers and the Motion Pictures.* New York: Frederick Ungar Publishing.

The development of the film was nurtured and inspired by the nineteenth-century drama and novel. In the twentieth century, however, the cinematic imagination has influenced the drama and novel.

The book is split into two parts: first, an analysis
of the influence of film on dramatists like Shaw, Piran-
dello, O'Neill, Brecht, Williams, Gertrude Stein, Arthur
Miller, Ionesco and Beckett; second, the influence of
film on novelists Thomas Mann, Kafka, Dreiser, Joyce,
Woolf, Faulkner, Dos Passos, Fitzgerald, West, Wolfe,
Robert Penn Warren, Hemingway, Greene, Steinbeck, Sartre,
Henry Miller and Robbe-Grillet.

650. Pickard, Roy. "Novels into Films" and "Plays into Films."
      *A Companion to the Movies: From 1903 to the Present
      Day*. New York: Hippocrene Books, pp. 219-36; 237-46.

      Provides select lists of famous novels and plays that
      have been adapted to film.

651. Probst, Robert E. "Visual to Verbal." *The English Journal*
      61: 71-75.

      Film, which provides a fixed text, can be read and
      discussed as literature can.

652. Richie, Donald, ed. *Focus on "Rashomon."* Englewood Cliffs,
      New Jersey: Prentice-Hall.

      Examines Kurosawa's film by means of reviews, commen-
      taries and essays. Includes a plot synopsis, content out-
      line, extract from the script and a reprinting of the
      Ryonosuke Akutagawa stories, "Rashomon" and "In a Grove,"
      which inspired the film.

653. Robinson, W.R., and Mary McDermott. "'2001' and Literary
      Sensibility." *The Georgia Review* 26: 21-37.

      Kubrick's "new story [*2001: A Space Odyssey* (1969)]
      looks beyond exhausted verbal sources and values. It
      takes as its province visual relations, connections too
      subtle for verbal articulation."

654. Rosenbaum, Jonathan. "The Voice and the Eye. A Commentary
      on 'The Heart of Darkness' Script." *Film Comment* 8, 4:
      27-32.

      Commentary on the genesis and content of Welles'
      script based on the Joseph Conrad story. Includes a num-
      ber of shot descriptions and some dialogue.

655. Samuels, Charles Thomas. "The Context of *A Clockwork
      Orange*." *The American Scholar* 41: 439-43. Reprinted in
      Mastering the Film and Other Essays. Ed. Lawrence

Graver. Knoxville: The University of Tennessee Press, 1977, pp. 171-78.

"Kubrick seems intent merely on showing us how to embody filmically a world first imagined in words. His expertise is undeniable, but it is also narrow and unedifying."

656. Sargent, Seymour H. "*Julius Caesar* and the Historical Film." *The English Journal* 61: 230-33, 245.

Shows similarity between Shakespeare's recreation of history in *Julius Caesar* and the treatment of history typical of American historical films.

657. Sharples, Win, Jr. "The Art of Filmmaking: An Analysis of 'Slaughterhouse Five.'" *Filmmakers Newsletter* 6, 1: 24-28.

A careful analysis of editing techniques in the film adaptation of Vonnegut's *Slaughterhouse-Five* which reveals the virtuosity of film editor Dede Allen, who succeeded in capturing the sense of dislocation of time and space in the novel.

658. Taylor, Henry. "A Panel of Experts on 'Blind Alley' [a television show] Discuss the Influence of Cinema on Modern Poets." *The Film Journal* 1, 3-4: 36-49.

A discussion of the various ways poets have treated the movies.

659. Trimmer, Joseph F. "*The Virginian*: Novel and Films." *Illinois Quarterly* 35, 2: 5-18. Reprinted in *The Classic American Novel and the Movies*. Ed. Gerald Peary and Roger Shatzkin. New York: Frederick Ungar Publishing, 1977, pp. 176-91.

The novel and its 1929 and 1945 film versions have "documented the alteration in the character of the Western myth and our attitude toward it.... Gradually, the virtues of the West have been exchanged for Victorian seriousness, cultural rigidity, and the emerging corporate executive."

660. Truffaut, François. "Adapting *Shoot the Piano Player*." *Focus on "Shoot the Piano Player."* Ed. Leo Braudy. Englewood Cliffs, New Jersey: Prentice-Hall, pp. 123-26.

On the film adaptation of the David Goodis novel *Down There*. "I couldn't adapt a film from a book I hated."

661. Walker, Alexander. *Stanley Kubrick Directs*. New York:
      Harcourt Brace Jovanovich.

      Not seen.

662. Weisstein, Ulrich. "Translations and Adaptations of
      Heinrich Mann's Novel in Two Media." *The Film Journal*
      1, 3-4: 53-61.

      Mann's novel *Professor Unrat* was so successfully adapted
      to film in *The Blue Angel* (1930) that its author's name
      has come to be associated with the film, not the novel
      on which it is based.

663. Wilmington, Michael. "*The Fugitive.*" *The Velvet Light
      Trap* 5: 33-55.

      "It is not slighting Graham Greene to say that, although
      his novel [*The Power and the Glory*] is incomparably better
      than the film [*The Fugitive* (1947)] Ford made of it, the
      director's very inability to reconcile Greene's theologi-
      cal obsessiveness probably shows why Ford is the greater
      artist."

664. Zambrano, Ana Laura. "*Great Expectations*: Dickens' Style
      in Terms of Film." *Hartford Studies in Literature* 4:
      104-13.

      Brings film terminology into use to discuss the cinematic
      qualities of the novel.

                                1973

665. Abele, Rudolph Von. "Film as Interpretation: A Case
      Study of *Ulysses.*" *The Journal of Aesthetics and Art
      Criticism* 31: 487-500.

      "I shall name and discuss ten ways in which the film
      Ulysses [(1967)] may be said to interpret the novel, and
      try to draw a few conclusions from what I find."

666. Appel, Alfred, Jr. "The Eyehole of Knowledge: Voyeuristic
      Games in Film and Literature." *Film Comment* 9, 3: 20-26.

      Voyeurism and eroticism in Nabokov, Hitchcock and
      Rohmer.

667. Appel, Alfred, Jr. "Nabokov's Dark Cinema: A Diptych."
      TriQuarterly 27: 196-273. Revised and printed as Chap-
      ter 2, "Negative Images," and Chapter 4, "Positive

Images," in *Nabokov's Dark Cinema*. New York: Oxford University Press, 1974, pp. 29-59; 153-59.

Nabokov's attitude toward popular cinema.

668. Armour, Robert. *"Deliverance*. Four Variations of the American Adam." *Literature/Film Quarterly* 1: 280-85.

The Adam theme (described by R.B. Lewis in *The American Adam*) in James Dickey's novel, *Deliverance*, is purposely accented in the film adaptation.

669. Atwell, Lee. "Two Studies in Space-Time." *Film Quarterly* 26, 2: 2-9.

George Roy Hill successfully presented the "fractured time concept" present in Kurt Vonnegut's novel *Slaughterhouse-Five*.

670. Baldanza, Frank. *"Sons and Lovers*: Novel to Film as a Record of Cultural Growth." *Literature/Film Quarterly* 1: 64-70.

The tightening of the plot in the movie version of D.H. Lawrence's novel "did aesthetic violence to the looseness and random impulsiveness that is at the heart of Lawrence."

671. Ball, Robert Hamilton. "The Beginnings of Shakespeare Sound Films." *Shakespeare Newsletter* 23: 48.

Though the 1929 *Taming of the Shrew* was the first feature-length sound film adaptation of a Shakespeare play, pre-sound film excerpts accompanied by sound from wax cylinders or actors behind screens were presented in movie houses.

672. Ball, Robert Hamilton. "On Shakespeare Filmography." *Literature/Film Quarterly* 1: 299-306.

Survey and criticism of several Shakespeare filmographies.

673. Ball, Robert Hamilton. "Tree's *King John* Film: An Addendum." *Shakespeare Quarterly* 24: 455-59. See 233.

Corrects and modifies statements concerning the silent film adaptation of *King John* made by Herbert Beerbohm Tree in 1899-1900.

674. Bancroft, David. "Cocteau--Orphée: Film-maker--Poet."
      Meanjin Quarterly 32: 73-79.

      "Cocteau--painter, musician, architect and poet--brought
      all his talents together to construct a work of collective
      creation which can be assessed finally as a complete
      vindication of the ideal of the synthesis of the arts--
      an ideal which, it is claimed, only the cinema medium
      can approach so nearly, and towards which the evolution
      of Cocteau's entire aesthetic as an artist had moved."

675. Barrett, Gerald. "Andrew Sarris Interview: October 16,
      1972 (Part One)." *Literature/Film Quarterly* 1: 195-
      205. See 788.

      Sarris on the *auteur* theory.

676. Barrett, Gerald R. "Graham Greene's *Ministry of Fear*:
      The Transformation of an Entertainment." *Literature/
      Film Quarterly* 2: 316-23. See 775.

      "The film's greatest delights are found in Lang's
      skillful and creative treatment of his formal materials
      rather than in the philosophic equivocations noticeably
      evident in its denouement."

677. Barrett, Gerald. "Jonas Mekas Interview: October 10,
      1972." *Literature/Film Quarterly* 1: 103-12.

      The two interests in the interview are the origin of
      the New American Cinema and the use of literature in
      film.

678. Barrett, Gerald R., and Thomas Erskine, eds. *From Fiction
      to Film: Ambrose Bierce's "An Occurrence at Owl Creek
      Bridge."* Encino, California: Dickenson Publishing.

      A casebook designed as a "new approach to the teach-
      ing of short stories, films, and the art of adaptation,"
      which contains the reprinted story, a shot analysis
      of two film adaptations of the story and several critical
      essays.

679. Becker, Henry, III. "*The Rocking-Horse Winner*: Film as
      Parable." *Literature/Film Quarterly* 1: 55-63.

      The 1949 film version of D.H. Lawrence's story is
      "a carefully and skillfully made tragic film."

680. Bedard, B.J. "Reunion in Havana." *Literature/Film
      Quarterly* 2: 352-58.

This third collaboration between Carol Reed and Graham Greene, *Our Man in Havana* (1959), "is ultimately the least satisfying of the trio."

681. Berlin, Norman. "*Macbeth*: Polanski and Shakespeare." *Literature/Film Quarterly* 1: 291-98.

"How Polanski sees (or reads) *Macbeth* indicates the rich suggestiveness of Shakespeare's art; it also indicates Polanski's personal vision of the modern world."

682. Blades, Joe. "The Evolution of *Cabaret*." *Literature/Film Quarterly* 1: 226-38.

Traces changes in Isherwood's work from novella, *Goodbye to Berlin*, to straight play, *I Am a Camera*, to musical book, *Cabaret*.

683. Bobrow, Andrew C. "The Making of *Dillinger*." *Filmmakers Newsletter* 7, 1: 20-25.

Screenwriter-director John Milius talks about his experiences making the film *Dillinger*.

684. Brody, Alan. "The Gift of Realism: Hitchcock and Pinter." *Journal of Modern Literature* 3: 149-72.

"Besides reflecting the very individual vision of their authors, Alfred Hitchcock's *Shadow of a Doubt* (1943) and Harold Pinter's *The Birthday Party* are representative, in certain crucial ways, of the contemporary history and development of the film and theater themselves."

685. Chaplin, William. "Our Darker Purpose: Peter Brook's *King Lear*." *Arion* n.s. 1: 168-87.

Brook's film is informed by "a vigorous exploratory aesthetic," which challenges us to rethink the play, and which indicates his own search for a means of translating the play into a powerful film.

686. Clarke, Arthur C. "Son of Dr. Strangelove: Or, How I Learned to Stop Worrying and Love Stanley Kubrick." *Report on Planet Three and Other Speculations*. New York, Evanston, San Francisco: Harper & Row, pp. 238-46. Reprinted in *Turning Points: Essays on the Art of Science Fiction*. Ed. Damon Knight. New York: Harper & Row, 1977, pp. 277-84.

On the genesis of, and Clarke's collaboration with
Kubrick in the making of, *2001: A Space Odyssey* (1968).

687. Collier, John. "The Apology." *Milton's "Paradise Lost":
Screenplay for Cinema of the Mind.* New York: Alfred
A. Knopf.

This screenplay "is a parade of scenes based on Milton's
glorious and appalling images, peopled with hideous or
radiant monsters, and with archetypes of human beings
caught in the pregnant situations of the fable."

688. Coulthard, Ron. "From Manuscript to Movie Script: James
Dickey's *Deliverance.*" *Notes on Contemporary Literature*
3, 5: 11-12.

In the screenplay, Dickey alters the character of Ed,
whose character development is at the center of the novel,
for the sake of "cheap suspense."

689. Crump, G.B. "Lawrence and the *Literature/Film Quarterly.*"
The D.H. Lawrence Review 6: 326-32.

A critical review of the first issue of the journal
Literature/Film Quarterly, which was devoted to film
adaptations of several of D.H. Lawrence's works.

690. Daniel, Wendell. "A Researcher's Guide and Selected
Checklist of Film as Literature and Language." *Journal
of Modern Literature* 3: 323-50.

Part I lists six reference books which are basic to
any research project regarding film. Part II cites
bibliographies and filmographies which are most useful
in researching the topic of film and literature and
language. Part III is a checklist of periodical bibliographies. Part IV annotates a list of indexes useful for
locating articles published in periodicals. Part V cites
theoretical studies. Part VI offers a selection of read-
ings on film and language.

691. Degenfelder, E. Pauline. "The Film Adaptation of
Faulkner's *Intruder in the Dust.*" *Literature/Film
Quarterly* 1: 138-48.

"*Intruder in the Dust* [(1949)] is probably the most
outstanding cinematic adaptation of Faulkner's fiction."

692. Demby, Betty Jeffries. "An Interview with Robert Bolt."
Filmmakers Newsletter 6, 12: 28-33.

Bolt talks about both the different obligations of playwrighting and screenwriting and his adaptations of his play *A Man for All Seasons* and Pasternak's *Doctor Zhivago*.

693. Demby, Betty Jeffries. "The Making of 'Godspell': An Interview with Director David Greene." *Filmmakers Newsletter* 6, 7: 32-35.

Problems encountered in adapting the musical to the screen.

694. Dempsey, Michael. "*Deliverance*/Boorman: Dickey in the Woods." *Cinema* 8, 1: 10-17.

Though Dickey wrote the screenplay of his novel, a consideration of the film shows the great influence of director Boorman on the completed film.

695. De Vries, Daniel. "*2001: A Space Odyssey*." *The Films of Stanley Kubrick*. Grand Rapids, Michigan: William B. Eerdmans Publishing, pp. 45-56.

Points out the differences in Kubrick's and A.C. Clarke's conceptions of the story that became *2001: A Space Odyssey* (1968).

696. Dimeo, Steven. "Reconciliation: *Slaughterhouse-Five*-- The Film and the Novel." *Film Heritage* 8, 2: 1-12.

"In many instances screenwriter Stephen Geller catches the flavor of the novel so well that he clarifies and enhances its purpose."

697. Dimeo, Steven. "The Ticking of an Orange." *Riverside Quarterly* 5: 318-21.

Not seen.

698. Dreyer, Carl. "A Little on Film Style." *Dreyer in Double Reflection: Translation of Carl Th. Dreyer's Writings about the Film (On Filmen)*. Ed. and with Essays and Annotations by Donald Skoller. New York: E.P. Dutton, pp. 122-42.

Not seen.

699. Eidsvik, Charles. "Demonstrating Film Influence." *Literature/Film Quarterly* 1: 113-21.

"The media-awareness of modernist literature makes any
claim about 'the cinematic' quality of literature a
tricky endeavor."

700. Eikhenbaum, Boris. "Literature and Cinema (1926)."
*Russian Formalism: A Collection of Articles and Texts
in Translation.* Ed. Stephen Bann and John E. Bowlt.
Edinburgh: Scottish Academic Press, pp. 122-27.

"Film is gradually creating its own styles and genres,
its own stylistics and semantics. It is with this goal
that it is tapping literature. It has its methods of
shooting (photography) and editing, but it needs material.
It takes literature and translates it into filmic language."

701. Eskin, Stanley G. *"The Garden of the Finzi-Continis."*
Literature/Film Quarterly 1: 171-77.

The film "provides examples of homologies (that is,
techniques and effects more or less identical in the
novel and film), of analogies (that is, equivalencies
achieved by translating into terms appropriate to film
effects obtained differently in the novel), and of
divergences (that is, changes, additions or omissions
in the film resulting in significant differences of
structure, meaning or emphasis)."

702. Fagin, Steven. "Narrative Design in *Travels with My
Aunt.*" *Literature/Film Quarterly* 2: 379-83.

Analyzes Graham Greene's novel and George Cukor's
film "in terms of narrative structure."

703. Fisher, James E. "Olivier and the Realistic *Othello.*"
Literature/Film Quarterly 1: 321-31.

"In its essentials, in the interpretation of character and the evocation of freshly illumined responses
of the mind and heart, this film [of the British National
Theatre's 1965 production of the play] amounts to a
great *Othello.*"

704. Fisher, Richard. "'Under Milkwood': A Film Critique."
Filmmakers Newsletter 6, 9-10: 30-31.

"At the very beginning of his film adaptation of Dylan
Thomas's *Under Milkwood*, Andrew Sinclair draws up the
battle lines. The film is a war between sight and
sound, between recorded word and depicted image."

705. Fletcher, John. "Bergman and Strindberg." *Journal of
      Modern Literature* 3: 173-90.

      "In spite of the fact that the cultural influences
      [on Bergman] are largely literary," he has not made
      films "that were little more than screen adaptations of
      Strindberg's plays."

706. French, Warren. *Filmguide to "The Grapes of Wrath."*
      Bloomington: Indiana University Press.

      Besides notes on Outline, The Director, The Production,
      Analysis, Ford Filmography, and Bibliography, the volume
      contains an Appendix in which the novel, screenplay
      and film are compared.

707. Fuegi, John. "Brecht and the Film Medium." *Expression,
      Communication and Experience in Literature and Language.*
      Ed. Ronald G. Popperwell. London: Modern Humanities
      Research Association, pp. 223-25.

      Brecht never saw the potential of film as an instrument
      for political change.

708. Geduld, Carolyn. *Filmguide to "2001: A Space Odyssey."*
      Bloomington: Indiana University Press.

      Provides notes on the film in the form of an Outline,
      short essays on the Director and the Producer, and an
      Analysis of the film. Includes a Bibliography.

709. Geduld, Harry. *Filmguide to "Henry V."* Bloomington:
      Indiana University Press.

      The guide outlines the film and gives information con-
      cerning director Laurence Olivier, the production of
      the film, an analysis of the film itself and bibliograph-
      ical materials.

710. Gerlach, John. "*The Last Picture Show* and One More Adap-
      tation." *Literature/Film Quarterly* 1: 161-66.

      "What *The Last Picture Show* [(1971)] does demonstrate
      is the sad limitation of the filmed novel. The best ones
      are made from second-rate novels."

711. Gerlach, John. "Shakespeare, Kurosawa, and *Macbeth*: A
      Response to J. Blumenthal." *Literature/Film Quarterly*
      1: 352-59. See 401.

Revises Blumenthal's too optimistic critical appraisal of the Kurosawa adaptation of *Macbeth*.

712. Gill, Richard. "The Soundtrack of *Madame Bovary*: Flaubert's Orchestration of Aural Imagery." *Literature/Film Quarterly* 1: 206-17.

"The best way to appreciate the complex function of sound in his novel is to keep in mind the technical device of the soundtrack on which all types of sound are recorded and arranged in order to achieve certain special effects that will enhance the film as a whole."

713. Gomez, Joseph A. "*The Entertainer*: From Play to Film." *Film Heritage* 8, 3: 19-26.

"Although certainly flawed, Richardson's *The Entertainer* [(1960)] employs a significant 'aural/visual patterning' which alters the structure of the play, but which is appropriate to the film medium."

714. Gomez, Joseph A. "*The Third Man*: Capturing the Visual Essence of Literary Conception." *Literature/Film Quarterly* 2: 332-39.

Carol Reed "preserves the themes and tone of Greene's literary treatment but through 'aural/visual patterning' rather than through dependence on excessive dialogue or narrative devices peculiar to literary genres."

715. Gregory, Charles. "Knight Without Meaning?" *Sight and Sound* 42: 155-59.

Modern Hollywood filmmakers seem unable to create the atmosphere and kind of hero typical of the works of Raymond Chandler, Dashiell Hammett, Graham Greene and James M. Cain.

716. Guzzetti, Alfred. "Christian Metz and the Semiology of the Cinema." *Journal of Modern Literature* 3: 292-308.

"Metz's effort to excise from cinema process of signification and, in the name of language, to set it in a realm of abstract logical relations is in the end meaningless and futile."

717. Halio, Jay. "Three Filmed *Hamlets*." *Literature/Film Quarterly* 1: 316-20.

Of the three different filmed versions of *Hamlet*, with
Olivier (1948), Richard Burton (1964) and Richard Chamber-
lain (1970), only the first is "a true *film* version."

718. Hayman, Ronald. "Grigori Kozintsev, Talking About His
      'Lear' and 'Hamlet' Films." *Transatlantic Review*
      46/47: 10-15.

      A short but enlightening interview/conversation.

719. Hirsch, Foster. "Tennessee Williams." *Cinema* 8, 1: 2-7.

      A review of some film adaptations of Tennessee Williams'
      works.

720. Isaacs, Neil D. "Unstuck in Time: *Clockwork Orange* and
      Slaughterhouse-Five." *Literature/Film Quarterly* 1:
      122-31.

      "Given the sci-fi conventions and their contributions
      to the mythos of our culture, both *A Clockwork Orange*
      and *Slaughterhouse-Five* could have been made into movies
      of the first rank. Kubrick succeeded admirably by using
      the full sight-and-sound repertory of the film rhetoric
      to propel his reconception of the narrative and its
      meanings. Hill failed by copping out, diminishing the work
      and narrowing the scope of his approach and his art."

721. James, F. "Getting in Through 'The Open Window.'" *Today's
      Filmmaker* 2: 20-22.

      Not seen.

722. Jones, Edward T. "Summer of 1900: A la recherche of
      The Go-Between." *Literature/Film Quarterly* 1: 154-60.

      Joseph Losey and Harold Pinter successfully collaborated
      in translating the late L.P. Hartley's novel *The Go-Be-
      tween* into "a film of comparable quality remarkably true
      to its literary source."

723. Jorgens, Jack J. "A Course in Shakespeare on Film." *The
      Shakespeare Newsletter* 23: 43.

      A short evaluation of a college course on Shakespeare
      and film.

724. Jorgens, Jack J. "Image and Meaning in the Kozintsev
      Hamlet." *Literature/Film Quarterly* 1: 307-15.

"The Kozintsev *Hamlet* is remarkable for its powerful
realization of important moments in the play." See foot-
note 8 for a synopsis of differences between the play
and film.

725. Keyser, Les. "England Made Me." *Literature/Film Quarterly*
      2: 364-72.

      The film adaptation of Graham Greene's novel *England
      Made Me* "will endure" because its director, Peter Duffell,
      understood the differences between the novel and film.

726. Kiley, Frederick T., and Walter McDonald, eds. *A "Catch-
      22" Casebook*. New York: Crowell.

      Not seen.

727. Koch, Howard. "The Making of *Casablanca*" and "In Con-
      clusion: What Happened to Story in the Contemporary
      Film?" *"Casablanca": Script and Legend*. Woodstock,
      New York: The Overlook Press, pp. 17-27; 208-23.

      Besides Koch's two essays--one on the problems he faced
      while working on the screenplay, the second lamenting
      the decreased emphasis on the use of the script in
      Hollywood filmmaking--the book contains the script of
      Casablanca (1942), an analysis of the film by Richard
      Corliss and two reviews.

728. Kramer, Victor A. "Agee's Projected Screenplay for
      Chaplin: 'Scientists and Tramps.'" *Southern Humanities
      Review* 7: 357-64.

      Agee did write parts of a scenario for Chaplin. "The
      sketch for 'Scientists and Tramps' is only a beginning;
      yet its insight into the difficulty of maintaining one's
      integrity in a society such as ours remains important."

729. Lambert, Gavin. *GWTW: The Making of "Gone with the Wind."*
      Boston-Toronto: Little, Brown.

      An account of the scripting, casting, shooting and
      successful reception of the film, with emphasis placed
      on David O. Selznick's role as producer.

730. Lansbury, Coral. "A Cry from Bergman--A Whisper of
      Dickens." *Meanjin Quarterly* 32: 323-27.

      "The Dickensian references give the film [*Cries and
      Whispers* (1972)] distance and permit us to endure the
      ritual of death."

731. Lenfest, David S. *"Brighton Rock/Young Scarface."*
      Literature/Film Quarterly 2: 373-78.

      Graham Greene's adaptation of his novel *Brighton Rock*
      for film "shows his ability to work with new styles in
      fiction and film, and yet remain true to his own reli-
      gious principles."

732. Linden, George W. "Five Views of *Rashomon.*" *Soundings*
      56: 393-411.

      Examines *Rashomon* as a commercial venture, a work of
      art, a cultural allegory, a film, and as a philosophic
      statement.

733. McCracken, Samuel. "Novel into Film: Novelist into Critic:
      A Clockwork Orange ... Again." *The Antioch Review* 32:
      427-36.

      The film is clearly Kubrick's interpretation of Anthony
      Burgess' novel.

734. McGlynn, Paul D. "Point of View and the Craft of Cinema:
      Notes on Some Devices." *The Journal of Aesthetics and
      Art Criticism* 32: 187-95.

      An analysis of devices used to effect the film director's
      point of view in a number of feature films.

735. McGugan, Ruth E. *"The Heart of the Matter."* *Literature/
      Film Quarterly* 2: 359-63.

      The adaptation of Graham Greene's novel to film was
      not successful.

736. McNeir, Waldo R., and Michael Payne. "Feature Length
      Sound Films Adapted from Shakespeare's Plays Available
      for Distribution in the U.S." *The Shakespeare News-
      letter* 23: 44.

      Lists 41 films and the distributors that handle them.

737. Madsen, Roy Paul. "Adaptation: Novels and Stage Plays
      into Cinema-Television." *The Impact of Film: How
      Ideas Are Communicated Through Cinema and Television*.
      New York: Macmillan, pp. 244-64.

      Discusses various aspects of the adaptation of literary
      works to film.

738. Mamber, Stephen. *"A Clockwork Orange."* *Cinema* 7, 3: 49-57.

"Kubrick, like Burgess, sees violence everywhere, and if there are no purely innocent victims, there are no completely evil villains."

739. Manchel, Frank. "Dickens in the Film: The Adaptation of Three Books." *Film Study: A Resource Guide.* Rutherford, Madison, Teaneck: Fairleigh Dickinson University Press, pp. 149-56. Condensed and slightly revised in *Exercise Exchange* 19 (Fall 1974): 20-28. [Not seen.]

Briefly compares each of the following films: *Great Expectations* (1946), *A Tale of Two Cities* (1935) and *David Copperfield* (1935), with its literary source.

740. Mass, Roslyn. "The Presentation of the Character of Sarah Miles in the Film Version of *The End of the Affair*." *Literature/Film Quarterly* 2: 347-51.

In Graham Greene's novel, the center of attention is the character Maurice Bendrix; in the film, however, the balance of interest shifts to the character of Sarah Miles.

741. Mellen, Joan. "Film and Style: The Fictional Documentary." *The Antioch Review* 32: 403-25.

"Both nonfiction novel and fictional documentary aspire to revitalize their art in implicit protest against the retreat from commitment to a moral asceticism epitomized by Susan Sontag's influential essay, 'Against Interpretation.'"

742. Mellen, Joan. "Outfoxing Lawrence: Novella into Film." *Literature/Film Quarterly* 1: 17-27. Reprinted in *Women and Their Sexuality in the New Film.* New York: Horizon Press, 1973, pp. 216-28.

"In his adaptation of D.H. Lawrence's novella, 'The Fox,' director Mark Rydell has so far departed from the original that he has produced a caricature, almost a cartoon version of the story."

743. Moore, Harry T. "D.H. Lawrence and the Flicks." *Literature/Film Quarterly* 1: 3-11.

A survey of film versions of Lawrence's work.

744. Morris, Peter. "Shakespeare on Film." *Films in Review* 24: 132-63. See J.B. Sewell, *Films in Review* 24: 317.

An international survey of sound film adaptations of Shakespeare's plays which also includes commentary on methods of adaptation.

745. Morrissette, Bruce. "Aesthetic Response to Film and Novel: Parallels and Differences." *Expression, Communication and Experience in Literature and Language*. Ed. Ronald G. Popperwell. London: Modern Humanities Research Association, pp. 215-18. Also printed in *Symposium* 27: 137-51. [Not seen.]

Lists the "issues which would require detailed study to analyse the film-novel relationship," and surveys the ways in which "A joint evolution of film and novel appears to be in progress."

746. Mullin, Michael. "*Macbeth* on Film." *Literature/Film Quarterly* 1: 332-42.

Of the nine silent film versions and another nine sound film adaptations of *Macbeth*, only Kurosawa's *Throne of Blood* (1957) "was an artistic success."

747. Murray, Edward. "*In Cold Blood*: The Filmic Novel and the Problem of Adaptation." *Literature/Film Quarterly* 1: 132-37.

Richard Brooks' unsatisfactory adaptation of Truman Capote's *In Cold Blood* "fails to be either a very faithful translation of the original or, what is worse, a freshly conceived and compelling work of art on its own terms."

748. Naremore, James. "John Huston and *The Maltese Falcon*." *Literature/Film Quarterly* 1: 239-49.

Defends Huston from Andrew Sarris' charge that he is more an "adapter" then an *auteur* director.

749. Naremore, James. "The Walking Shadow: Welles' Expressionist *Macbeth*." *Literature/Film Quarterly* 1: 360-66.

Discussion of *Macbeth* (1948) "in terms of Welles' personality."

750. Nelson, Joyce. "*Slaughterhouse-Five*: Novel and Film." *Literature/Film Quarterly* 1: 149-53.

"By selecting and expanding the more visual aspects of Vonnegut's work (Valencia's wild ride to the hospital), and by leaving out the more verbal sections (such as

Rumfoord reading Truman's war speeches), Hill has perhaps
lessened the anti-war didacticism of the novel, but to
the film's advantage. For George Roy Hill's film con-
vinces us of the grief behind the transcendence, the
emotion which Vonnegut, 'the pillar of salt,' felt he
could not convey."

751. Page, Malcolm. "Charles Wood: *How I Won the War* and
Dingo." *Literature/Film Quarterly* 1: 256-62.

"The adaptor [of Patrick Ryan's novel *How I Won the
War*], Charles Wood, is a playwright of some distinction who is obsessed with war, armies and soldiers, and
who at the same time wrote a play, *Dingo*, which relates
closely to the subject of the film.... The director,
Richard Lester, shared some of these obsessions and did
much to shape the script."

752. Phillips, Gene. "Faulkner and the Film: Two Versions of
Sanctuary." *Literature/Film Quarterly* 1: 263-73.

"*Sanctuary* has been filmed twice in two versions that
both depart in different ways from Faulkner's original
story but which, nonetheless, capture in their own terms
the flavor of the original: *The Story of Temple Drake*
(1932), directed by Stephen Roberts, and *Sanctuary* (1961),
directed by Tony Richardson."

753. Pirie, David. *A Heritage of Horror: The English Gothic
Cinema 1946-1972*. London: Gordon Fraser.

There is a strong analogy to be drawn between the
preoccupation of the writers of Gothic fiction at the
end of the eighteenth century in England and the gothic
films made in England in the late 1950's and after.
Central concerns of artists of both periods were the
Persecuted Woman, the Fatal Woman, and the Fatal Man.
A swift recounting of "characteristics of English
Gothic literature" in the first chapter leads into the
analysis of films revealing manifestations of characteristic Gothic themes. Principal interests: Dracula,
Frankenstein, Science Fiction, Exoticism and Psychosis.

754. Purcell, James M. "Graham Greene and Others: The British
Depression Film as an Art Form." *Antigonish Review*
15: 75-82.

Not seen.

755. Reddington, John. "Film, Play and Idea." *Literature/Film Quarterly* 1: 367-71.

Discusses Peter Brook's *King Lear* (1970) and Roman Polanski's *Macbeth* (1971).
"No one seems quite sure how to respond to films of Shakespeare's plays. Whole-hearted approval of any movie made of a great stage work seems always to be checked by something like ethical considerations."

756. Reynolds, Lessie M. "Film as a Poetic Art and Contemporary Epic." *South Atlantic Bulletin* 38, 2: 8-14.

Film can assume "at least as many varieties of form as literature can." The feature film most often emulates the epic in vastness of scope and in episodic form, in the presentation of the hero and in the embodiment of an entire culture's ideals.

757. Ross, T.J. "Wild Lives." *Literature/Film Quarterly* 1: 218-25.

Discussion of François Truffaut's adaptation of *Fahrenheit 451* (1966) and *The Bride Wore Black* (1968).

758. Rothwell, Kenneth S. "Hollywood and Some Versions of *Romeo and Juliet*: Towards a 'Substantial Pageant.'" *Literature/Film Quarterly* 1: 343-51.

"The series of *Romeo* films may ... be seen as preliminary monitorings of Shakespeare's text on film. As the backlog of our experience with film grows, we grow closer to ideal cinematic versions of *Romeo*."

759. Rothwell, Kenneth S. "Roman Polanski's *Macbeth*: Golgatha Triumphant." *Literature/Film Quarterly* 1: 71-75. See in *Literature/Film Quarterly* articles by Silverstein, 2 (1974): 88-90; Rothwell, 2 (1974): 91-92; Jorgens, 3 (1975): 277-78.

Despite its "unbridled violence" the film is successful "because of attention to detail, technical skill, and overpowering and almost inexhaustible energy."

760. Ruhe, Edward. "Film: The 'Literary' Approach." *Literature/Film Quarterly* 1: 76-83. See 883.

A defense of the interdisciplinary study of literature and film.

761. Rutherford, Charles S. "A New Dog with an Old Trick:
      Archetypal Patterns in *Sounder*." *The Journal of Popular
      Film* 2: 155-63.

      Homeric elements in William H. Armstrong's novel
      Sounder were emphasized by screenwriter Lonne Elder III
      to give the film its universality.

762. Samuels, Charles Thomas. "How Not to Film a Novel." *The
      American Scholar* 42: 148-50, 152, 154. Reprinted in
      Mastering the Film and Other Essays. Ed. Lawrence
      Graver. Knoxville: The University of Tennessee, 1977,
      pp. 190-97.

      "Most filmed novels are illustrated paraphrases, with
      setting and characters pictured, and theme rendered
      through dialogue. *Fat City* [(1972)] exemplifies both
      this method and its cost." John Huston adapted Leonard
      Gardner's novel to the screen.

763. Scott, James F. "The Emasculation of *Lady Chatterley's
      Lover*." *Literature/Film Quarterly* 1: 37-45.

      The film version of D.H. Lawrence's novel "falls far
      short of being successfully cinematic."

764. Shklovsky, Viktor. "Poetry and Prose in Cinematography
      (1927)." *Russian Formalism: A Collection of Articles
      and Texts in Translation*. Ed. Stephen Bann and John
      E. Bowlt. Edinburgh: Scottish Academic Press, pp.
      128-30.

      Two types of film--prosaic and poetic--are defined
      with reference to the structure and resolution of prose
      and poetry in literature.

765. Silverstein, Norman. "Introduction." *Journal of Modern
      Literature* 3: 145-48.

      A short essay describing the articles in this issue
      of the *Journal of Modern Literature* devoted to "Film
      as Literature and Language."

766. Sinclair, Andrew. "The Making of 'Under Milkwood.'"
      Filmmakers Newsletter 6, 9-10: 32-34.

      The writer/director of the film adaptation of Dylan
      Thomas' play discusses his experiences making the film.

767. Slout, William L. "*Uncle Tom's Cabin* in American Film
      History." *The Journal of Popular Film* 2: 137-51.

A survey of the film adaptations of the Harriet
Beecher Stowe novel.

768. Smith, Julian. "Short Fiction on Film: A Selected
Filmography." *Studies in Short Fiction* 10: 397-409.

A list of films "taken from short stories and novellas
by writers whose works have been anthologized in literature texts--that is, writers who are generally considered
worthy of study."

769. Smith, Julian. "Vision and Revision: *The Virgin and the
Gypsy* as Film." *Literature/Film Quarterly* 1: 28-36.

The film version of D.H. Lawrence's novella is "a
model of how to make a free adaptation that inspires
a reconsideration of the literary source."

770. Solecki, Sam. "D.H. Lawrence's View of Film." *Literature/
Film Quarterly* 1: 12-16.

Lawrence "wasn't so much opposed to film itself as to
the misuse of film he had witnessed in his society."

771. Spiegel, Alan. "Flaubert to Joyce: Evolution of a
Cinematographic Form." *Novel* 6: 229-43.

In the ways in which they render the material world
in their novels "Flaubert and the novelists who follow
in his tradition--Conrad, Joyce, Faulkner, Nabokov and
Robbe-Grillet--operate in ways analogous to the operation
of the camera eye."

772. Van Wert, William F. "Narrative Structure in *The Third
Man*." *Literature/Film Quarterly* 2: 341-46.

"Where the narrative structure of the novel belongs
to the nineteenth century.... the film belongs clearly
to the twentieth century."

773. Wees, William C. "Dickens, Griffith and Eisenstein:
Form and Image in Literature and Film." *The Humanities
Association Review* 214: 266-76.

Those who argue that the film cannot reveal the "inner
world" of a character or allow the audience to "see
thought" are wrong, for in Dickens' novels one can find
cinematic expression and literary expression concurrently,
as both Griffith and Eisenstein well knew.

774. Weinberg, Herman G. "Novel into Film." *Literature/Film Quarterly* 1: 99-102.

"While the novel has served the film well, as indeed all published literary sources have, the best results have been obtained in the 'blood transfusions' from secondary, rather than primary, works into the veins of the film."

775. Welsh, James M. "Graham Greene's *Ministry of Fear*: The Transformation of an Entertainment." *Literature/Film Quarterly* 2: 310-16. See 676.

"Fritz Lang's *Ministry of Fear* (1944) is neither a faithful nor an entirely successful adaptation."

776. Welsh, James M. "The Sound of Silents: An Early *Shrew*." *The English Journal* 62: 754-58, 767-69.

Sam Taylor's 1929 adaptation of Shakespeare's play "is a tour-de-farce, but, even so, the farcical elements are well handled."

777. Willson, Robert F., Jr. "Which Is the Real 'Last Picture Show'?" *Literature/Film Quarterly* 1: 167-69.

Peter Bogdanovich's use of *Red River* instead of some "B" western movie as the "last picture" in his film *The Last Picture Show* (1971) is a sign that "the director has given in ... to an impulse to send Sam's last picture show to its grave with a final heroic surge." This impulse does violence to the tone and thematic concerns of the novel.

778. Zambrano, Ana Laura. "Greene's Visions of Childhood: 'The Basement Room' and *The Fallen Idol*." *Literature/ Film Quarterly* 2: 324-31.

Greene's ideas about the nature of good and evil were formed principally by Marjorie Bowen's *The Viper in Milan*, a book he read as a boy.

779. Zambrano, Ana Laura. "*Women in Love*: Counterpoint on Film." *Literature/Film Quarterly* 1: 46-54.

Ken Russell's film version of D.H. Lawrence's novel "provides masterful and penetrating insight into Lawrence's themes, and it enriches our appreciation of the beauty and complexity of the style of both artists."

780. Zlotnick, Joan. "*The Day of the Locust*, a Night at the Movies." *Film Library Quarterly* 6, 1: 22-26.

    Nathanael West's movie scripts indicate that he was familiar with film techniques before he wrote *The Day of the Locust*.

1974

781. "*Kuhle Wampe*." *Screen* 15, 2: 41-73. See George Hoellering, "Making *Kuhle Wampe*: An Interview." *Screen* 5, 4: 71-79.

    A list of screen credits for the film is provided, along with commentary on the film by Bertolt Brecht, James Pettifer and Bernard Eisenschitz.

782. Allyn, John. "Hawthorne on Film--Almost." *Literature/Film Quarterly* 2: 124-28.

    Donald Fox's thirty-minute film version of "Young Goodman Brown," "despite some imaginative cinematic touches ... as a whole is distorted and diminished."

783. Appel, Alfred. "The End of the Road: Dark Cinema and *Lolita*." *Film Comment* 10, 5: 25-31. Revised for publication in 784.

    "Nabokov's *mise-en-scène*, his prose equivalent of deep-focus, creates a veritable dark cinema ..., for the most evocative aural and visual descriptions in *Lolita* are in the manner of classic Forties *films noirs*."

784. Appel, Alfred, Jr. *Nabokov's Dark Cinema*. New York: Oxford University Press.

    "Certain pervasive attitudes, effects, and techniques in [Nabokov's] fiction could not have been achieved without a knowledge of cinema, and this book will argue that popular forms have exerted a positive influence on a body of work whose themes are not exclusive to high art."

785. Armes, Roy. "Film and the Modern Novel." *Film and Reality: An Historical Survey*. Baltimore: Penguin Books, pp. 209-14.

    A brief discussion of the work of Robbe-Grillet and Pasolini. "Thanks to writer-directors like these two, film and literature are becoming more closely related as equal and modern forms of artistic expression."

786. Atkins, Irene Kahn. "In Search of the Greatest Gatsby."
      Literature/Film Quarterly 2: 216-28.

      Three film adaptations of F. Scott Fitzgerald's novel
      The Great Gatsby evaluated.

787. Atkins, Thomas R. "The Illustrated Man." *Sight and Sound*
      43: 96-100. Reprinted in *The Classic American Novel
      and the Movies*. Ed. Gerald Peary and Roger Shatzkin.
      New York: Frederick Ungar Publishing, 1977, pp. 42-51.

      An interview in which Ray Bradbury discusses the films
      made from his books, stories and screenplays.

788. Barrett, Gerald. "Andrew Sarris Interview, Part II."
      Literature/Film Quarterly 2: 3-15. See 675.

      Contains commentary on adaptation of literary works
      to film.

789. Barrett, Gerald R., and Thomas L. Erskine, eds. *From
      Fiction to Film: D.H. Lawrence's "The Rocking-Horse
      Winner."* Encino, California: Dickenson Publishing.

      A casebook on the film adaptation of Lawrence's short
      story. It contains the text of the story, the final
      shooting script of the film adapted by Anthony Pelissier
      and several critical essays.

790. Blatty, William Peter. *William Peter Blatty on "The
      Exorcist": From Novel to Film*. New York: Bantam Books.

      Not seen.

791. Brater, Enoch. "Pinter's *Homecoming* on Celluloid." *Modern
      Drama* 17: 443-48.

      The film version of the play, with a script by Pinter,
      provides the viewer an opportunity to observe "the
      writer's changing concept of the same characters and the
      same situation" with which his imagination has been
      working.

792. Brewster, Ben, and Colin MacCabe. "Brecht and the Revo-
      lutionary Cinema?" *Screen* 15, 2: 4-6.

      Brecht helped in the production of the film *Kuhle
      Wampe* (1931), "which is an exemplary revolutionary film
      in its use of montage ... and in its demonstration of
      the application of Brecht's theatrical techniques to
      the very different conditions of the cinema."

793. Campbell, Gregg M. "Beethoven, Chopin and Tammy Wynette:
      Heroines and Archetypes in *Five Easy Pieces*." *Literature/
      Film Quarterly* 2: 275-83.

      Bobby Dupea, the hero in the film, is compared with
      archetypal characters in American fiction.

794. Ciment, Michael. *Kazan on Kazan*. New York: The Viking
      Press.

      Printed in the form of an interview, the book records
      Kazan discussing his ideas and accomplishments in
      directing films and plays. Discussed at some length are
      A Streetcar Named Desire (1951) and *Baby Doll* (1956),
      both made in collaboration with Tennessee Williams.

795. Clayton, Jack. "I'm Proud of That Film: Jack Clayton
      Interviewed by Marjorie Rosen." *Film Comment* 10, 4:
      49-51.

      A discussion of the film adaptation of F. Scott
      Fitzgerald's novel *The Great Gatsby*, which was directed
      by Clayton.

796. Clayton, Thomas. "Aristotle on the Shakespearean Film:
      or, Damn Thee, William, Thou Art Translated." *Litera-
      ture/Film Quarterly* 2: 183-89.

      Considers the place of the plot and the text in film
      adaptations of Shakespeare's plays.

797. Corliss, Richard. *Talking Pictures: Screenwriters in
      the American Cinema*. Woodstock, New York: The Overlook
      Press.

      A critical survey of Hollywood screenwriters.
      "My aim has been to avoid facile generalizations by
      confronting specific films, thus not merely pinpointing
      a writer's themes but discovering how he related his
      preoccupations to the job at hand."

798. Cunningham, Frank R. "Lindsay Anderson's *O Lucky Man!*
      and the Romantic Tradition." *Literature/Film Quarterly*
      2: 256-61.

      "Anderson's film is a rich example of the tradition
      of literary and cinematic Romanticism, that mode of
      perceiving reality that celebrates man's unique signi-
      ficance in terms of his potential for enduring (and,
      when he is a lucky man, prevailing) in a cosmos that is
      seen as continually expanding, dynamic, and thus pur-
      posive."

799. Dawson, Jan. "The Continental Divide." *Sight and Sound*
     43: 12-15. The interview with Peter Bogdanovich, pp.
     14-15, has been revised and reprinted in *The Classic
     American Novel and the Movies*. Ed. Gerald Peary and
     Roger Shatzkin. New York: Frederick Ungar Publishing,
     1977, pp. 83-89.

     Interviews with Claude Chabrol and Peter Bogdanovich
     discussing their adaptations of works by Henry James.

800. Demby, Betty Jeffries. "The Art of Screenwriting: An
     Interview with Wolf Mankowitz." *Filmmakers Newsletter*
     7, 4: 26-29.

     Mankowitz reflects on his screenwriting work, and
     particularly on his adaptation of L.P. Hartley's novel
     The Hireling.

801. Demby, Betty Jeffries. "The Making of *Conrack*: An Inter-
     view with Martin Ritt." *Filmmakers Newsletter* 7, 6:
     27-31.

     The film remains faithful to Pat Conroy's novel *The
     Water Is Wide*.

802. Dworkin, Martin S. "The Writing on the Screen." *Graham
     Greene: The Films of His Fiction*. By Gene D. Phillips,
     S.J. New York and London: Teachers College Press, pp.
     vii-xviii.

     "The arts once were not separated from each other, or
     from either the paramount or the least concerns and
     activities of the people who created them and lived
     their meaning. Even now, their distinctiveness, as
     created media and as experiences to have and to share,
     may be more truly a matter of conventional attitudes,
     or of limited abstraction for philosophical analysis,
     than of essential differentiation."

803. Edel, Leon. "Novel and Camera." *The Theory of the Novel:
     New Essays*. Ed. John Halperin. New York: Oxford
     University Press, pp. 177-88.

     "The issue is that the novel, in trying so desperately
     to become a camera, has ceased to be on the whole any-
     thing else, has ceased to be itself."

804. Eidsvik, Charles. "Soft Edges: The Art of Literature,
     the Medium of Film." *Literature/Film Quarterly* 2:
     16-21.

"No other critic has more to say about the narrative cinema than the critic trained in both literature and the medium of film."

805. Esselman, Kathryn C. "From Camelot to Monument Valley: Dramatic Origins of the Western Film." *Focus on "The Western."* Ed. Jack Nachbar. Englewood Cliffs, New Jersey: Prentice-Hall, pp. 9-18.

"The filmed Western, because of its visual nature and defined iconography, incorporates material from the Arthurian tradition and its descendants the romance and the melodrama."

806. Estrin, Mark W. "'Triumphant Ignominy': *The Scarlet Letter* on Screen." *Literature/Film Quarterly* 2: 110-22. Partially reprinted in *The Classic American Novel and the Movies.* Ed. Gerald Peary and Roger Shatzkin. New York: Frederick Ungar Publishing, 1977, pp. 20-29.

"*The Scarlet Letter* of 1926 is a film whose flashes of brilliance do not quite make up for its failure to come to grips with so much that is already available in Hawthorne, but it justifies a viewer's belief in the possibilities for the novelist's transference to the screen."

807. Fell, John L. *Film and the Narrative Tradition.* Norman: University of Oklahoma Press.

A discussion of the historical origins and development of narrative film from 1886 to 1911.
"I believe that in the motion picture there surfaced an entire tradition of narrative techniques which had been developing unsystematically for a hundred years" in the novel, theater, prints, optical amusements and "shows," and graphics.

808. Fiedler, Leslie A. "The Death and Rebirth of the Novel." *The Theory of the Novel: New Essays.* Ed. John Halperin. New York: Oxford University Press, pp. 189-209.

The "authentic (i.e., mythic) novel" and the cinema, being true popular art forms, have a "special affinity" for each other, because both have the power to reach an audience "on the level of dream and nightmare."

809. France, Richard. "The 'Voodoo' *Macbeth* of Orson Welles." *yale/theatre* 5, 3: 66-78.

The article contains a short but effective comparison
of the stage and screen versions of *Macbeth*, both
directed by Orson Welles, who substituted the spectacle
of the horror movie for the catharsis of the portrayal
of tragic destiny.

810.   Gordon, Lois. "*The Go-Between*--Hartley and Pinter."
       Kansas Quarterly 4, 2: 81-92.

       "What prompted Pinter's interest in *The Go-Between?*
       The answer, in terms of style, is an easy one. Since
       1969, Pinter has clearly moved away from the stripping
       of character, from sparse dialogue, from juxtapositions
       of comedy and terror--from all the characteristics
       mentioned above--to a more poetic and lyric form."

811.   Gow, Gordon. "Pursuit of the Falcon." *Films and Filming*
       20 (March): 57-58.

       Comparison of the three film adaptations of Dashiell
       Hammett's *The Maltese Falcon* with each other and also
       with the novel.

812.   Holden, David F. "Three Literary Sources for *Through
       a Glass Darkly.*" *Literature/Film Quarterly* 2: 22-29.

       The film is "significantly indebted" to Charlotte
       Gilman's short story "The Yellow Wallpaper," Anton
       Chekhov's play *The Sea Gull* and Strindberg's play
       Easter.

813.   Hutchinson, Alexander. "Luchino Visconti's *Death in
       Venice.*" *Literature/Film Quarterly* 2: 31-43.

       "Form as a dimension of meaning has little to do with
       morality; and yet as the prize of discipline it is
       invested with ethical character. This is the central
       paradox of Visconti's *Death in Venice* [(1971)] just as
       it is of Mann's novella."

814.   Jensen, Paul. "Film Noir: The Writer; The World You Live
       In. Raymond Chandler." *Film Comment* 10, 6: 18-22, 24-26.

       "Chandler's movie career was limited, but his influ-
       ence as screenwriter (especially on *Double Indemnity*,
       1944) and as adapted novelist figured prominently in
       establishing the tone" of the *film noir* period of the
       1940's.

815. Jensen, Paul. "From Fiction to Fantasy with Howard Hawks." *Film Comment* 10, 6: 23.

Brief look at the two extant scripts written for Chandler's novel *The Big Sleep*.

816. Jones, Edward T. "Green Thoughts in a Technicolor Shade: A Revaluation of *The Great Gatsby*." *Literature/Film Quarterly* 2: 229-36.

"Paramount's latest *Gatsby* [(1974)] fulfills itself less as art perhaps but as an entertaining advertisement for F. Scott Fitzgerald."

817. Joyaux, Georges. "*The Bridge on the River Kwai*: From the Novel to the Movie." *Literature/Film Quarterly* 2: 174-82.

"Still, despite the many modifications the novel [by Pierre Boulle] underwent at the hands of the film makers, the movie met with tremendous success."

818. Kaminsky, Stuart M. "Literary Adaptation and Change: *The Killers*--Hemingway, Film Noir, and the Terror of Daylight." *American Film Genres: Approaches to a Critical Theory of Popular Film*. Dayton, Ohio: Pflaum Publishing, pp. 43-59.

Hemingway's short story "The Killers" is compared with its two film adaptations in 1946 and 1964. The first film adaptation appropriated and fitted the story to the conventions of the *film noir*. The second adaptation reflects a social and political world alien both to the original story and to the earlier film.

819. Kolker, Robert Phillip. "Night to Day." *Sight and Sound* 43: 23-39.

Discussion of adaptations of Edward Anderson's novel *Thieves Like Us*, by Nicholas Ray as *They Live by Night* (1949) and by Robert Altman as *Thieves Like Us* (1974).

820. Korte, Walter. "Godard's Adaptation of Moravia's *Contempt*." *Literature/Film Quarterly* 2: 284-89.

Godard's "most neglected" film, *Le Mepris* (*Contempt*, 1963), based on Moravia's *Il Disprezzo*, "affords us an example, not only of his moving cinematic narrative in new directions, but of how a novel may serve as the *pre-text* which provides the catalytic elements for an entirely new creation."

821. Laurence, Frank M. "Death in the Matinée: The Film End-
     ings of Hemingway's Fiction." *Literature/Film Quarterly*
     2: 44-51.

     "In some way the final emotional effect of every
     Hemingway film was significantly different from that of
     the novel or story on which it was based--the only
     exception being Leland Hayward's 1958 production of *The
     Old Man and the Sea* [(1958)], the script of which Heming-
     way had carefully supervised."

822. Linden, George W. "Films and a Novel Future." *The Journal
     of Aesthetic Education* 8, 1: 55-64.

     "Since I believe that both films and novels have a
     future, I shall look briefly at some of their relations
     in our time."

823. Lodge, David. "Thomas Hardy and the Cinematographic Form."
     Novel 7: 246-54.

     "Thomas Hardy is a more cinematographic writer" than
     Flaubert, Conrad, Joyce, Faulkner and Robbe-Grillet be-
     cause "the artistry with which he controls the reader's
     perspective on the relationship between character and
     environment, through shifts of focus and angle, ... makes
     him a powerful and original novelist, rather than his
     insight into human motivation, or his rendering of con-
     sciousness, or his philosophic wisdom. This of course
     makes him no less of a *writer*--quite the contrary, since
     he must do through language what the filmmaker can do
     by moving his camera and adjusting his lens."

824. Maas, Roslyn. "A Linking of Legends: *The Great Gatsby*
     and *Citizen Kane*." *Literature/Film Quarterly* 2: 207-15.

     The influence of Joseph Conrad on Orson Welles and
     F. Scott Fitzgerald may be seen in their respective
     works.

825. MacCabe, Colin. "Realism and Cinema: Notes on Some
     Brechtian Theses." *Screen* 15, 2: 7-27.

     A "set of digressions" on the subjects of "realism"
     and "cinema" derived from the writings of Bertolt
     Brecht.

826. McNally, Judith. "The Filming of *Jonathan Livingston
     Seagull*: An Interview with Director Hall Bartlett."
     Filmmakers Newsletter 7, 3: 22-27.

Explains how the director made a film "from a problematical book, some magnificent scenery, and 6000 temperamental birds."

827. Peary, Gerald. "Selected Sound Westerns and Their Novel Sources." *The Velvet Light Trap* 12 (Spring): 15-18.

Not seen.

828. Petrie, Graham. "Theater Film Life." *Film Comment* 10, 3: 38-43.

Ernst Lubitsch's *To Be or Not To Be* (1942), Jean Renoir's *The Golden Coach* (1952) and Ingmar Bergman's *The Magician* (1958) all exploit the audience's learned response to conventions of the stage. All three films can be seen as "forerunners" of Alain Resnais' *Last Year at Marienbad* (1961).

829. Phillips, Gene D., S.J. *Graham Greene: The Films of His Fiction*. New York: Teachers College Press.

Many of Greene's "entertainments" and his works of "serious fiction" adapted to film both by others and by himself are examined first as works of fiction, then as film adaptations. Included in this study are: *Orient Express* (1933); *Went the Day Well?* (US title: *Forty-Eight Hours*) (1942); *This Gun for Hire* (1942); *Ministry of Fear* (1944); *The Confidential Agent* (1945); *The Stranger's Hand* (1954); *Across the Bridge* (1957); *Travels with My Aunt* (1972); *The Fallen Idol* (1948); *The Third Man* (1949); *Our Man in Havana* (1959); *Loser Takes All* (1956); *The Man Within* (US title: *The Smugglers*) (1947); *The Fugitive* (1947); *The Heart of the Matter* (1953); *The End of the Affair* (1955); *The Quiet American* (1957); *Brighton Rock* (US title: *Young Scarface*) (1947); *The Comedians* (1967).

830. Purdy, Strother B. "Can the Novel and the Film Disappear?" *Literature/Film Quarterly* 2: 237-41.

An "excess of familiarity with the form" of film may already be bringing about a "diminution of consciousness" in our society.

831. Riley, Michael M. "Dickens and Film: Notes on Adaptation." *Dickens Studies Newsletter* 5 (December): 110-12.

A response to 544 arguing that a "Dickens film is not a Dickens novel, and if it succeeds it must do so on its own artistic terms."

832. Riley, Michael M., ed. "Interview with Jack Pulman,
      English Screenwriter." *Southern Humanities Review* 8:
      471-84.

      A writer for stage and screen, Pulman has had consider-
      able success with adaptations of novels for film and
      television.

833. Silver, Alain. "The Untranquil Light: David Lean's
      Great Expectations." *Literature/Film Quarterly* 2:
      140-52.

      In his adaptation of Dickens' novel, David Lean "re-
      tains the character of the novel" while making Dickens'
      hero, Philip Pirrip, "more dynamic."

834. Silver, Alain, and James Ursini. "The Dickens Adaptations:
      Great Expectations (1946), *Oliver Twist* (1948)."
      David Lean and His Films. London: Leslie Frewin
      Publishers, pp. 53-84.

      An examination of Lean's successful adaptation of both
      novels.

835. Simonet, Thomas. "Filming Inner Life: The Works of Robert
      Enrico." *Cinema Journal* 14, 1: 51-59.

      A study of Enrico's *In the Midst of Life* (1962), a
      trilogy based on Bierce's short stories "Chicamauga,"
      "The Mockingbird" and "An Occurrence at Owl Creek
      Bridge," designed to gauge the success of Enrico's tech-
      niques of rendering the inner or psychological reality
      of Bierce's characters.

836. Skerrett, Joseph T., Jr. "Graham Greene at the Movies:
      A Novelist's Experience with the Film." *Literature/
      Film Quarterly* 2: 293-301.

      A study of the "various Graham Greenes--moviegoer,
      film reviewer, screenwriter, and novelist."

837. Smith, Julian. "Hester, Sweet Hester Prynne--*The Scarlet
      Letter* in the Movie Market Place." *Literature/Film
      Quarterly* 2: 100-09.

      The 1926 film adaptation of Nathaniel Hawthorne's
      novel "was doomed from the start--doomed by the studio's
      desire that it should in no way give offense to any
      group strong enough to affect its commercial success."

838. Smith, Julian. "Orson Welles and the Great American Dummy—Or, The Rise and Fall and the Regeneration of Benjamin Franklin's Model American." *Literature/Film Quarterly* 2: 196-206.

   Benjamin Franklin's concept of the American man is compared with Welles' Charles Foster Kane and George Minafer in *The Magnificent Ambersons* (1942).

839. Sobchack, Vivian C. "Tradition and Cinematic Allusion." *Literature/Film Quarterly* 2: 59-65.

   "We can no longer write off the use of cinematic allusion as pretentious. We can no longer consider allusion a device belonging primarily to literature."

840. Stacy, Paul H. "Lawrence and Movies: A Postscript." *Literature/Film Quarterly* 2: 93-95.

   Examination of the cinematic aspects of D.H. Lawrence's novel *The Boy in the Bush* and of his attitudes towards film in selected poems.

841. Standiford, Les. "Novels into Film: *Catch-22* as Watershed." *Southern Humanities Review* 8: 19-25.

   "Nichols has created a work of his own, and a work that stands as an enviable example to filmmakers everywhere who would be drawn toward novel-to-film translation."

842. Toliver, Harold. "Mixed Modes: Cinematic Narrative." *Animate Illusions: Explorations of Narrative Structure*. Lincoln: University of Nebraska Press, pp. 189-206.

   "Cinematic narrative" requires the mixing of linear and pictorial arts. It cannot be realized unless there is "a balance between composition and decomposition," that is, "the balancing of a psychology of linear tension and the psychology of visual gestalts." Only with a balancing of these elements can a sense of reality be conveyed.

843. Willson, Robert F., Jr. "*Deliverance* from Novel to Film: Where Is Our Hero?" *Literature/Film Quarterly* 2: 52-58.

   In the novel, Ed Gentry, as narrator, becomes the hero of the story. This narrative point of view is, unfortunately, lost in the film.

844. Winston, Douglas Garrett. *The Screenplay as Literature*.
      Cranbury, New Jersey: Fairleigh Dickinson University
      Press.

      Not seen.

845. Zambrano, Ana Laura. "Feature Motion Pictures Adapted
      from Dickens: A Checklist--Part I." *Dickens Studies
      Newsletter* 5 (December): 106-09. "Feature Motion
      Pictures Adapted from Dickens: A Checklist--Part II."
      Dickens Studies Newsletter 6 (March 1975): 9-13.

      The list of film adaptations proceeds in alphabetical
      order by title of the Dickens novel. Television shows
      and films made primarily as educational aids have been
      excluded.

846. Zambrano, Ana Laura. "*Great Expectations*: Dickens and
      David Lean." *Literature/Film Quarterly* 2: 154-61.

      Lean's adaptation succeeded because he retained the
      "fairy tale" elements in the novel, subordinated plot
      to theme, and made the camera "become a means of sub-
      jective interpretation and introspection."

847. Zambrano, Ana Laura. "The Styles of Dickens and Griffith:
      A Tale of Two Cities and *Orphans of the Storm*."
      Language and Style 7: 53-61.

      A comparison of each artist's treatment of similar
      material designed to show that "both are ... creative
      individuals who adapted their arts to their medium and
      interpreted it in their own way."

848. Zambrano, Ana Laura. "*Throne of Blood*: Kurosawa's
      Macbeth." *Literature/Film Quarterly* 2: 262-74.

      Although he is thought of as the most "Western" of
      Japanese film directors, Kurosawa's adaptation of *Macbeth*
      "evolves not in the traditions of Elizabethan theatre
      but in a purely Japanese context."

                                1975

849. Abel, Richard. "The Contribution of the French Literary
      Avant-Garde to Film Theory and Criticism (1907-1924)."
      Cinema Journal 14 (Spring): 8-10.

"Clearly the cinema--especially the American cinema--
had a tremendous impact on the two generations of the
Parisian literary avant-garde during the early decades
of this century."

850. Anderegg, Michael A. "Conrad and Hitchcock: *The Secret
Agent* Inspires *Sabotage*." *Literature/Film Quarterly*
3: 215-25.

"An intelligent and creative director may, while
ignoring such matters as plot, characters, and even theme,
find in his source inspiration ... that will influence
his own creation in unexpected and fruitful ways."

851. Atkins, Irene Kahn. "Agatha Christie and the Detective
Film: A Timetable for Success." *Literature/Film
Quarterly* 3: 205-12.

A brief survey of some film adaptations of Dame Agatha
Christie's works, concluding with an analysis of Sidney
Lumet's adaptation of *Murder on the Orient Express*.

852. Ball, Robert Hamilton. "*The Taming of the Shrew*--with
'Additional Dialogue'?" *The Triple Bond: Plays, Mainly
Shakespearean, in Performance*. University Park and London:
The Pennsylvania State University Press, pp. 203-20.

Account of the 1929 film directed by Sam Taylor.

853. Bobrow, Andrew C. "John Schlesinger and 'The Day of the
Locust.'" *Filmmakers Newsletter* 8, 9: 28-32.

Schlesinger discusses his adaptation of Nathanael West's
novel.

854. Broughton, James. "What Magic in the Lanterns? Notes on
Poetry and Film." *Film Culture* 61: 35-40.

"Modern poetry has been deeply influenced by film.
Modern film has not sufficiently returned the compliment."

855. Burch, Noel. "Fictional Subjects." *Theory of Film Practice*. New York, Washington: Praeger Publishers, pp.
139-55.

An analysis of contemporary film form and its relationship to the "subject" of film. The chapter includes an
examination of Robbe-Grillet's contribution to literature
and cinema.

856. Carringer, Robert L. "*Citizen Kane, The Great Gatsby*, and Some Conventions of American Narrative." *Critical Inquiry* 2: 307-25.

A comparison of the film and the novel, showing that there are "remarkably extensive structural and conceptual parallels" between them.

857. Charney, Hanna. "Images of Absence in Flaubert and Some Contemporary Films." *Style* 9: 488-501.

Three examples of Flaubert's "evocation of absence" are examined in order to show that "Flaubert's vision is sometimes as close to that of film as a novelist's can be."

858. Childs, James. "Interview with John Hancock." *Literature/ Film Quarterly* 3: 109-16.

John Hancock adapted and directed the film of Mark Harris' novel *Bang the Drum Slowly*.

859. Cohen, Mitchell S. "Odd Jobs and Subsidies: Nathanael West in Hollywood." *Film Comment* 11, 3: 44-46.

West's unsuccessful career as Hollywood screenwriter.

860. DeFelice, James. *Filmguide to "Odd Man Out."* London, Bloomington: Indiana University Press.

Carol Reed's film, adapted from a novel by F.L. Green, is carefully examined. Contents include an outline of the film, comments on the director and the production, an analysis of and a summary critique of the film and a Carol Reed filmography.

861. Degenfelder, E. Pauline. "McMurtry and the Movies: *Hud* and *The Last Picture Show*." *Western Humanities Review* 29: 81-91.

"The purpose of this paper is to identify the modes in two film adaptations, *Hud* [(1963), adapted from McMurtry's novel *Horseman, Pass By*] and *The Last Picture Show* [(1971)], and to suggest how McMurtry's participation in *The Last Picture Show* contributes to its success as an adaptation."

862. DeMarco, Norman, comp. "Bibliography of Books on Literature and Film." *Style* 9: 593-607.

A selected bibliography.

863. Devlin, Francis P. "A 'Cinematic' Approach to Tennyson's Descriptive Art." *Literature/Film Quarterly* 3: 132-44.

A better understanding of Alfred, Lord Tennyson's poetry may be gained by examining it with cinematic terminology in mind.

864. Dick, Bernard. "Narrative and Infra-Narrative in Film." *Literature/Film Quarterly* 3: 124-30.

"A novel has its infra-structure, ... its narrative structure. But only film has infra-narrative in the sense of a visual plot unfolding concurrently with a verbal one."

865. D'Lugo, Marion. "Signs and Meaning in *Blow-Up*: From Cortázar to Antonioni." *Literature/Film Quarterly* 3: 23-29.

Relationship between Antonioni's film *Blow-Up* (1966) and the Julio Cortázar short story "Las babas del diablo," which inspired it.

866. Eidsvik, Charles. "Toward a '*Politique des Adaptations.*'" *Literature/Film Quarterly* 3: 255-63.

The effect of film adaptation on the growth of the art of the film has been seriously neglected by film historians.

867. Felheim, Marvin. "Criticism and the Films of Shakespeare's Plays." *Comparative Drama* 9: 147-55.

A survey of problems inherent in the critical approaches to films of Shakespeare's plays.

868. Fell, John L. "Film and Other Media." *Film: An Introduction*. New York: Praeger Publishers, pp. 28-40.

Draws general comparisons between film and theater and film and prose.

869. Fiore, Robert L. "The Picaresque Tradition in *Midnight Cowboy*." *Literature/Film Quarterly* 3: 270-76.

Understanding the picaresque tradition in literature gives the viewer a special insight into John Schlesinger's film *Midnight Cowboy* (1969).

870. Flamini, Roland. *Scarlett, Rhett, and a Cast of Thousands. The Filming of "Gone with the Wind."* New York: Macmillan.

On the making of *Gone with the Wind* (1939).

871. Giannetti, Louis D. "Cinematic Metaphors." *Godard and
      Others: Essays on Film Form*. Cranbury, New Jersey:
      Fairleigh Dickinson University Press, pp. 89-131.

      A refutation of film theorists who claim that film is
      incapable of emphasizing the complex uses of metaphor
      available to the literary artist. The essay concludes
      with an analysis of the metaphors used in Hitchcock's
      Psycho (1960) and Bergman's *Persona* (1966).

872. Giannetti, Louis. "The Gatsby Flap." *Literature/Film
      Quarterly* 3: 13-22.

      Though no "masterpiece," Jack Clayton's *The Great
      Gatsby* (1974), adapted from the F. Scott Fitzgerald
      novel, "abounds in intelligence, delicacy, and grace."

873. Giles, Dennis. "Kurosawa's Heroes." *Arion* n.s. 2: 270-99.

      Considers the films *Ikiru* (1952), *Seven Samurai* (1954)
      and *Rashomon* (1950).

874. Glaser, Carol. "Using Film Language to Understand Poetry."
      Media & Methods 11, 7: 38-40.

      Examines the effectiveness of using film techniques
      to approximate several verbal effects in poetry.

875. Guiles, Fred Lawrence. *Hanging in Paradise*. New York:
      McGraw-Hill Book Company.

      An overview of life in Hollywood for writers and
      screenwriters.

876. Guzzetti, Alfred. "Narrative and the Film Image." *New
      Literary History* 6: 379-92.

      In the "classical style" of filmmaking, the image
      is subordinated to the narrative requirement of the
      story; in the "modernist style" the image need not be
      linked to the narrative requirements of the film. There-
      fore, it is essential in film criticism "to treat the
      image plane as significant, even when the style insists
      that it is not, and understand that such significance
      originates not in style alone but in the relation of
      the film image both to the space to which it refers and
      to the conditions that bound its presentation to the
      spectator."

877. Hammond, Robert M. "The Authenticity of the Filmscript: Cocteau's *Beauty and the Beast*." *Style* 9: 514-32.

"This ... study exemplifies the kind of study in authenticity that any film and its shooting script should undergo, and at the same time makes an actual exemplary study of the problems involved specifically with *Beauty and the Beast* [(1946)]."

878. Handzo, Stephen. "Old Hollywood: John Houseman Interview. The Producer's Signature." *Film Comment* 11, 2: 18-21.

Houseman produced a number of films adapted from literature.

879. Hargrave, Harry A. "Film as Literature." *Southern Humanities Review* 9: 233-39.

Encourages the study of film as a form of literature.

880. Hartley, Dean Wilson. "'How Do We Teach It?': A Primer for the Basic Literature/Film Course." *Literature/Film Quarterly* 3: 60-69.

The problems that can arise in teaching the basic course in film adaptation and solutions to them are treated.

881. Heath, Stephen. "Film and System: Terms of Analysis, Part I." *Screen* 16, 1: 7-77. Part II appears in *Screen* 16, 2: 91-113. See Jonathan Rosenbaum, *Sight and Sound* 44 (1975): 217-18.

An analysis of Orson Welles' *Touch of Evil* (1958).

882. Heinz, Linda, and Roy Huss. "*A Separate Peace*: Filming the War Within." *Literature/Film Quarterly* 3: 160-71.

"*A Separate Peace* [(1972)], then, while it reveals physical activity brilliantly, is not true to the novel in its more important, psychological aspects."

883. Hodgkinson, Anthony W. "Film--A Central Discipline." *Literature/Film Quarterly* 3: 327-33. A response to 760.

"In the central discipline of Film ... production education must take its place as an essential aspect of practical aesthetics. That is to say, education *by means of* production, not instruction *in* production."

884. Isaacs, Neil D. "Lubitsch and the Filmed-Play Syndrome."
      Literature/Film Quarterly 3: 299-308.

      Lubitsch was skilled in finding "cinematic equivalents
      and enrichments of dramatic business."

885. Kauffmann, Stanley. *"Way Down East." Living Images: Film
      Comment and Criticism.* New York, Evanston, San Francisco,
      London: Harper & Row, pp. 281-89.

      A consideration of Griffith's use in the film of the
      material adapted from the Lottie Blair Parker play com-
      bined with a discussion of his own experience in the
      theater and his cinematic genius.

886. Kelman, Ken. "Naturalism Transcended: Von Stroheim's
      *Greed." The Essential Cinema: Essays on the Films in
      the Collection of Anthology Film Archives.* Ed. P. Adams
      Sitney. Vol. 1. New York: Anthology Film Archives and
      New York University Press, pp. 55-57.

      "Stroheim's obsession was precisely to realize fully
      the book *McTeague*, at any cost, down to the last detail."

887. Khatchadourian, Haig. "Film as Art." *The Journal of
      Aesthetics and Art Criticism* 33: 271-84.

      "The art-form which the filmmaker must be most care-
      ful not to imitate is, in my opinion, literature, and
      specifically fiction. It must also carefully avoid imi-
      tating theatrical productions."

888. LeSage, Julia. "Teaching the Comparative Analysis of
      Novels and Films." *Style* 9: 453-68.

      Provides both a theoretical framework and a course
      procedure which proved successful in the college class-
      room.

889. MacCann, Richard Dyer. "Appendix II: Reference Works
      for Film Study." *Cinema Journal* 14 (Special Issue),
      2: 72-79. See John L. Fell, *Cinema Journal* 9, 1 (1969):
      43-48. The MacCann bibliography reprinted in *Perform-
      ing Arts Resources.* Ed. Ted Perry. New York: Drama
      Book Specialists, Theatre Library Association, II, 57-68.

      An excellent bibliography of reference works for film
      study.

890. McConnell, Frank D. *The Spoken Seen: Film & the Romantic Imagination*. Baltimore & London: The Johns Hopkins University Press.

   A collection of essays designed to examine the individual's various unconscious and conscious reactions to the "reality" of the film. Considers the reaction to: the animated cartoon and the photograph, the use of language, the representation of society, the kinds of narrative genre and, finally, the reality "above tradition and inherited meaning" created by the viewer himself.
   The book is based on "the assumption that a truly accurate description of the art of film must include a sense of the two hundred years of imaginatively revolutionary thinking and writing that precede and parallel its own development."

891. McDougal, Stuart Y. "Mirth, Sexuality and Suspense: Alfred Hitchcock's Adaptation of *The Thirty-Nine Steps*." *Literature/Film Quarterly* 3: 232-39.

   "Hitchcock's principal concerns--the development of suspense, and the explorations of man's elemental fears and his relationships with women--are clearly not those of Buchan, and yet he has transformed the story in accordance with his own interests."

892. McDougal, Stuart Y. "Visual Tropes: An Analysis of *The Fallen Idol*." *Style* 9: 502-13.

   "Through an imaginative use of cinematic tropes, *The Fallen Idol* [(1948)] brilliantly captures the feelings of a little boy confronted for the first time with the complexities of the adult world." The film was based on Graham Greene's novel.

893. McGinnis, Wayne D. "*Chinatown*: Roman Polanski's Contemporary Oedipus Story." *Literature/Film Quarterly* 3: 249-51.

   An examination of parallels between the film and the plays of Sophocles which reveals "enough similarities to warrant a comparison and a possible attribution."

894. McNally, Judith. "The Art of Screenwriting: Neil Simon Discusses 'Prisoner of Second Avenue.'" *Filmmakers Newsletter* 8, 7: 27-32.

   Playwright-screenwriter Simon talks about his experience working in theater and in film.

895. McWilliams, Dean. "The Novelist as Filmmaker: Marguerite
      Duras' *Destroy, She Said.*" *Literature/Film Quarterly*
      3: 264-69.

      Marguerite Duras' success in bringing her novel *Détruire,
      dit-elle* to the screen is "achieved by disregarding a
      number of the conventional distinctions between litera-
      ture and film."

896. Mayersberg, Paul. "The Story So Far ... 'The Man Who
      Fell to Earth': A Commentary by the Screenwriter."
      Sight and Sound 44: 225-31.

      The screenwriter explains how he adapted Walter Tevis'
      novel to film.

897. Monaco, James. "Notes on 'The Big Sleep'/Thirty Years
      After." *Sight and Sound* 44: 34-38.

      The success of this film adaptation resulted from the
      perfect combination of director Hawks's style, Raymond
      Chandler's themes and the whole set of prevailing
      American cultural attitudes.

898. Morrissette, Bruce. "Post-Modern Generative Fiction:
      Novel and Film." *Critical Inquiry* 2: 253-62.

      Presents "a synchronic, contemporary analysis of genera-
      tive theory and practice in post-modern literature and
      film."

899. Morsberger, Robert E., ed. *"Viva Zapata!" The Original
      Screenplay by John Steinbeck*. New York: The Viking
      Press.

      Steinbeck's script for Elia Kazan's film *Viva Zapata!*
      (1952). Included is a short essay, "Steinbeck's Screen-
      plays and Productions," and a list of films written by
      Steinbeck or adapted for film by him and by others from
      his work.

900. Morsberger, Robert E., and Katharine M. Morsberger.
      "Screenplays as Literature: Bibliography and Criticism."
      Literature/Film Quarterly 3: 45-54; Bibliography, 55-59.

      The screenplay has too long been a neglected aspect
      of film study and criticism.

901. Muir, Kenneth. "The Critic, the Director, and Liberty
      of Interpreting." *The Triple Bond: Plays, Mainly*

> *Shakespearean, in Performance*. University Park and
> London: The Pennsylvania State University Press, pp.
> 20-29.
>
> Kozintsev's adaptation of *King Lear* is a successful
> recreation of the play.

902. Murray, D.M. "Faulkner, Silent Comedies, and the Animated
     Cartoon." *Southern Humanities Review* 9: 241-57.

     "There is no evidence that the novelist was consciously
     influenced by the comic films or that, conversely, his
     farcical humor influenced them. But recognition of the
     similarities between his humor and that of Sennett and
     Disney should add another dimension to our appreciation
     of his great art."

903. Oliver, Bill. "*The Long Goodbye* and *Chinatown*: Debunking
     the Private Eye Tradition." *Literature/Film Quarterly*
     3: 240-48.

     Robert Altman's film adaptation of Raymond Chandler's
     novel and Roman Polanski's *Chinatown* (1974) take a
     modern attitude toward the tradition of the private eye,
     drawing the conclusion that there is no value in positive
     action.

904. Perlmutter, Ruth. "Add Film to Rhetoric." *Literature/
     Film Quarterly* 3: 316-26.

     The attempts by artists to destroy, through literature
     and film, the "comforting schemata" of traditional
     rhetoric reveals only the impossibility of the effort.
     One cannot escape rhetoric. "The essential irony of
     literature and cinema without fiction is that, in the
     end, perforce, a grand metaphor evolves."

905. Petrie, Graham. "Dickens, Godard, and the Film Today."
     The Yale Review 64: 185-201.

     Though Dickens' influence on Griffith and Eisenstein
     may not have been as direct and formative as these film-
     makers claim, his influence remains "vital" and can be
     seen again in the style and vision of Godard.

906. Pointer, Michael. "A Dickens Garland: From Griffith on,
     the Eminent Victorian Has Captivated Film Directors
     and Public." *American Film* 1 (December): 14-19.

     Survey of film adaptation of Dickens' work.

907. Poteet, G. Howard. "Film Scripts." *Published Radio,*
      Television, and Filmscripts: A Bibliography. Troy,
      New York: The Whitston Publishing Company, pp. 169-231.

      A listing of screenplays by film title. "The book lists
      only screenplays which have been published in script
      form. Both complete works and fragments have been in-
      cluded."

908. Powell, Dilys. "The Film of the Book." *Essays by Divers*
      Hands 38: 93-111.

      Astute comments on a number of adaptations, among them
      Olivier's *Henry V* (1955) and *Hamlet* (1948); Welles'
      Othello (1951); Ken Russell's *Women in Love* (1969); and
      Cukor's *David Copperfield* (1935).

909. Pratt, George. "Early Stage and Screen: A Two-Way Street."
      Cinema Journal 14, 2: 16-19.

      Instances from around the turn of the century illustrate
      ways in which the stage borrowed techniques from the film.

910. Pryluck, Calvin. "The Film Metaphor Metaphor: The Use
      of Language-Based Models in Film Study." *Literature/*
      Film Quarterly 3: 117-23.

      "In the analysis of film, language-based units,
      terminology, and analysis can by reduction divert atten-
      tion from those aspects that may be unique to film."

911. Riley, Michael. "Gothic Melodrama and Spiritual Romance:
      Vision and Fidelity in Two Versions of *Jane Eyre.*"
      Literature/Film Quarterly 3: 145-59.

      Comparison of Robert Stevenson's version (1944) of the
      Charlotte Brontë novel with Delbert Mann's 1971 adapta-
      tion.

912. Rollins, Peter C., and Harry W. Menig. "Regional Litera-
      ture and Will Rogers: Film Redeems a Literary Form."
      Literature/Film Quarterly 3: 70-82.

      "Almost all of Rogers' films were adapted from works
      of the regional genre."

913. Ross, Harris. "A Selected Bibliography of the Relation-
      ship of Literature and Film." *Style* 9: 564-92.

      A selected bibliography of articles on the subject.

914. Schneider, Harold W. "Literature and Film: Marking Out Some Boundaries." *Literature/Film Quarterly* 3: 30-44.

    All teachers of literature and language must "for the sake of their own disciplines know much about the aesthetics of film, of the way a film works, of the history of film."

915. Silva, Edward T. "From *Candide* to *Candy*: Love's Labor Lost." *Journal of Popular Culture* 8: 783-91.

    "Where the book *Candy* was underdeveloped in character and incident, the movie *Candy* [(1968)], as all films, was necessarily over-developed in concrete images of physical reality."

916. Simone, Thomas R. "The Mythos of 'The Sickness Unto Death': Kurosawa's *Ikiru* and Tolstoy's *The Death of Ivan Ilych*." *Literature/Film Quarterly* 3: 2-12.

    The film and novella are related "analogically," for they are "among the most profound meditations on death and rebirth in the modern world."

917. Simper, DeLoy. "Poe, Hitchcock, and the Well-wrought Effect." *Literature/Film Quarterly* 3: 226-31.

    Considers *The Birds* (1963) "as an example of the well-wrought film."

918. Sobchack, Thomas. "Genre Film: A Classical Experience." *Literature/Film Quarterly* 3: 196-204.

    "The genre film is a classical mode in which imitation not of life but of conventions is of paramount importance."

919. Stone, Edward. "Ahab Gets Girl, or Herman Melville Goes to the Movies." *Literature/Film Quarterly* 3: 172-81.

    Discusses alterations made in *Moby Dick* when it was adapted for the screen in *The Sea Beast* (1926) and in *Moby Dick or The White Whale* (1930).

920. Sturhahn, Larry. "*One Flew Over the Cuckoo's Nest*: An Interview with Director Milos Forman." *Filmmakers Newsletter* 9, 2: 26-31.

    Forman's feeling for the Kesey novel greatly eased his efforts adapting it to film.

921. Suhor, Charles. "The Film/Literature Comparison."
      Media & Methods 12, 4: 56-59.

      Provides a chart devised "to compare film and three
      literary forms--the novel, the short story, and drama--in
      terms of their capacity for achieving numerous artistic
      effects."

922. Taylor, John Russell. "Stanley Kubrick." *Directors and
      Directions: Cinema for the Seventies.* New York: Hill
      and Wang, pp. 100-35.

      Comments on Kubrick's *Lolita* (1962) and *2001: A Space
      Odyssey* (1968).

923. Tiessen, Paul. "A Comparative Approach to the Form and
      Function of Novel and Film: Dorothy Richardson's
      Theory of Art." *Literature/Film Quarterly* 3: 83-90.

      Elucidates Richardson's definition of the "essential
      nature of the film experience," especially in relation
      to her views on the "'function' of art in general and
      the novel in particular."

924. Wagner, Geoffrey. *The Novel and the Cinema.* Cranbury,
      New Jersey: Fairleigh Dickinson University Press.

      A study of the relationship between novel and film.
      "Film saw in narrative fiction, rather than in poetry
      or drama, imagistic techniques and strategies which
      contributed to its own rapid development. In this sense
      only does the present book propose any dependence of
      cinema on fiction."
      Part One, "The Problem of Popularity," reviews some
      of the origins of the novel and the cinema, showing
      the effects on form produced by the need to appeal to
      the popular taste. Included are considerations of
      Citizen Kane (1941) and *Les Liaisons Dangereuses* (1959).
      Part Two, "History," examines the ways in which the
      cinema "mechanically reproduces, and therefore quali-
      fies, reality." Considered in this part: *Greed* (1923),
      The Blue Angel (1930), *The House of Usher* (1960) and
      Face to Face (1953).
      Part Three, "Methods," examines "three principal
      manners by means of which novels to date have been adapted
      for the screen: transposition, commentary, and analogy."
      Films used to illustrate transposition are *Wuthering
      Heights* (1939), *Jane Eyre* (1944), *Madame Bovary* (1949),
      Lord Jim (1965), *Hunger* (1966), *Last Year at Marienbad*
      (1961), *1984* (1956). Films used to illustrate commentary:

The Heiress (1949), *Catch-22* (1970), *A Clockwork Orange* (1971), *The Stranger* (1967). Films used to illustrate analogy: *Candide* (1960), *The Trial* (1962), *Cabaret* (1972), *Death in Venice* (1971) and *Contempt* (1963).

925. Wexman, Virginia Wright. "The Transfer from One Medium to Another: *The Maltese Falcon* from Fiction to Film." *The Library Quarterly* 45: 46-55.

The three film versions of Dashiell Hammett's novel, the 1931 *Maltese Falcon* (sometimes called *Dangerous Female*) directed by Roy Del Ruth, *Satan Met a Lady* by William Dieterle (1936) and John Huston's *The Maltese Falcon* (1941), are compared with each other and with the novel. The success of the 1941 film is due "to the confluence of first-rate screen material, hospitable social conditions, technical advances within the medium itself, and creative genius."

926. White, William. *Nathanael West: A Comprehensive Bibliography*. Kent, Ohio: The Kent State University Press, pp. 41-44.

Section D lists films on which West worked as a screen-writer.

927. Wiese, Epi. "Visconti and Renoir: Shadowplay." *The Yale Review* 64: 202-17.

A study of the use and effect of "ambiguity" in Visconti's *Death in Venice* (1971) based on the Thomas Mann novella and Jean Renoir's *A Day in the Country* (1936) based on Guy de Maupassant's "Une Partie de Campagne."

928. Willeford, Charles. "From *Cockfighter* to *Born to Kill*." *Film Quarterly* 29, 1: 20-24.

Novelist Willeford talks about writing the screenplay adaptation of his book.

929. Wojciechowska, Maia. "Give Your Fiction the 'Movie Treatment.'" *The Writer* 88 (September): 18-19.

"Within the nature of a movie treatment there are all the elements a writer needs to develop his idea visually. And visual writing is what the best modern writing is all about in our visually oriented age."

930.   Zambrano, Ana Laura. "Charles Dickens and Sergei Eisen-
       stein: The Emergence of Cinema." *Style* 9: 469-87.

       Though stimulated by Griffith's editing techniques,
       Eisenstein found in Dickens' novels "a vital link between
       the traditions of literature, theatre, and film; and it
       was the rhythm of montage in Dickens that greatly in-
       fluenced his own works."

931.   Zambrano, Ana Laura. *Horror: Film & Literature.* New
       York: Gordon Press.

       Not seen.

                              1976

932.   "Folger Film Archive Ready for Research." *Shakespeare
       Newsletter* 26: 29.

       Twenty-seven feature films, eight feature-length adap-
       tations, eight short films available for study at the
       Folger.

933.   Anderegg, Michael A. "Shakespeare on Film in the Class-
       room." *Literature/Film Quarterly* 4: 165-75.

       Explores what one "gains or loses" in the teaching of
       Shakespeare and film.

934.   Armes, Roy. "Film Narrative in the 1960s." *The Ambiguous
       Image: Narrative Style in Modern European Cinema.*
       Bloomington & London: Indiana University Press, pp.
       108-18.

       Literary influence can be seen in the films of Susan
       Sontag, Marguerite Duras and Agnès Varda.

935.   Ashton, Jean. "Reflecting Consciousness: Three Approaches
       to Henry James." *Literature/Film Quarterly* 4: 230-39.

       Survey of films adapted from Henry James's works,
       particularly Bogdanovich's *Daisy Miller* (1974) and
       Chabrol's *The Bench of Desolation* (1974).

936.   Bachmann, Gideon. "Pasolini on de Sade: An Interview
       during the Filming of 'The 120 Days of Sodom." *Film
       Quarterly* 29: 39-45.

       "It is the first time I am making a film about the
       modern world."

937. Baldwin, James. "Growing Up with the Movies." *American
      Film* 1, 7: 8-18. Reprinted as Part I of *The Devil
      Finds Work: An Essay.* New York: The Dial Press, 1976.

      Baldwin relates his reactions to film to the develop-
      ment of his writer's sensibility.

938. Borges, Jorge Luis. "Borges as Film Critic." Trans.
      Gloria Waldman and Ronald Christ. *Sight and Sound* 45:
      230-33.

      Collection of articles on film including *The Informer*
      (1935) and *The Petrified Forest* (1936).

939. Bowles, Stephen E. "*The Exorcist* and *Jaws.*" *Literature/
      Film Quarterly* 4: 196-214.

      Discusses first some of the assumptions and techniques
      of the new horror-suspense film, then takes up the
      question of what changes from novel to film "were re-
      quired to generate suspense."

940. Brewster, Ben. "Brecht and the Film Industry (on *The
      Threepenny Opera* film and *Hangmen Also Die*)." *Screen*
      16, 4: 16-29.

      Brecht's interest in and efforts on behalf of both
      film projects.

941. Brock, D. Heyward. "Dürrenmatt's *Der Besuch der alten
      Dame*: The Stage and Screen Adaptations." *Literature/
      Film Quarterly* 4: 60-67.

      "Generally, critics have found [*The Visit* (1964)] to
      be unsatisfactory despite the original play and its
      English adaptation."

942. Brunette, Peter, and Gerald Peary. "Tough Guy: James
      M. Cain Interviewed." *Film Comment* 12, 3: 50-57.

      Cain, a well-known novelist of "hard-boiled fiction,"
      has remained largely unacknowledged as a screenwriter.

943. Christensen, Jerome C. "Versions of Adolescents: Robert
      Bresson's *Four Nights of a Dreamer* and Dostoyevsky's
      "White Nights." *Literature/Film Quarterly* 4: 222-29.

      Both Bresson's film and the story by Dostoevsky that
      inspired it "investigate the ways a dreamer may try to
      use reality to maintain and enrich a fragile fantasia."

944. Cook, Bruce. "The Saga of Bingo Long and the Traveling
      All-Stars." *American Film* 1, 9: 9-13.

      The adaptors of William Brashler's novel *The Bingo
      Long Traveling All-Stars and Motor Kings*, Hal Barwood
      and Matt Robbins, took great liberties with the book.

945. Cozarinsky, Edgardo. "Borges on and in Film." *Sight and
      Sound* 45: 41-45.

      A survey of Borges' attitude toward and involvement
      with film.

946. Crain, Mary Beth. "The Ox-Bow Incident Revisited."
      Literature/Film Quarterly 4: 240-48.

      "It is hard to say how much [of Walter Van Tilburg
      Clark's] novel was changed in the film because of the
      personal preferences of the film makers or the dictates
      of mass appeal."

947. Crittenden, Anne. "'Picnic at Hanging Rock': A Myth and
      Its Symbols." *Meanjin Quarterly* 35: 167-74.

      A symbolic reading of the film's key images [which
      were derived from Joan Lindsay's novel] designed to
      illuminate the meanings "of the confrontation of civili-
      zation and nature that occur in the film."

948. Crowl, Samuel. "Chain Reaction: A Study of Roman Polanski's
      Macbeth." *Soundings* 59: 226-33.

      Shows the influence of Jan Kott's *Shakespeare Our
      Contemporary* on recent film adaptations of Shakespeare
      plays, and particularly on Polanski's *Macbeth* (1971).

949. Dardis, Thomas. "James Agee: The Man Who Loved the Movies."
      American Film 1, 8: 62-67.

      Agee as film critic and screenplay writer.

950. Dardis, Thomas. *Some Time in the Sun*. New York: Charles
      Scribner's Sons.

      Examines the lives and products of five acknowledged
      novelists during their screenwriting days in Hollywood.
      "Fitzgerald, Huxley, and West were not as lucky as
      Faulkner and Agee in finding directors with whom they
      could work so profitably, but all five of these writers
      found screenwriting in Hollywood to be at the very center
      of their lives for years. Some of the work these men
      did there is superb, and some of it is quite bad by any
      standard; but nearly all of it is interesting."

951. Degenfelder, E. Pauline. "The Four Faces of Temple Drake: Faulkner's *Sanctuary*, *Requiem for a Nun*, and the Two Film Adaptations." *American Quarterly* 28: 544-60.

The comparison of the novel and the two film adaptations, *The Story of Temple Drake* (1932) and *Sanctuary* (1961), shows changing treatments of women in literature and film.

952. Dietrich, Richard F. "Beckett's Goad: From Stage to Film." *Literature/Film Quarterly* 4: 83-89.

In adapting Beckett's play *Act Without Words II* in the film *The Goad* (1970) Paul Joyce captures the essential ambiguity that is characteristic of Beckett's work.

953. Duffy, Robert A. "Gade, Olivier, Richardson: Visual Strategy in *Hamlet* Adaptation." *Literature/Film Quarterly* 4: 141-52.

An examination of the visual techniques in three *Hamlet* films--Svend Gade's (1920), Olivier's (1948), Richardson's (1969)--shows that the three "widely variant visual strategies hint that a 'comprehensive' *Hamlet* may be beyond the reach of the cinema."

954. Dumont, Lillian, and Sandi Silverberg. "An Interview with Alain Robbe-Grillet." *Filmmakers Newsletter* 9, 9: 22-25.

Novelist-director Robbe-Grillet discusses his theories of filmmaking.

955. Feldstein, Elayne P. "From Novel to Film: The Impact of Harold Pinter on Robin Maugham's *The Servant*." *Studies in the Humanities* 5 (October): 9-14.

Not seen.

956. Ferrua, Pietra. "*Blow-Up* from Cortázar to Antonioni." *Literature/Film Quarterly* 4: 68-75.

Antonioni gives "the essence of Cortázar's short story in his beautiful and perfect film."

957. Friel, Joseph C. "Ustinov's Film *Billy Budd*, A Study in the Process of Adaptation: Novel, to Play, to Film." *Literature/Film Quarterly* 4: 271-84.

Collaborators on the screenplay for the film, Ustinov and Robert Rossen, depended substantially on a dramatized version of the novel by Herman Melville, *Uniform of Flesh*, written by Louis O. Coxe and Robert Chapman.

958. Gerlach, John. *"The Diary of a Country Priest*: A Total Conversion." *Literature/Film Quarterly* 4: 39-45.

"Bernanos develops his work with methods rooted in the ability of the novel to investigate the convergence of a number of complex social issues and viewpoints, while Bresson emphasizes the significance of particular instants, a method more suited to film."

959. Giannetti, Louis D. "The Member of the Wedding." *Literature/Film Quarterly* 4: 28-38.

Though it is based on the Carson McCullers play, and its script, by Edward and Edna Anhalt, is "virtually a transcription of the stage play," Fred Zinnemann's film is, nevertheless, more than "mere canned theatre."

960. Gomez, Joseph A. *"Women in Love*: Novel into Film." *Ken Russell: The Adaptor as Creator*. London: Frederick Muller Limited.

The book itself provides a study of the sources of Ken Russell's films, focussing on Russell's particular method or style of adaptation.
"Russell possesses a unique style and personal vision which stamps nearly every frame of his films, and he also depends almost exclusively on adapting his films from literary sources. In a sense, he is the film world's adaptor *par excellence*."
Chapter 4, on *Women in Love* (1969), examines the evolution of the film script, discusses D.H. Lawrence's novel, and explains Russell's methods of adapting it to film. "By any standard the film is a good one, but given the entire Russell canon, its importance as a motion picture is not as great as is casually supposed."

961. Grant, Barry K. "Whitman and Eisenstein." *Literature/Film Quarterly* 4: 264-70.

"Eisenstein thought of Whitman's poetry in terms of montage."

962. Green, Martin. "The Dialectic of Adaptation: *The Canterbury Tales* of Pier Paolo Pasolini." *Literature/Film Quarterly* 4: 46-53.

"In a way not always apparent in conventional cinematic adaptations of literary classics, there is a relationship of mutual and reciprocal illumination between Pasolini's film and Chaucer's masterpiece."

963. Guiliano, Edward, and Richard C. Keenan. "Browning Without Words: D.W. Griffith and the Filming of *Pippa Passes*." *Browning Institute Studies* 4: 125-59. See 60.

The cinematic qualities in Browning's poem made it readily accessible as material for Griffith. A shot-by-shot transcription of the film is included.

964. Harrington, John. *Film and/as Literature*. Englewood Cliffs, New Jersey: Prentice-Hall.

This anthology of essays treats the relationship between film and literature in seven sections: Adaptation; Film and Theater; Film and Novel; Film and Poetry; Authorship and Auteurship; Message, Medium, and Literary Art; and Film's Literary Resources.

965. Haver, Ronald. "Finally, the Truth about *Casablanca*." *American Film* 1, 8: 10-16.

Outlines the origin and production of the film, adapted from a three-act play, *Everybody Comes to Rick's*, by Murray Burnett and Joan Alison.

966. Heath, Stephen. "From Brecht to Film: Theses, Problems (on *History Lessons* and *Dear Summer Sister*)." *Screen* 16, 4: 34-44.

An examination of two films--*History Lessons* was adapted from Brecht's *The Business Deals of Mr. Julius Caesar*-- in light of Brecht's theory of film.

967. Heath, Stephen. "*Touch of Evil*, the Long Version--a Note." *Screen* 17, 1: 115-17.

A description of the cuts made to shorten Welles' film by fourteen minutes.

968. Hilenski, Ferdinand Alexi. "D.W. Griffith's Film Version of Browning's *Pippa Passes*: Some Problems in Early Literature to Film Adaptation." *Literature/Film Quarterly* 4: 76-82.

Griffith's *Pippa Passes* (1909) shows several film
techniques suggested by Browning's poem that Griffith
used later with great success.

969. Hodgdon, Barbara. "'The Mirror Up to Nature': Notes on
Kozintsev's *Hamlet*." *Comparative Drama* 9: 305-17.

A "look at Kozintsev's reality, that is, how he sees
and how he photographs objects and the natural world;
at his uses of spaces and rhythms; at his conception of
Ophelia; and at his cinematic translation of the ritual
and improvisational occasions of Shakespeare's play."

970. Homan, Sidney. "A Cinema for Shakespeare." *Literature/
Film Quarterly* 4: 176-86.

Review of "successes, failures and things in between"
in a college course called "The Movies and Shakespeare."

971. Jorgens, Jack J. "The Cinematic Bard." *Washingtonian*
(May): 272, 274-77.

Not seen.

972. Jorgens, Jack J. "Laurence Olivier's *Richard III*."
Literature/Film Quarterly 4: 99-107. Reprinted in
1043.

"His *Richard III* [(1955)] properly remains one of the
most admired and popular of Shakespeare films."

973. Jorgens, Jack J. "Shakespeare on Film: A Selected Checklist." *Literature/Film Quarterly* 4: 191-93.

Lists selected criticism of film adaptations of
Shakespeare.

974. Jorgens, Jack J. "Welles' *Othello*: A Baroque Translation." *Focus on Orson Welles*. Ed. Ronald Gottesman.
Englewood Cliffs, New Jersey: Prentice-Hall, pp. 146-
56. Reprinted in 1043.

"Orson Welles' *Othello* [(1951)] is one of the few
Shakespeare films in which the images on the screen
generate enough beauty, variety, and graphic power to
stand comparison with Shakespeare's poetic images, in
which the visual imagery compensates for the inevitable
loss of complexity and dramatic voltage accompanying
heavy alterations in the text."

975. Kinder, Marsha. "Establishing a Discipline for the
      Teaching of Film: Criticism and the Literary Analogue."
      Quarterly Review of Film Studies 1 (November): 424-29.

      Several ways in which film can be studied within the
      context of the study of literature without sacrificing
      the integrity of the cinematic medium are briefly
      described and include: Comparison of a Filmmaker and
      Writer, Comparison of Genre in Film and Literature,
      Writers Influenced by Film, Films Rich with Literary
      Allusions, Comparison between Literary and Film Criticism.

976. Koszarski, Richard. *Hollywood Directors 1914-1940*. New
      York: Oxford University Press.

      Comments by directors on their work reprinted from a
      variety of magazines and periodicals. Insightful refer-
      ences to film adaptations of literature abound. See
      particularly comments by Allan Dwan, pp. 154-59, and
      George Cukor, pp. 322-31.

977. Kovács, Katherine Singer. "Georges Méliès and the
      Féerie." *Cinema Journal* 16, 1: 1-13.

      The *féerie*, "a type of melodrama in which acrobatics,
      music, and mime were the main elements," was "the
      single most important theatrical influence in the devel-
      opment of Méliès' film style."

978. LaValley, Albert. "The Emerging Screenwriter." *Quarterly
      Review of Film Studies* 1: 19-44.

      The screenwriter's relation to the film.

979. Lehman, Ernest. "Dialogue on Film: Ernest Lehman."
      American Film 2, 1: 33-48.

      An interview in which screenwriter Lehman discusses
      several of his adaptations of literary works for film,
      including Albee's *Who's Afraid of Virginia Woolf?* and
      Roth's *Portnoy's Complaint*.

980. Lopez, Daniel. "Novel into Film: Bertolucci's *The
      Conformist*." *Literature/Film Quarterly* 4: 303-12.

      "Bertolucci has succeeded fully in adapting the
      literary work [Alberto Moravia's *The Conformist*] to the
      screen."

981. McNally, Judith. "*India Song*: An Interview with Marguerite
      Duras." *Filmmakers Newsletter* 9, 3: 18-21.

Writer-director Duras talks about the making of *India Song* (1975).

982. MacShane, Frank. "The Golden Graveyard." *The Life of Raymond Chandler.* New York: E.P. Dutton, pp. 104-28.

An account of Raymond Chandler's experiences as a screenwriter for Paramount Pictures.

983. MacShane, Frank. "Stranger in a Studio: Raymond Chandler and Hollywood: Part II." *American Film* 1, 7: 54-60.

How Chandler adapted Patricia Highsmith's novel *Strangers on a Train* for the Hitchcock film.

984. Miller, Mark Crispin. "Kubrick's Anti-Reading of *The Luck of Barry Lyndon.*" *Modern Language Notes* 91: 1360-79.

Comparison of novel and film shows that "Like *2001* [(1968)] and *A Clockwork Orange* [(1971)], *Barry Lyndon* [(1975)] deals with the inadequacy of language itself; and like those earlier films, it makes simple judgements impossible."

985. Morsberger, Robert E. "Adrift in Steinbeck's *Lifeboat.*" *Literature/Film Quarterly* 4: 325-38.

A comparison of Steinbeck's original, unpublished novel with the film. *Lifeboat* (1944) "is an uneven conglomeration of Hitchcock suspense, Steinbeck philosophy, and Swerling situation and dialogue."

986. Morsberger, Robert E. "The Hemingway Kind of Love: Macomber at the Movies." *Literature/Film Quarterly* 4: 54-59.

"The most nearly faithful and successful screen version of a Hemingway short story" is Zoltan Korda's adaptation of "The Short Happy Life of Francis Macomber" in 1947.

987. Mullin, Michael. "Orson Welles' *Macbeth*: Script and Screen." *Focus on Orson Welles.* Ed. Ronald Gottesman. Englewood Cliffs, New Jersey: Prentice-Hall, pp. 136-45.

"Welles' *Macbeth* [(1948)] remains interesting both for what it can tell us about the artist and for what it can tell us about the subject."

988. Palmer, James W. "Fiction into Film: Delbert Mann's
      Jane Eyre (An Edited Interview)." *Studies in the
      Humanities* 5 (October): 3-8.

      Not seen.

989. Pendo, Stephen. *Raymond Chandler on Screen: His Novels
      into Film*. Metuchen, New Jersey: The Scarecrow Press.

      The study deals with the six of seven Chandler novels
      adapted to the screen in which the character Philip
      Marlowe appears.
      "The purpose of this book primarily lies in comparing
      the literary character of Philip Marlowe, as Chandler
      created him, with the film character, as scriptwriters
      and directors have interpreted him." A "plot comparison"
      of each novel with the film adaptation appears at the
      end of each appropriate chapter.

990. Pendo, Stephen. "Raymond Chandler's Philip Marlowe:
      His Metamorphoses in Film." *Films in Review* 27:
      129-36.

      Traces the different treatments of Chandler's hero
      in film adaptations of his fiction.

991. Perlmutter, Ruth. "Malcolm Lowry's Unpublished Film-
      script of *Tender Is the Night*." *American Quarterly*
      28: 561-74.

      "Not only a brilliant amplification of Fitzgerald's
      intent in the novel, the script is also a culmination
      of Lowry's own aspirations, of his lifelong interest
      in films and the impact of film on his own fiction."

992. Scholes, Robert. "Narration and Narrativity in Film."
      Quarterly Review of Film Studies 1 (August): 283-96.

      Unlike literature, which "must exert extraordinary
      pains to achieve some impression of the real" in the
      process of narration, film easily renders material
      objects and the actions of characters. For this reason,
      a successful narrative film must encourage and achieve
      "some level of reflection, of conceptualization," in
      the viewer.

993. Schultheiss, John. "George Jean Nathan and the Dramatist
      in Hollywood." *Literature/Film Quarterly* 4: 13-27.

Survey of the failures and successes of dramatists who also wrote for Hollywood films. Includes an appendix listing representative films and plays by dramatists who wrote for the film.

994.   Spiegel, Alan. *Fiction and the Camera Eye: Visual Consciousness in Film and the Modern Novel*. Charlottesville: University Press of Virginia.

In the work of Flaubert and Joyce, in particular, and of other novelists writing in the modern tradition—Zola, James, Conrad, Faulkner, Nabokov, Robbe-Grillet and others—there is a way of recording experience in narrative form that can be called cinematographic. Part I examines the origins of cinematographic form in the work of Flaubert, then traces the evolution of this form as it branches into two related but essentially different directions. The first of these is the "noncinematographic antitype, interior form," which is to be found in the works of Zola, Lawrence and Woolf; the second is the "cinematographic form," found in the works of James, Conrad and Joyce. Part II explores the "various components of cinematographic form in the fiction of Joyce and numerous other twentieth-century novelists." Some of these components are "adventitiousness, anatomization, depthlessness, and montage."

995.   Spiegel, Alan. "The Mud on Napoleon's Boots: The Adventitious Detail in Film and Fiction." *The Virginia Quarterly Review* 52: 249-64.

Distinguishes between the "adventitious" versus the "artistically necessary" fact in fiction and film, asserting that the "adventitious" facts, which do "not signify nor connect with anything else in the narrative context beyond their own phenomenal appearances" preserve the "modern" way one views the world.

996.   Welsh, James M. "To See It Feelingly: *King Lear* Through Russian Eyes." *Literature/Film Quarterly* 4: 153-58.

"One is not likely to encounter a more haunting film of Shakespeare for a good many years to come."

997.   Wilder, Billy, and I.A.L. Diamond. "Dialogue on Film." *American Film* 1, 9: 33-48.

Director and writer have been collaborators on numerous projects. Includes a Wilder filmography and list of script collaborations with Diamond.

998. Wilds, Lillian. "One *King Lear* for Our Time: A Bleak
      Film Vision by Peter Brook." *Literature/Film Quarterly*
      4: 159–64.

      "From the first shot to the last, Brook's film is
      nothing if not coherent; it has in fact a persuasive
      and terrifying unity."

999. Williams, Linda L. "Stendhal and Bertolucci: The Sweet-
      ness of Life Before the Revolution." *Literature/Film
      Quarterly* 4: 215–21.

      Comparison of Bertolucci's *Before the Revolution* (1964)
      and the source of its inspiration, Stendhal's *La
      Chartreuse de Parme.*

1000. Willson, Robert F., Jr. "Lubitsch's *To Be or Not To Be*
      or Shakespeare Mangled." *Shakespeare on Film Newsletter*
      1, 1: 2–3, 6.

      Not seen.

1001. Wood, Robin. "Welles, Shakespeare and Webster." *Personal
      Views: Explorations in Film.* London and Bedford: The
      Gordon Fraser Gallery, pp. 136–52.

      An analysis of *Touch of Evil* (1958), suggesting that
      where before one sought to compare Welles with Shake-
      speare it now seems more appropriate to invoke John
      Webster, "in whose plays the Elizabethan creativity de-
      generates into morbidity and decadence."

1002. Zambrano, Ana Laura. *Dickens and Film.* New York: Gordon
      Press.

      Not seen.

1977

1003. Allen, Jeanne Thomas. *"Turn of the Screw* and *The
      Innocents*: Two Types of Ambiguity." *The Classic Ameri-
      can Novel and the Movies.* Ed. Gerald Peary and Roger
      Shatzkin. New York: Frederick Ungar Publishing, pp.
      132–42.

      Jack Clayton's film tries with some success to retain
      the ambiguity in James's story.

1004. Altman, Charles F. "Towards a Historiography of American
       Film." *Cinema Journal* 16, 2: 1-25.

       An examination of "the modes of historical explana-
       tion commonly employed in dealing with the American
       film." Contains a useful section on film and the other
       arts, pp. 8-10.

1005. Armour, Robert. "Poetry and Film for the Classroom."
       The English Journal 66, 1: 88-91.

       A general discussion of differences and similarities
       between poetry and film.

1006. Atkins, Irene Kahn. "Hollywood Revisited: A Sad Home-
       coming." *Literature/Film Quarterly* 6: 105-11.

       The film adaptation of Fitzgerald's *The Last Tycoon*
       fails largely because the material in the book has
       been stretched too thinly into a film "too filled with
       static moments lacking in emotional involvement."

1007. Bazerman, Charles. "Time in Play and Film: *Macbeth* and
       Throne of Blood." *Literature/Film Quarterly* 5: 333-37.

       The sense of time in the play is altered in the
       Kurosawa film.

1008. Berlin, Norman. "Peter Brook's Interpretation of *King
       Lear*: 'Nothing Will Come of Nothing.'" *Literature/
       Film Quarterly* 5: 299-303.

       Finds the film unfaithful to the original, owing to
       a distorting treatment designed to minimize "everything
       that is positive in the play."

1009. Bevan, David G. "Pasolini and Boccaccio." *Literature/
       Film Quarterly* 5: 23-24.

       The film of *The Decameron* "reveals Pasolini's own
       imaginary experience derived from a particular reading."

1010. Bodeen, DeWitt. "F. Scott Fitzgerald and Films." *Films
       in Review* 28: 285-94.

       Survey of film adaptations of Fitzgerald's fiction.

1011. Bodeen, DeWitt. "Films and Edith Wharton." *Films in
       Review* 28: 73-81.

       Survey of film adaptations of Edith Wharton's fiction.

1012. Bodeen, DeWitt. "Henry James into Film." *Films in Review*
       28: 163-70.

       Survey of film adaptations of Henry James's fiction.

1013. Bodeen, DeWitt. "Joseph Hergesheimer and Films." *Films
       in Review* 28: 538-45.

       Survey of film adaptations of Hergesheimer's fiction.

1014. Brandes, David. "An Interview with John Huston." *Film-
       makers Newsletter* 10, 9: 20-24.

       Huston's attitudes towards filmwriting, directing
       and acting.

1015. Brewster, Ben. "The Fundamental Reproach (Brecht)."
       Cine-Tracts 1, 2: 44-53.

       Brecht's fundamental reproach to the cinema is stated
       in a diary entry quoted in the text of this essay. For
       Brecht, cinema could not by itself establish a "distance"
       between performance and viewer.

1016. Brooks, Richard. "Dialogue on Film." *American Film*
       3, 1: 33-48.

       Discussion of several of his film adaptations from
       literature. Also includes a history of films to which
       Brooks contributed as screenwriter and as screenwriter-
       director.

1017. Brunette, Peter. "Faces in the Mirror: Twain's Pauper,
       Warners' Prince." *The Classic American Novel and
       the Movies*. Ed. Gerald Peary and Roger Shatzkin.
       New York: Frederick Ungar Publishing, pp. 105-13.

       Warner Brothers' 1937 adaptation of Twain's *The Prince
       and the Pauper* "betters" the book.

1018. Carlson, Jerry W. "*Washington Square* and *The Heiress*:
       Comparing Artistic Forms." *The Classic American Novel
       and the Movies*. Ed. Gerald Peary and Roger Shatzkin.
       New York: Frederick Ungar Publishing, pp. 94-104.

       The Heiress, William Wyler's 1949 film of James's
       novel *Washington Square*, was not directly adapted from
       the novel but rather from the Broadway play *The Heiress*,
       written by Ruth and Augustus Goetz.

1019. Clandfield, David. "The Onomastic Code of Stagecoach."
       Literature/Film Quarterly 5: 174-80.

       Examines the significance of character and place
       names in the film.

1020. Cohen, Keith. "Eisenstein's Subversive Adaptation."
       The Classic American Novel and the Movies. Ed. Gerald
       Peary and Roger Shatzkin. New York: Frederick Ungar
       Publishing, pp. 239-56.

       Eisenstein's finished treatment of An American
       Tragedy, his projected film adaptation of Theodore
       Dreiser's novel, was rejected by Paramount. Where
       Dreiser had simply depreciated American society, Eisen-
       stein had produced "a vividly anticapitalist document."

1021. Crick, Philip. "Toward an Aesthetic of Film Narrative."
       The British Journal of Aesthetics 17: 185-88.

       Refutes Kracauer's theory about the "unstaged reality"
       of documentary film: "Unscripted film may indeed present
       unscripted human movement. However ... that movement
       will be seen by a viewer from Western culture as having
       been narrated anyway, without the help of actors. 'That
       which happens next' is the basis of narration; and in
       any film, however bad, things are always happening
       next."

1022. Degenfelder, Pauline. "Sirk's The Tarnished Angels:
       Pylon Recreated." Literature/Film Quarterly 5: 242-51.

       Sirk's adaptation of Faulkner's novel does not dupli-
       cate but recreates the literary source: the spirit of
       the film is closer to the 1950s than to the 1930s; its
       interest is in character, not period; and Faulkner's
       criticism of technology is muted.

1023. Dick, Bernard F. "The Passenger and Literary Existen-
       tialism." Literature/Film Quarterly 5: 66-74.

       Finds correspondences between Antonioni's film and
       the philosophies of Sartre and Camus.

1024. Dworkin, Martin J. "'Stay Illusion!': Having Words
       about Shakespeare on Screen." The Journal of Aesthetic
       Education 11, 1: 51-61.

       An indictment of the interpretations of Shakespeare
       in Zeffirelli's Romeo and Juliet (1968) and Richardson's
       Hamlet (1969). For very different reasons each inter-

pretation suffers from "warped meanings" imposed on the
material for reasons of accommodating "some notion of
topicality" or "fashionable 'relevance.'"

1025. Ellis, Kate. "Life with Marmee: Three Versions." *The
       Classic American Novel and the Movies.* Ed. Gerald
       Peary and Roger Shatzkin. New York: Frederick Ungar
       Publishing, pp. 62-72.

       The George Cukor adaptation (1933) and the Mervyn
       Le Roy remake (1949) of Louisa May Alcott's *Little
       Women* discussed.

1026. Evans, Arthur B. *Jean Cocteau and His Film of Orphic
       Identity.* Philadelphia: The Art Alliance Press.

       A reevaluation of Jean Cocteau as an early film-poet
       based upon studies of three films: *Le Sang d'un Poète*
       (1930), *Orphée* (1950) and *Le Testament d'Orphée* (1959).
       Included are a discussion of "Narrative Versus Poetic
       Film" and an extensive "initiation" into Cocteau's
       artistic vocabulary.
       These three films "stand as a threefold cinematic
       legacy to the Orphic identity of their creator, and
       offer perhaps the clearest and most succinct portrait
       of Jean Cocteau-the-poet, as he had wished himself to
       be known for all time. Their story is his story, their
       composite identity is his identity, and their truths
       his truths."

1027. Firestone, Bruce M. "A Rose Is a Rose Is a Columbine:
       Citizen Kane and William Styron's *Nat Turner.*"
       Literature/Film Quarterly 5: 118-23.

       Styron's use of the columbine incident in his novel
       to explain his hero's first two decades of growth might
       well have been suggested by "Rosebud" in *Citizen Kane*
       (1941).

1028. Flinn, Tom, and John Davis. "Warners' War of the Wolf."
       The Classic American Novel and the Movies. Ed. Gerald
       Peary and Roger Shatzkin. New York: Frederick Ungar
       Publishing, pp. 192-205.

       Michael Curtiz's 1941 version of Jack London's *The
       Sea Wolf* differed from the original "not for the usual
       reasons of length or conflict with a production code
       or directorial style, but because of the possible
       political implications of a major character."

1029.   French, Brandon. "Lost at Sea." *The Classic American Novel and the Movies*. Ed. Gerald Peary and Roger Shatzkin. New York: Frederick Ungar Publishing, pp. 52-61.

Ray Bradbury's screenplay for John Huston's *Moby Dick* (1956) accounts largely for the failure of the film.

1030.   Fuller, Dan. "*Tom Sawyer*: Saturday Matinee." *The Classic American Novel and the Movies*. Ed. Gerald Peary and Roger Shatzkin. New York: Frederick Ungar Publishing, pp. 73-82.

Paramount's 1930 adaptation of Mark Twain's novel suffers from the studio's desire to keep the film fit for a juvenile audience.

1031.   Geduld, Carolyn. "Wyler's Suburban Sister: *Carrie* 1952." *The Classic American Novel and the Movies*. Ed. Gerald Peary and Roger Shatzkin. New York: Frederick Ungar Publishing, pp. 152-64.

The social implications and moral ambiguity in Dreiser's novel *Sister Carrie* "had to be cleaned up by scriptwriters Ruth and Augustus Goetz, before it could be brought to the screen by William Wyler as *Carrie* [(1952)]."

1032.   Gill, Brendan. "Novels into Movies." *Film Comment* 13, 2: 44-45.

Movie makers would do well to avoid using a "risky" novel like *Islands in the Stream* by Ernest Hemingway for a film; bankable novels, "pre-tested" in the marketplace, are best suited for making successful movies.

1033.   Halio, J.L. "Zeffirelli's *Romeo and Juliet*: The Camera *Versus* the Text." *Literature/Film Quarterly* 5: 322-25.

The film, which cuts almost 60% of the text, remains popular with critics and a young audience alike.

1034.   Harmetz, Aljean. *The Making of "The Wizard of Oz."* New York: Alfred A. Knopf.

This fascinating book examines the scripting, casting and production of the film adapted from the story by L. Frank Baum.

1035. Herman, Jay. "Hollywood and American Literature: The American Novel and the Screen." *The English Journal* 66, 1: 82-86.

Novels and film adaptations of them belong to two distinct genera; the film cannot reproduce the novel from which it is made.

1036. Higashi, Sumiko. "*Jane Eyre*: Charlotte Brontë Vs. the Hollywood Myth of Romance." *Journal of Popular Film* 6, 1: 13-31.

"Given the characterization of Jane in the novel and the social and economic context of the [nineteen] forties, it could have been a meaningful film. But instead, the movie emerged as a misrepresentation of Charlotte Brontë's work and an amassed set of Hollywood industry conventions."

1037. Hodgdon, Barbara. "Kozintsev's *King Lear*: Filming a Tragic Poem." *Literature/Film Quarterly* 5: 291-98.

A careful description of the film designed to show the director's success "in balancing subjective with objective vision" through the use of close and long shots.

1038. Hollyman, Burns. "Alexander Black's Picture Plays: 1893-1894." *Cinema Journal* 16, 2: 26-33.

Black's work, influenced by other nineteenth-century art forms, "is unique in that it spans the gap in film history between the pre-cinematic period of 1860-1896 and what we presently regard as the beginning of modern narrative form."

1039. Homan, Sidney R. "Criticism for the Filmed Shakespeare." *Literature/Film Quarterly* 5: 282-90.

Useful discussion of "types ... of current criticism of the filmed Shakespeare," with "reflections on the problems and possibilities common to all criticism on Shakespeare film."

1040. Horak, Jan-Christopher. "Maurice Tourneur's Tragic Romance." *The Classic American Novel and the Movies*. Ed. Gerald Peary and Roger Shatzkin. New York: Frederick Ungar Publishing, pp. 10-19.

"It is *The Last of the Mohicans* [(1920)] that stands as Maurice Tourneur's greatest work, and certainly one of the great films of the silent period."

1041. Horrigan, William. "Dying Without Death: Borzage's *A Farewell to Arms*." *The Classic American Novel and the Movies*. Ed. Gerald Peary and Roger Shatzkin. New York: Frederick Ungar Publishing, pp. 297-304.

Frank Borzage's film (1932), adapted from Hemingway's novel *A Farewell to Arms*, bears the earmarks of Borzage's not Hemingway's style and values.

1042. Iden, Peter. "The Sensation Maker: Rainer Werner Fassbinder and the Theater." *Wide Angle* 2, 1: 4-13.

Similarities in Fassbinder's film and stage direction can be seen in his use of political themes.

1043. Jorgens, Jack J. *Shakespeare on Film*. Bloomington and London: Indiana University Press.

A temperate, brilliant analysis of major film adaptations of Shakespeare's plays.
Detailed analysis of seventeen films: Reinhardt's *A Midsummer Night's Dream* (1935); Hall's *A Midsummer Night's Dream* (1969); Zeffirelli's *The Taming of the Shrew* (1966) and *Romeo and Juliet* (1968); Mankiewicz's *Julius Caesar* (1953); Welles' *Chimes at Midnight* (1965); Olivier's *Henry V* (1944) and *Richard III* (1955); Welles' *Macbeth* (1948); Kurosawa's *The Castle of the Spider's Web* (1957); Polanski's *Macbeth* (1971); Welles' *Othello* (1951); Burge's *Othello* (1965); Olivier's *Hamlet* (1948); Kozintsev's *Hamlet* (1964); Brook's *King Lear* (1970); and Kozintsev's *King Lear* (1970). The order followed is comedy, history, tragedy; films are discussed in terms of theatrical presentation, realistic interpretation and filmic adaptation. Film credits and notes keying film scripts to the Shakespeare texts are provided in an appendix.

1044. Juhnke, Janet. "A Kansan's View." *The Classic American Novel and the Movies*. Ed. Gerald Peary and Roger Shatzkin. New York: Frederick Ungar Publishing, pp. 165-75.

Recounts stories about the making of MGM's 1939 adaptation of L. Frank Baum's *The Wonderful Wizard of Oz*.

1045. Kaplan, E. Ann. "Hawthorne's 'Fancy Pictures' on Film." *The Classic American Novel and the Movies*. Ed. Gerald Peary and Roger Shatzkin. New York: Frederick Ungar Publishing, pp. 30-41.

Joe May and Lester Cole's adaptation (1940) of
Nathaniel Hawthorne's novel *The House of the Seven
Gables* stresses the social and political aspects of
the novel.

1046.   Karman, Mal. "The Art of the Screenwriter: William
        Goldman." *Filmmakers Newsletter* 10, 12: 20-22.

Goldman, "a novelist who writes screenplays," explains
his philosophy of screenwriting and his treatment of
the screenplay for the film *A Bridge Too Far* (1977)
adapted from the Cornelius Ryan novel.

1047.   Kawin, Bruce F. *Faulkner and Film.* New York: Frederick
        Ungar Publishing.

Faulkner's connection with Hollywood is examined
from four perspectives: Faulkner's fiction abounds in
"cinematic" techniques, making him "the most cinematic
of novelists"; films adapted from Faulkner's fiction,
except *Intruder in the Dust* (1949) and *Tomorrow* (1971),
are seriously flawed; Faulkner's career as a screenwriter; and Faulkner's contribution to film.

1048.   Kawin, Bruce F. "A Faulkner Filmography." *Film Quarterly*
        30: 12-21.

A list of all the screenwriting Faulkner did between
1932 and 1954.

1049.   Kinder, Marsha. "*Throne of Blood*: A Morality Dance."
        Literature/Film Quarterly 5: 339-45.

In place of the text, "a number of highly patterned
visual polarities" are used in a kind of dance "to
develop the moral conflicts" in the film.

1050.   Kliman, Bernice. "An American Tragedy: Novel, Scenario,
        and Films." *Literature/Film Quarterly* 5: 258-68.

Discussion of Sergei Eisenstein's 1930 scenario, and
film versions by Josef von Sternberg *(An American
Tragedy;* 1931), and George Stevens *(A Place in the Sun;*
1951), of Theodore Dreiser's novel *An American Tragedy.*

1051.   Kliman, Bernice. "Olivier's *Hamlet*: A Film-Infused Play."
        Literature/Film Quarterly 5: 305-14.

Olivier deliberately created the film hybrid, the
"film-infused play," as the best possible means of
presenting "the heightened language of Shakespeare."

1052. Koszarski, Richard. *Hollywood Directors 1941-1976*.
       London, New York: Oxford University Press.

       An anthology of interviews with a number of film
       directors who discuss, among other things, the process
       of film adaptation of literature.

1053. Kozintsev, Grigori. *"King Lear": The Space of Tragedy.
       The Diary of a Film Director*. Berkeley and Los
       Angeles: University of California Press.

       Kozintsev's diary, which he kept during the making
       of the film, "unfolds a day-to-day meditation on the
       play." A main theme running through the diary is the
       influence of other forms of theater, of the early Sergei
       Eisenstein and of nineteenth-century Russian literature
       on Kozintsev's approach to and execution of his project.

1054. LaValley, Albert J. "The Virtues of Unfaithfulness."
       The Classic American Novel and the Movies. Ed. Gerald
       Peary and Roger Shatzkin. New York: Frederick Ungar
       Publishing, pp. 272-85.

       A comparative examination of Sinclair Lewis's novel
       Dodsworth, the play version written primarily by Sidney
       Howard and the 1936 film adaptation directed by William
       Wyler.

1055. Leyda, Jay, ed. *Voices of Film Experience, 1894 to the
       Present: Talking About Films*. New York: Macmillan.

       A massive anthology of commentary by directors,
       screenwriters, actors and actresses, producers and
       others who work in the filmmaking business taken mainly
       from interviews.

1056. Luhr, William, and Peter Lehman. "Narrative Comparison,
       Part One"; "Narrative Comparison, Part Two: Films
       Using Stevenson's *The Strange Case of Dr. Jekyll
       and Mr. Hyde* as a Source." *Authorship and Narrative
       in Cinema*. New York: Capricorn Books, G.P. Putnam's
       Sons, pp. 197-219; 221-80.

       Chapter 6 analyzes the "narrative elements" in
       Robert Louis Stevenson's story in order to establish
       its structure as an "individuated aesthetic object."
       Chapter 7 discusses the use of these "narrative
       elements" by filmmakers, showing in the process "the
       essential dissimilarity present in the so-called similar
       elements," which suggests that all works of art must
       be approached and evaluated on their own aesthetic
       terms.

1057. McCreadie, Marsha. "*Henry V*: Onstage and on Film."
       Literature/Film Quarterly 5: 316-21.

       Most modern staged versions of Shakespeare's
       Henry V reveal the influence of Laurence Olivier's
       1944 film adaptation.

1058. McCreadie, Marsha. "*One Flew Over the Cuckoo's Nest*:
       Some Reasons for One Happy Adaptation." *Literary/
       Film Quarterly* 5: 125-31.

       Despite a number of changes in the adaptation, the
       film enjoys a popular and critical success equal to
       that of the novel.

1059. Marcus, Fred. *Short Story/Short Film*. Englewood Cliffs,
       New Jersey: Prentice-Hall.

       "How film and fiction function as storytelling modes."
       Investigates the various concerns of adaptation:
       "Film, Fiction, and Criticism"; "Film and Fiction:
       Contrasts in Media"; "Point of View and Tone in Film
       and Fiction"; "The Art of Animation"; "Stories Adapted
       to Film." Includes a list of short films adapted from
       short fiction.

1060. Maslin, Janet. "Ballantine's Scotch, Glemby Haircuts,
       White Suits, and White Teflon: Gatsby 1974." *The
       Classic American Novel and the Movies*. Ed. Gerald
       Peary and Roger Shatzkin. New York: Frederick Ungar
       Publishing, pp. 261-67.

       Jack Clayton's adaptation of F. Scott Fitzgerald's
       novel *The Great Gatsby* fails principally because the
       screenplay by Francis Ford Coppola "is worse than
       merely clumsy."

1061. Mast, Gerald. "Form and Language." *Film/Cinema/Movie:
       A Theory of Experience*. New York, Hagerstown, San
       Francisco, London: Harper & Row, pp. 15-23.

       The tendency among theorists who "have tended toward
       an exclusive concern for the film material and the
       cinematic process without a proper concern for the
       cinema's various forms, frequently dismissing such
       formal issues as impure borrowings from other (usually
       literary) arts," is "unwarranted and dangerous."

1062. Michel, Sonya. "*Yekl* and *Hester Street*: Was Assimila-
       tion Really Good for the Jews?" *Literature/Film
       Quarterly* 5: 142-46.

The film *Hester Street* (1975) remains faithful to its source, *Yekl, A Tale of the Ghetto*, by Abraham Cahan.

1063. Millard, Barbara C. "Shakespeare on Film: Towards an Audience Perceived and Perceiving." *Literature/Film Quarterly* 5: 352-56.

With film, "our culture has created, in effect, a 'new' theatre for Shakespeare, with a new audience," which "differs markedly in response and expectations from the traditional audiences of readers and theatre-goers."

1064. Moffat, Ivan. "On the Fourth Floor of Paramount: Interview with Billy Wilder." *The World of Raymond Chandler.* Ed. Miriam Gross. London: Weidenfeld and Nicholson.

Wilder talks about his collaboration with Raymond Chandler in writing the screenplay for the film adaptation of James M. Cain's short story "Double Indemnity."

1065. Monaco, James. "Film and the Novel" and "Film and Theatre." *How to Read a Film: The Art, Technology, Language, History and Theory of Film and Media.* New York: Oxford University Press, pp. 29-33; 33-37.

A concise analysis of differences between film and the novel and film and the theater.

1066. Mulvey, Laura. "Notes on Sirk and Melodrama." *Movie* 25: 53-56.

"While the Western and the gangster film celebrate the ups and downs endured by men of action, the melodrama of Douglas Sirk, like the tragedies of Euripides, probing pent-up emotion, bitterness and disillusion well known to women, act as a corrective."

1067. Nadeau, Robert. "Melville's Sailor in the Sixties." *The Classic American Novel and the Movies.* Ed. Gerald Peary and Roger Shatzkin. New York: Frederick Ungar Publishing, pp. 124-31.

Peter Ustinov's 1962 film adaptation of Herman Melville's novel *Billy Budd* tends to avoid "the more profound and disturbing aspects of the Melville masterpiece."

1068. Palmer, James W. "Cinematic Ambiguity: James's *The Turn of the Screw* and Clayton's *The Innocents*." *Literature/ Film Quarterly* 5: 198-215.

Jack Clayton's adaptation (1962) of Henry James's
story succeeds in retaining the novel's ambiguous
treatment of the "governess' reliability" and the "be-
lievability of the ghost."

1069. Palmer, R. Barton. "*Chinatown* and the Detective Story."
Literature/Film Quarterly 5: 112-17.

"An exploration of the parallels between *Chinatown*
[(1974)] and *Oedipus* will show ... how profoundly
Polanski has transformed the detective story genre into
a vehicle for the expression of a much different theme."

1070. Parish, James Robert, and Michael R. Pitts. *The Great
Science Fiction Pictures*. Metuchen, New Jersey: The
Scarecrow Press.

List of science fiction films, many adapted from
novels and short stories, with screen credits, description of action and background information.

1071. Paroissien, David. "*The Life and Adventures of Nicholas
Nickleby*: Alberto Cavalcanti Interprets Dickens."
Hartford Studies in Literature 9: 17-28.

"By suggesting that we view the life and adventures
of the Nickleby family allegorically, Cavalcanti both
adapts the novel to film and provides imaginative insight into the text itself."

1072. Peary, Gerald. "Rico Rising: Little Caesar Takes Over
the Screen." *The Classic American Novel and the
Movies*. Ed. Gerald Peary and Roger Shatzkin. New
York: Frederick Ungar Publishing, pp. 289-96.

In the film *Little Caesar* (1930), adapted from W.R.
Burnett's novel, the character of Rico Bandello has
been changed to make him resemble Al Capone.

1073. Pellow, G. Kenneth. "The Transformation of *The Sterile
Cuckoo*." *Literature/Film Quarterly* 5: 252-57.

The film is in a great many ways inferior to the
novel by John Nichols.

1074. Perebinossoff, Phillipe R. "Theatricals in Jean Renoir's
The Rules of the Game and *Grand Illusion*." *Literature/
Film Quarterly* 5: 50-56.

In *The Rules of the Game* (1939) theatricals suggest
"the breakdown of the aristocracy," while in *Grand*

Illusion (1937) they suggest the "imbalance in society during wartime."

1075. Poague, Leland. *"As You Like It* and *It Happened One Night*: The Generic Pattern of Comedy." *Literature/ Film Quarterly* 5: 346-50.

Both works, Shakespeare's play and Frank Capra's film, "share a common comic movement, a comic pattern of action and imagery, a common set of concerns, and a comic conclusion."

1076. Potamkin, Harry Alan. "The Film in the Theater." *The Compound Cinema: The Film Writings of Harry Alan Potamkin.* Selected, Arranged, and Introduced by Lewis Jacobs. New York and London: Teachers College Press, pp. 579-82.

Use of film as a backdrop in the theater in Russia and America.

1077. Przybylska, Krystyna Korvin. "An Interview with Andrzej Wajda." *Literature/Film Quarterly* 5: 2-16.

Includes thoughtful commentary on differences between film and theater.

1078. Richmond, Hugh M. "The Synergistic Use of Shakespeare Film and Videotape." *Literature/Film Quarterly* 5: 362-64.

Describes the program at the University of California, Berkeley, that uses interdisciplinary techniques to teach Shakespeare.

1079. Robbe-Grillet, Alain. "Order and Disorder in Film and Fiction." *Critical Inquiry* 4: 1-20.

Robbe-Grillet describes his own experiences dealing with problems and definitions of order and disorder as they relate to his own work. As a writer and filmmaker, he has found himself opposed to the "established order," endeavoring as an artist to establish the "created order," that is, "the movement of organization created by the very work of the writer."

1080. Rothwell, Kenneth S. "Zeffirelli's *Romeo and Juliet*: Words into Pictures and Music." *Literature/Film Quarterly* 5: 326-331.

From its opening, the film "ransacks cinematic art for pictorial and musical equivalents of Shakespeare's words."

1081. Safer, Elaine B. "'It's the Truth Even If It Didn't Happen': Ken Kesey's *One Flew Over the Cuckoo's Nest.*" *Literature/Film Quarterly* 5: 132-41.

The mythical dimension which R.P. McMurphy gains from being portrayed from Chief Bromden's point of view in the novel is lost when, in the film, Milos Forman supplants "Bromden's interior monologue with concrete detailed scenes."

1082. Samuels, Charles Thomas. "Carol Reed and the Novelistic Film." *Mastering the Film and Other Essays.* Ed. Lawrence Graver. Knoxville: The University of Tennessee Press, pp. 12-41.

The "novelistic cinema is a cinema in which plot predominates, in which the chief goal is satisfactory fulfillment of narrative expectations." Reed's *The Third Man* approaches the perfect "novelistic" film because the plot and the film's visual style are equally balanced and effective.

1083. Samuels, Charles Thomas. "Jean Renoir and the Theatrical Film." *Mastering the Film and Other Essays.* Ed. Lawrence Graver. Knoxville: The University of Tennessee Press, pp. 42-68.

"Novelistic films define themselves aesthetically because they contain visual description; theatrical films, which rely more heavily on dialogue and acting, must modify their dramatic borrowings or they become a recording medium rather than an art." Includes analyses of *A Day in the Country* (1936), *Grand Illusion* (1937) and *Rules of the Game* (1939).

1084. Schwartz, Nancy L. "From American Tragedy to Small-Town Dream-Come-True." *The Classic American Novel and the Movies.* Ed. Gerald Peary and Roger Shatzkin. New York: Frederick Ungar Publishing, pp. 218-25.

George Stevens' *Alice Adams* (1935), adapted from the Booth Tarkington novel, ended as a fairy tale where the novel had ended as a tragedy.

1085.   Silva, Fred. "Uncivil Battles and Civil War." *The
        Classic American Novel and the Movies*. Ed. Gerald
        Peary and Roger Shatzkin. New York: Frederick Ungar
        Publishing, pp. 114-23.

        "John Huston's 1951 adaptation of Stephen Crane's
        novel, *The Red Badge of Courage*, represents an instance
        of a talented, sympathetic director reworking a widely
        heralded classic novel that in filmic terms is highly
        problematic."

1086.   Silver, Charles, and Mary Corliss. "Hollywood Under
        Water: Elia Kazan on *The Last Tycoon*." *Film Comment*
        13, 1: 40-44.

        Elia Kazan discusses the way he filmed Harold Pinter's
        script of F. Scott Fitzgerald's unfinished novel.

1087.   Simons, John L. "Henry on Bogie: Reality and Romance
        in 'Dream Song No. 9' and *High Sierra*." *Literature/
        Film Quarterly* 5: 269-71.

        The film is a "key to understanding" John Berryman's
        poem.

1088.   Smoller, Sanford J. "The 'Booboisie' and Its Discontents."
        The Classic American Novel and the Movies. Ed. Gerald
        Peary and Roger Shatzkin. New York: Frederick Ungar
        Publishing, pp. 226-38.

        Both movie versions of Sinclair Lewis' novel *Babbitt*,
        by Warner Brothers in 1924 and by First National (a
        subsidiary of Warner Brothers) in 1934, failed as social
        criticism and at the box office.

1089.   Snyder, John R. "The Spy Story as Modern Tragedy."
        Literature/Film Quarterly 5: 216-34.

        "I shall try to supplement the notion of the realistic
        spy story as reflector of modern problems with a theory
        of its meaning—a 'metaphysics' of the genre."
        Includes close analyses of Joseph Conrad's story
        Secret Agent and Sir Carol Reed's film *The Third Man*
        (1949) and several other stories and films.

1090.   Staton, Shirley F. "Shakespeare Redivivus: Supplementary
        Techniques for Teaching Shakespeare." *Literature/
        Film Quarterly* 5: 358-61.

        Film and videotape can be used successfully to teach
        Shakespeare.

1091. Stowell, H. Peter. "John Ford's Literary Sources: From
       Realism to Romance." *Literature/Film Quarterly* 5:
       164-73.

       John Ford is an *auteur* director who "blends what
       romance and film do best: he fuses, in Hawthorne's
       terms, the 'real' with the 'marvelous.'"

1092. Styan, J.L. "Sight and Space: The Perception of Shake-
       speare in Stage and Screen." *Educational Theatre Journal*
       29: 18-28.

       The danger of seeing the film version of Shakespeare
       rather than seeing the play performed live on the stage
       is that the camera necessarily will have to select what
       the viewer sees in a given scene, thereby reducing his
       participation in the complete action unfolding on the stage.

1093. Turin, Maureen. "*I Married a Doctor*: Main Street Meets
       Hollywood." *The Classic American Novel and the Movies*.
       Ed. Gerald Peary and Roger Shatzkin. New York:
       Frederick Ungar Publishing, pp. 206-17.

       Warner Brothers' 1936 adaptation of Sinclair Lewis'
       Main Street "hoped to attract the old devotees of *Main
       Street*, while appealing to a different audience who
       identified the film through its new title as a 'woman's
       film.'"

1094. Turner, John W. "*Little Big Man*: the Novel and the Film:
       A Study of Narrative Structure." *Literature/Film
       Quarterly* 5: 154-63.

       "Novels and films can be compared on the basis of
       their narrative structure, on *how* they tell a story and
.   not on *what* they tell."

1095. Vidal, Gore; Hollis Alpert; and Jan Kadar. "Dialogue
       on Film: Gore Vidal." *American Film* 2, 6: 33-48.

       Vidal's attitude toward and involvement with film.

1096. Wead, George. "Frank Norris: His Share of *Greed*." *The
       Classic American Novel and the Movies*. Ed. Gerald
       Peary and Roger Shatzkin. New York: Frederick Ungar
       Publishing, pp. 143-51.

       Defends Frank Norris' stature as a novelist from
       those who claim that Erich von Stroheim's film *Greed*
       (1923) transformed and enriched its source, Norris'
       McTeague.

1097.   Weaver, Mike. "Edgar Allan Poe and the Early Avant-
        Garde Film." *Essays and Studies* 30: 73-85.

        Two silent film versions of *The Fall of the House
        of Usher* made in the late 1920's "were important con-
        tributions to the avant-garde film in its first phase,
        but they may also be considered as creative criticism
        of Poe's original story, illuminating not only its
        theme but also the presentation of those themes, as
        the transfer takes place from one medium to another."

1098.   White, Robert J. "Myth and Mise-en-Scène: Pasolini's
        Epido Re." *Literature/Film Quarterly* 5: 30-37.

        "Pasolini has ... attempted to place Oedipus outside
        of time and history by deliberately creating a tension
        between the prologue/epilogue of the film (which, set
        in modern times, is personal and autobiographical) and
        the central portion of the film (which is shot in
        Morocco and is designed to look primitive and pre-his-
        toric)."

1099.   Yacowar, Maurice. *Hitchcock's British Films*. Hamden,
        Connecticut: Archon Books, pp. 85-98; 116-22.

        A study of twenty-four Hitchcock films made in
        England between 1925 and 1939. Though many were adapted
        from works of literature, the author attends princi-
        pally to Hitchcock's cinematic development. All the
        films receive lengthy plot summaries but only two are
        discussed from the aspect of adaptation with any
        thoroughness: *The Manxman* (1929) from the novel by Sir
        Hall Caine and *Juno and the Paycock* (1930) from the
        Sean O'Casey play.

1100.   Yacowar, Maurice. *Tennessee Williams and Film*. New York:
        Frederick Ungar Publishing.

        An examination in chronological order of release of
        every film adapted from Tennessee Williams' works,
        undertaken with two questions in mind: "How well has
        Williams weathered the adaptation? How accurate is
        one's sense of Williams if it comes from his films?"
        Films examined include: *The Glass Menagerie* (1950);
        A Streetcar Named Desire (1951); *The Rose Tattoo* (1955);
        Baby Doll (1956); *Cat on a Hot Tin Roof* (1958); *Suddenly
        Last Summer* (1959); *The Fugitive Kind* (1960); *Summer
        and Smoke* (1961); *The Roman Spring of Mrs. Stone* (1961);
        Sweet Bird of Youth (1962); *Period of Adjustment* (1962);
        The Night of the Iguana (1964); *This Property Is Con-
        demned* (1966); *Boom* (1968); *Last of the Mobile Hot-
        shots* (1969).

1101. Zambrano, Ana Laura. "*David Copperfield*: Novel and Films." *Hartford Studies in Literature* 9: 1-16.

Considers the differing ways in which the Dickens novel has been adapted to film, focusing first on George Cukor's 1935 film and then on Delbert Mann's 1970 adaptation.

1102. Zito, Stephen. "*Dog Soldiers*: Novel into Film." *American Film* 2, 10: 8-15.

Robert Stone, author of *Dog Soldiers*, talks about his attempts to write the screenplay for the film adaptation that became *Who'll Stop the Rain?* (1978).

DISSERTATIONS

1939

1103. Whitehead, Edgar Harlan. "An Investigation of the Theory and Technique of Adapting the Novel to the Motion Picture." University of Southern California. [Not seen.]

1940

1104. Clapis, Joseph A. "Film and Book: An Analytic Comparison." Columbia University. [Not seen.]

1950

1105. Asheim, Lester. "From Book to Film: A Comparative Analysis of the Content of Novels and Motion Pictures Based Upon Them." University of Chicago.

1106. Gaupp, Charles John. "A Comparative Study of the Changes in Fifteen Film Plays Adapted from Stage Plays." The University of Iowa.

1107. North, Joseph H. "The Early Development of the Motion Picture (1887-1909)." Cornell University. Printed in book form by Arno Press, New York, 1973.

1951

1108. Runden, Charity E. "Film and Poetry: Some Interrelationships." Indiana University.

1952

1109. Grady, Marion B. "A Comparison of Motion Pictures and
       Books as Resource Materials." University of Chicago.

1956

1110. Bluestone, George. "Film Versions of the Novel." The
       Johns Hopkins University.

1957

1111. Chenoworth, Stuart Curran. "A Study of the Adaptation
       of Acting Technique from Stage to Film, Radio and
       Television in the United States, 1900-1951." North-
       western University.

1959

1112. Sidney, George. "Faulkner and Hollywood: A Study of
       His Career as a Scenarist." *DA* 20: 2810. The Univer-
       sity of New Mexico.

1961

1113. Asral, Ertem. "Tennessee Williams on Stage and Screen."
       DA 22: 1169-70. University of Pennsylvania.

1962

1114. Hurtgen, Charles Livermore. "Film Adaptations of
       Shakespeare's Plays." University of California,
       Berkeley.

1963

1115. Costello, Donald P. "George Bernard Shaw and the Motion
       Picture: His Theory and Practice." University of
       Chicago.

1116. See, Carolyn. "The Hollywood Novel: An Historical and
       Critical Survey." *DA* 24: 5418. University of Cali-
       fornia, Los Angeles.

1117. Selby, Stuart Alan. "The Study of Film as Art Form in
       American Secondary Schools." Columbia University.

1118. Warren, Clifton Lanier. "Tennessee Williams as a Cine-
       matic Writer." *DA* 25: 489-90. Indiana University.

1964

1119. Spatz, Jonas. 'Hollywood in Fiction: Some Versions of
       the American Myth." *DA* 25: 6637. Indiana University.

1120. Wolfe, Glenn Joseph. "Vachel Lindsay: The Poet as Film
       Theorist." *DA* 26: 1222-23. State University of Iowa.
       Printed in book form by Arno Press, New York, 1972.

1966

1121. Gollub, Judith Podselver. "Nouveau Roman et nouveau
       cinéma." *DA* 26: 6712-13. University of California,
       Los Angeles. French text.

1122. Manchel, Frank. "Film Literature: A Resource Study for
       Secondary School English Teachers." *DA* 27: 3875A.
       Columbia University.

1967

1123. Baird, James Lee. "The Movies in Our Heads: An Analysis
       of Three Film Versions of Theodore Dreiser's *An
       American Tragedy*." *DA* 28: 557A. University of Wash-
       ington.

1968

1124. King, Katherine Viola. "Film: Narrative and Post-Narra-
       tive Mode." University of California, Los Angeles.
       [Not seen.]

1125. Skoller, Donald S. "Problems of Transformation in the
       Adaptations of Shakespeare's Tragedies from Play-
       Script to Cinema." *DA* 29: 2830A. New York University.

1969

1126. Battle, Barbara Helen. "George Cukor and the American
       Theatrical Film." *DAI* 30: 439A. Columbia University.

1127. Blumenberg, Richard. "The Manipulation of Time and Space
       in the Novels of Alain Robbe-Grillet and in the Narra-
       tive Films of Alain Resnais, with Particular Refer-
       ence to *Last Year at Marienbad*." *DAI* 30: 4051A. Ohio
       University.

1128. Estrin, Mark Walter. "Dramatizations of American Fic-
       tion: Hawthorne and Melville on Stage and Screen."
       DAI 30: 3428A. New York University.

1129. Margolies, Alan. "The Impact of Theatre and Film on
       F. Scott Fitzgerald." *DAI* 30: 3467A. New York Univer-
       sity.

1130. Nulf, Frank Allen, Jr. "Luigi Pirandello and the Cinema:
       A Study of His Relationship to Motion Pictures and
       the Significance of That Relationship to Selected
       Examples of His Prose and Drama." *DAI* 30: 4055-56A.
       Ohio University.

1131. Snyder, John J. "James Agee: A Study of His Film
       Criticism." *DAI* 30: 3477-78A. St. Johns University
       (Canada). Printed in book form by Arno Press, New
       York, 1977.

1132. Storrer, William Allen. "A Comparison of Edward Albee's
       Who's Afraid of Virginia Woolf? as Drama and as Film."
       DA 29: 3544-45A. Ohio University.

1970

1133. Eidsvik, Charles Vernon. "Cinema and Literature." *DAI*
       31: 6601A. University of Illinois at Urbana-Champaign.

1134. Latham, John Aaron. "The Motion Pictures of F. Scott
       Fitzgerald." *DAI* 31: 6617-18A. Princeton University.

1135. Laurence, Frank Michael. "The Film Adaptations of
       Hemingway: Hollywood and the Hemingway Myth." *DAI*
       31: 5411A. University of Pennsylvania.

1136. Merritt, Russell LaMonte. "The Impact of D.W. Griffith's
       Motion Pictures from 1908 to 1914 on Contemporary
       American Culture." Harvard University.

1137. Van Wert, William. "The Theory and Practice of the
       Ciné-Roman." *DAI* 36: 4816A. Indiana University.

1971

1138. Chittister, Sister Joan, O.S.B. "The Perception of
      Prose and Filmic Fiction." *DAI* 32: 6508A. The Penn-
      sylvania State University.

1139. Embler, Jeffrey Brown. "A Historical Study of the Use
      of Film to Provide Additional Content to Theatrical
      Productions on the Legitimate Stage." University
      of Pittsburgh.

1140. Flanders, Mark Wilson. "Film Theory of James Agee."
      DAI 33: 3687-88A. The University of Iowa. Printed
      in book form by Arno Press, New York, 1977.

1141. Olf, Julian M. "The Play as Moving Picture: Toward a
      Phenomenology of Theatre." New York University.

1142. Podeschi, John Battista. "The Writer in Hollywood."
      DAI 32: 4629A. University of Illinois at Urbana-
      Champaign.

1143. Schweitzer, Robert Fred. "The Biblical Christ in
      Cinema." *DAI* 32: 5387A. University of Missouri--
      Columbia.

1972

1144. Andrew, James Dudley. "Realism and Reality in Cinema:
      The Film Theory of André Bazin and Its Source in
      Recent French Thought." *DAI* 33: 1711-12A. The Univer-
      sity of Iowa.

1145. Barrow, Craig Wallace. "Montage in James Joyce's
      Ulysses." *DAI* 33: 1713A. University of Colorado.

1146. Degenfelder, E. Pauline Sutta. "Essays on Faulkner:
      Style, Use of History, Film Adaptations of His Fic-
      tion." *DAI* 33: 5169A. Case Western Reserve University.

1147. Gill, June Marian. "The Films of Alain Robbe-Grillet."
      University of California, Berkeley.

1148. Holladay, John McKinley. "Trends in the Use of Film
      Among English Teachers at Selected Colleges and
      Universities in Michigan." *DAI* 33: 6235-36A. The
      University of Michigan.

1149.   Knoll, John Francis. "Malcolm Lowry and the Cinema."
        DAI 34: 5181A. St. Louis University.

1150.   Lewis, William Joseph. "A Comparison of Responses of
        Adolescents to Narrative and Lyric Literature and
        Film." *DAI* 33: 2221A. The Florida State University.

1151.   MacDonald, George Buchanan. "An Application of New
        Critical Methodology to the Study of the Narrative
        Fictional Film." *DAI* 32: 6435A. Lehigh University.

1152.   Michalczyk, John Joseph. "Malraux's 'Espoir': A
        Critical and Historical Analysis of the Film."
        Harvard University.

1153.   Quinn, Theodore Kinget. "W.S. Merwin: A Study in Poetry
        and Film." *DAI* 33: 3665-66A. The University of Iowa.

1154.   Savarese, Sister Paul Christi, C.S.J. "Cinematic Tech-
        niques in the Novels of William Faulkner." *DAI* 33:
        1179A. St. Louis University.

                                1973

1155.   Barr, Stephen Ronald. "Novel to Film: The Adaptation
        of American Renaissance Symbolic Fiction." *DAI* 34:
        4186A. University of Utah.

1156.   Belson, James Ira. "Maps of Consciousness: Creating
        an Inner Life for Character in Film and Novel."
        DAI 34: 4242A. University of Southern California.

1157.   Buzzard, David Bruce. "Humanizing the Secondary English
        Curriculum Through the Use of Film." *DAI* 34: 2155A.
        The Ohio State University.

1158.   Goodwin, James Edward. "I. Sergei Eisenstein's
        Ideological Aesthetics: The Silent Films. II. American
        Autobiography and the Writing Life. III. Transcen-
        dental Politics: Thoreau and John Brown." *DAI* 34:
        2624A. Rutgers University, The State University of
        New Jersey.

1159.   Haseloff, Cynthia. "Formative Elements of Film: A
        Structural Comparison of Three Novels and Their
        Adaptations by Irving Ravetch and Harriet Frank,
        Jr." *DAI* 33: 458A. University of Missouri--Columbia.

1160. Hudlin, Edward Warrington. "The Poetics of the Cinema."
       DAI 37: 376-77A. Columbia University.

1161. Losano, Wayne A. "The Horror Film and the Gothic Narra-
       tive Tradition." *DAI* 34: 5221A. Rensselaer Polytechnic
       Institute.

1162. Pearse, James Allen. "Montage in Modern Fiction: A
       Cinematographic Approach to the Analysis of Ironic
       Tone in Joyce Cary's 'The Horse's Mouth.'" *DAI* 34:
       3596-97A. The University of Arizona.

1163. Schultheiss, John Edward. "The 'Eastern' Writer in
       Hollywood in the 1930's." *DAI* 34: 4473A. University
       of Southern California.

1164. Silber, Joan Ellyn Frager. "Cinematic Techniques and
       Interpretations in Film and Television Adaptations
       of Shakespeare's *Hamlet*." *DAI* 34: 5370A. The Univer-
       sity of Michigan.

1165. Sweet, Frederick Joseph. "Narrative in the Films of
       Alain Resnais and Contemporary Fiction." *DAI* 34:
       1870A. The University of Michigan.

1166. Zambrano, Ana Laura. "The Novels of Charles Dickens
       and the Modern Film: A Study in the Aesthetics of the
       Visual Imagination." *DAI* 34: 3682A. University of
       California, Los Angeles.

                              1974

1167. Bishoff, Robert Earl, Jr. "Changing Perspectives: 'An
       American Tragedy' from Literature to Film." *DAI* 35:
       440A. University of Massachusetts.

1168. Bradt, David Richard. "From Fiction to Film: An
       Analysis of Aesthetic and Cultural Implications in
       the Adaptations of Two American Novellas." *DAI* 35:
       3671-72A. Washington State University.

1169. DeSchepper, Gerald Richard. "Seeing Art as Something
       and Nothing: A Comparison of Structuralism and Her-
       meneutics in Relation to Selected Works of Poetry,
       Painting and Film." *DAI* 35: 5237A. Ohio University.

1170. Gibson, Christine Mary. "Cinematic Techniques in the
      Prose Fiction of Beatriz Guido." *DAI* 36: 310-11A.
      Michigan State University.

1171. Harlow, Nancy Rex. "Dickens' Cinematic Imagination."
      DAI 35: 7307A. Brown University.

1172. Pfaff, Roland Leonard. "Bullough's 'Psychical Distance,'
      the Aesthetic Attitude, and Appreciation of Theater
      and Film." *DAI* 35: 3064A. The University of Michigan.

1173. Schueneman, Warren. "Elia Kazan: Director." *DAI* 35:
      5571A. University of Minnesota.

1174. Tomek, James Joseph. "Relationship of Literature and
      Film in Cocteau." *DAI* 35: 3014-15A. Duke University.

                          1975

1175. Becvar, William Joseph. "The Stage and Film Career of
      Rouben Mamoulian." *DAI* 36: 3221A. University of Kansas.

1176. Budd, Michael Nathan. "A Critical Analysis of Western
      Films Directed by John Ford from *Stagecoach* to
      Cheyenne Autumn." *DAI* 36: 1869A. The University of
      Iowa.

1177. Carr, Gary Lee. "The Screen Writing of John Howard
      Lawson 1928-1947: Playwright at Work in Hollywood."
      DAI 36: 580A. The University of Texas at Austin.

1178. Davis, Gary Corbett. "John Steinbeck in Film: An
      Analysis of Realism in the Novel and the Film--A
      Nonteleological Approach." *DAI* 36: 3170A. University
      of Southern California.

1179. Gomez, Joseph A., Jr. "The Sources and Films of Ken
      Russell: The Adaptor as Creator." *DAI* 36: 2460A. The
      University of Rochester.

1180. Hope, Kenneth Weaver. "Film and Meta-Narrative." *DAI*
      36: 4814A. Indiana University.

1181. Hopkins, Leroy Taft, Jr. "Literary Technique and
      Political Engagement: Alfred Doblin's Work in Film
      and Radio." Harvard University.

1182. Jaffe, Ira Sheldon. "Aristotle and the Movies: A Critical Study of Unity in the Film." *DAI* 36: 5604A. University of Southern California.

1183. Leonard, Arthur Byron. "Poetry and Film: Aspects of the Avant-Garde in France (1918-1932)." *DAI* 36: 6085A. Stanford University.

1184. Maland, Charles John. "American Visions: The Films of Chaplin, Ford, Capra, and Welles, 1936-1941." *DAI* 36: 3171A. The University of Michigan.

1185. Miller, Judy Held. "The Development of Cinematographic Techniques in Three Novels of Jamie Torres Bodet." *DAI* 36: 2791A. State University of New York at Albany.

1186. Money, Mary Alice. "Evolution of the Popular Western in Novels, Films, and Television, 1950-1974." *DAI* 36: 2825-26A. The University of Texas at Austin.

1187. Ricci, Frederick. "An Analysis of the Directing Techniques of Elia Kazan in Theatre and Film as Illustrated in *A Streetcar Named Desire*." *DAI* 36: 35A. Columbia University.

1188. Saunders, Joseph Bacon. "Off-Screen Images: An Origin of Visual Style in Cinema." *DAI* 36: 7014A. University of Southern California.

1189. Vendetti, James Anthony. "A Critical Interpretation of Jack Clayton's Film *The Innocents*." *DAI* 36: 4816-17A. Columbia University.

1190. Walz, Eugene Paul. "The Light-Mare World of Recent Film Satire." *DAI* 36: 6092A. University of Massachusetts.

1191. Woodbury, Dorothy Joan. "Toward a Theory of Empathy: A Developmental Hierarchy Applied to Response to Filmed Literature." *DAI* 36: 3249-50A. University of Washington.

1976

1192. Adams, Dale Talmadge. "Film Study in the Discipline of English." *DAI* 37: 7373A. The University of Texas at Austin.

1193.   Allen, Jeanne Thomas. "Aspects of Narration in *The Turn
        of the Screw* and *The Innocents.*" *DAI* 37: 2846-47A.
        The University of Iowa.

1194.   Bartell, Shirley Miller. "The Chinese Bandit Novel
        and the American Gangster Film: A Theoretical Model
        for Crosscultural and Interdisciplinary Teaching."
        DAI 37: 5554A. Florida Atlantic University.

1195.   Boroff, Phil Dean. "Joshua Logan's Directorial Approach
        to the Theatre and Motion Pictures: A Historical
        Analysis." *DAI* 37: 3270A. Southern Illinois Univer-
        sity.

1196.   Brandt, Carole Ann. "A Critical Consideration of the
        Transference of Playscripts into Films, with Partic-
        ular Reference to the American Film Theatre's 1975
        Series." *DAI* 37: 5439A. Southern Illinois University.

1197.   Browne, Nicholas Kaptyn. "Toward a Theory of Filmic
        Narration." *DAI* 37: 3965A. Harvard University.

1198.   Cook, Bruce Randall. "Science Fiction and Film: A Study
        of the Interaction of Science, Literature, and the
        Growth of Cinema." *DAI* 37: 6810A. University of
        Southern California.

1199.   Crouch, William Pryor. "Satanism and Possession in
        Selected Contemporary Novels and Their Cinematic
        Adaptations." *DAI* 37: 3966A. Northwestern University.

1200.   Dayton, Joyce Arlene. "Literature and Film: An Inter-
        disciplinary Course for College Undergraduates."
        DAI 37: 6455-56A. State University of New York at
        Albany.

1201.   Fernandez, Henry Cecilio. "The Influence of Galdós on
        the Films of Luis Buñuel." *DAI* 37: 7735A. Indiana
        University.

1202.   Foster, Harold Mark. "The New Literacy: A Manual for
        High School Film Teachers." *DAI* 37: 783-84A. The
        University of Michigan.

1203.   Frank, Felicia Nina Liss. "The Magazines 'Workers
        Theatre,' 'New Theatre' and 'New Theatre and Film'
        as Documents of the American Left-Wing Theatre Move-
        ment of the Nineteen-Thirties." *DAI* 37: 3273A. City
        University of New York.

1204. Frost, Francis Patrick. "A Historical-Critical Study of
       the Films of Richard Brooks, with Special Attention
       to His Problems of Achieving and Maintaining Final
       Decision-Control." *DAI* 37: 1845A. University of
       Southern California.

1205. Giles, Dennis Leslie. "The Retrieve: A Theory of
       Narrative Structure with Application to Film." *DAI*
       37: 6810A. Northwestern University.

1206. Hedges, Inez Kathleen. "Temporal and Spatial Structures
       in Films and the Novel: A Comparison between Yasujiro
       Ozu's 'Kohayagawa-ke No Aki' and Michel Butor's
       'L'Emploi du Temps.'" *DAI* 37: 5805A. The University
       of Wisconsin--Madison.

1207. Kasdan, Margo Law. "The Metaphor of Spectacle as an
       Interpretive Model in Narrative Cinema." *DAI* 38: 3A.
       Brown University.

1208. Kaspers, Candace Brand. "Symbolism in the Film Adapta-
       tions and Novels of D.H. Lawrence's *Sons and Lovers*,
       Women in Love, and *The Virgin and the Gypsy*." *DAI*
       37: 6113-14A. The University of Michigan.

1209. Lee, Carolyn Ann. "An Analysis of the Cinematic Elements
       in Selected Films of Elia Kazan: 1952-62." *DAI* 37:
       3233A. The University of Michigan.

1210. Lellis, George Patrick. "From Formalism to Brecht: The
       Development of a Political and Aesthetic Sensibility
       in *Cahiers du Cinéma*." *DAI* 37: 4664A. The University
       of Texas at Austin.

1211. LeSage, Julia Lewis. "The Films of Jean-Luc Godard and
       Their Use of Brechtian Dramatic Theory." *DAI* 37:
       1845-46A. Indiana University.

1212. McCardell, William Paul. "The 'Existential' Films of
       Norman Mailer: A Comparison with His Fiction and
       Nonfiction." *DAI* 37: 2185A. Temple University.

1213. McMillen, Barbara Fialkowski. "A Study of the Formal
       and Thematic Uses of Film in the Poetry of Parker
       Tyler, Frank O'Hara and Adrienne Rich." *DAI* 37:
       1549-50A. Ohio University.

1214. Mancini, Marc Louis. "Jacques Prévert: Poetic Elements
       in His Scripts and Cinematic Elements in His Poetry."
       DAI 37: 1595-96A. University of Southern California.

1215. Navarro, Lenore Mary. "From Fiction to Film: A Critical
       Analysis of Graham Greene's *The Fallen Idol*, *The
       Third Man*, and *Our Man in Havana*, Directed by Carol
       Reed." *DAI* 37: 5405-06A. University of Southern California.

1216. Orlandello, John Richard. "Stage to Screen: Film Adap-
       tations of the Plays of Eugene O'Neill." *DAI* 37:
       1271A. The University of Michigan.

1217. Palmer, James Wentworth. "Film and Fiction: Essays in
       Narrative Rhetoric." *DAI* 37: 1-2A. Claremont Graduate
       School.

1218. Schenck, Mary-Low Taylor. "Action Writing: A Study of
       Selected Works of Twentieth-century Drama, Fiction
       and Film Whose Theme Is the Examination of Their
       Own Processes." *DAI* 38: 257A. Brown University.

1219. Silver, Alain Joël. "Visual and Narrative Style in the
       Films of David Lean." *DAI* 37: 1846A. University of
       California, Los Angeles.

1220. Stam, Robert Philip. "The Interrupted Spectacle: The
       Literature and Cinema of Demystification." *DAI* 38:
       776-77A. University of California, Berkeley.

1221. Ubans, Mara Isaks. "Expressionist Drama and Film: Filmic
       Elements in Dramas and Film Scripts by Selected
       Expressionist Authors." *DAI* 37: 5864-65A. University
       of Southern California.

1222. Wallace, Roger Dale. "Gregg Toland--His Contributions
       to Cinema." *DAI* 37: 1271-72A. The University of
       Michigan.

                            1977

1223. Adamson, Judith Emily. "Greene on Film." University
       of Montreal (Canada).

1224. Allen, Robert Clyde. "Vaudeville and Film 1895-1915:
       A Study in Media Interaction." *DAI* 38: 3773A. The
       University of Iowa.

1225. Bayton, Michael DeWitt. "Poe, the Critics and Film-
      makers." *DAI* 38: 5472A. Northwestern University.

1226. Castelli, Louis Phillip. "Film Epic, A Generic Examina-
      tion and an Application of Definitions to the Work
      of David Lean." *DAI* 38: 6363-64A. Northwestern Univer-
      sity.

1227. Cutler, Janet Klotman. "Eugene O'Neill on the Screen:
      Love, Hate, and the Movies." *DAI* 38: 3109A. Univer-
      sity of Illinois at Urbana-Champaign.

1228. Hoekzema, Dorothea B. "Verisimilitude as a Way of
      Beginning the Narrative: The Language of Fiction and
      Film." Ohio University. [Not seen.]

1229. Johnson, John Randal. "*Macnaíma*: From Modernism to
      Cinema Novo." *DAI* 38: 4193A. The University of Texas
      at Austin.

1230. Kramer, Karen. "Film Adaptations of Novels and Plays."
      University of Connecticut, Storrs. [Not seen.]

1231. Maldanado, Armando. "Manuel Puig: The Aesthetics of
      Cinematic and Psychological Fiction." *DAI* 38: 2156-
      57A. The University of Oklahoma.

1232. Norden, Martin Frank. "The Art of Anxiety: Principles
      of Suspense in Representative Narrative Films."
      DAI 38: 5762A. University of Missouri--Columbia.

1233. Poggi, Gregory Joseph. "From Dramatic to Cinematic
      Standards: American Silent Film Theory and Criticism
      to 1929." *DAI* 38: 1745A. Indiana University.

1234. Rowe, Carel. "The Baudelairean Cinema: Analysis and
      Definition of a Trend Within the American Avant-
      Garde Cinema." *DAI* 38: 4412A. Northwestern University.

1235. Williams, Linda Paglierani. "Perceptual Ambiguity in
      Selected Modern Plays and Films." *DAI* 38: 2099A.
      Boston University School of Education.

APPENDIX

Abbreviations

D:	director	Pm:	poem
F:	film	R:	release date
GB:	Great Britain	S:	source
N:	novel	Sc:	screenwriter
P:	producer	SS:	short story
Pl:	play		

ADAMS, SAMUEL HOPKINS

    SS: "Night Bus"
    F: *It Happened One Night*
    D: Frank Capra
    Sc: Robert Riskin
    P: Columbia
    R: 1934
    See items 142, 1075

AIKEN, CONRAD

    SS: "Silent Snow, Secret Snow"
    F: *Silent Snow, Secret Snow*
    D: Gene Kearney
    Sc: Gene Kearney
    P: Gene Kearney, Alexander Alland, Richard Tompkins
    R: 1968
    See item 618

AKUTAGAWA, RYUNOSUKE

    SS: "Rashomon" and "In a Grove"
    F: *Rashomon*
    D: Akira Kurosawa

Sc: Akira Kurosawa, Shinobu Hashimoto
P: Daiei
R: 1950
See items 273, 652, 732, 872

AKUTAGAWA, RYUNOSUKE

SS: "Rashomon" and "In a Grove"
F: *The Outrage*
D: Martin Ritt
Sc: Michael Kanin. Based on the Akira Kurosawa film
Rashomon and the play by Fay and Michael Kanin
P: MGM
R: 1964
See item 406

ALAIN-FOURNIER (ALAIN FOURNIER, HENRI)

N: *The Wanderer*
F: *The Wanderer* (*Le Grand Meaulnes*)
D: Jean-Gabriel Albicocco
Sc: Jean-Gabriel Albicocco
P: Madeleine Films-AWA Films of Paris
R: 1969
See item 602

ALBEE, EDWARD

Pl: *Who's Afraid of Virginia Woolf?*
F: *Who's Afraid of Virginia Woolf?*
D: Mike Nichols
Sc: Ernest Lehman
P: Warner Bros.
R: 1966
See items 979, 1132

ALBEE, GEORGE SUMNER

N: *The Next Voice You Hear*
F: *The Next Voice You Hear*
D: William A. Wellman
Sc: Charles Schnee
P: MGM
R: 1950
See item 216

ALCOTT, LOUISA MAY

    N: *Little Women*
    F: *Little Women*
    D: George Cukor
    Sc: Sarah Y. Mason, Victor Heerman
    P: David O. Selznick/RKO
    R: 1933
    See items 142, 1025

ALCOTT, LOUISA MAY

    N: *Little Women*
    F: *Little Women*
    D: Mervyn Le Roy
    Sc: Andrew Solt, Sarah Y. Mason, Victor Heerman
    P: MGM
    R: 1949
    See item 1025

ANDERSON, EDWARD

    N: *Thieves Like Us*
    F: *They Live by Night* (GB title: *The Twisted Road*)
    D: Nicholas Ray
    Sc: Charles Schnee
    P: RKO
    R: 1948
    See item 818

ANDERSON, EDWARD

    N: *Thieves Like Us*
    F: *Thieves Like Us*
    D: Robert Altman
    Sc: Calder Willingham, Joan Tewksbury, Robert Altman
    P: Jerry Bick/George Litto/United Artists
    R: 1974
    See item 818

ANDERSON, LINDSAY, and DAVID SHERWIN

    S: Original story
    F: *O Lucky Man!*

D: Lindsay Anderson
Sc: David Sherwin
P: Warner Bros.
R: 1973
See item 798

ANDERSON, MAXWELL

Pl: *Anne of the Thousand Days*
F: *Anne of the Thousand Days*
D: Charles Jarrott
Sc: Bridget Boland, John Hale, Richard Sokolove
P: Hal B. Wallis/Universal
R: 1970
See item 553

ANOUILH, JEAN

Pl: *Becket*
F: *Becket*
D: Peter Glenville
Sc: Edward Anhalt
P: Hal B. Wallis/Paramount
R: 1964
See item 551

ANTONIONI, MICHELANGELO

S: Original story
F: *The Passenger*
D: Michelangelo Antonioni
Sc: Mark Peploe, Peter Wollen, Michelangelo Antonioni
P: Carlo Ponti/MGM
R: 1976
See item 1023

ARMSTRONG, WILLIAM H.

N: *Sounder*
F: *Sounder*
D: Martin Ritt
Sc: Lonne Elder III
P: Twentieth Century-Fox
R: 1972
See item 761

AUSTEN, JANE

    N: *Pride and Prejudice*
    F: *Pride and Prejudice*
    D: Robert Z. Leonard
    Sc: Aldous Huxley, Jane Murfin. Based on a dramatization
       of the novel by Helen Jerome.
    P: MGM
    R: 1940
    See item 313

BACH, RICHARD

    N: *Jonathan Livingston Seagull*
    F: *Jonathan Livingston Seagull*
    D: Hall Bartlett
    Sc: Hall Bartlett, Richard Bach
    P: Paramount
    R: 1973
    See item 826

BARTH, JOHN

    N: *End of the Road*
    F: *End of the Road*
    D: Aram Avakian
    Sc: Dennis McGuire, Terry Southern, Aram Avakian
    P: Allied Artists
    R: 1969
    See item 552

BASSANI, GIORGIO

    N: *The Garden of the Finzi-Continis*
    F: *The Garden of the Finzi-Continis (Il Giardino dei*
       Finzi-Contini)
    D: Vittorio De Sica
    Sc: Cesare Zavattini, Vittorio Bonicelli, Ugo Pirro
    P: Documento/Filmkunst/Walter Reade
    R: 1972
    See item 701

BAUM, L. FRANK

    N: *The Wizard of Oz*
    F: *The Wizard of Oz*
    D: Victor Fleming
    Sc: Noel Langley, Florence Ryerson, Edgar Allan Wolfe
    P: MGM
    R: 1939
    See items 1034, 1044

BEACH, REX

    N: *Padlocked*
    F: *Padlocked*
    D: Allan Dwan
    Sc: Becky Gardiner
    P: Famous Players-Lasky/Paramount
    R: 1926
    See item 64

BECKETT, SAMUEL

    Pl: *Act Without Words II*
    F: *The Goad*
    D: Paul Joyce
    Sc: Samuel Beckett
    P: Grove Press
    R: 1970
    See item 952

BECKETT, SAMUEL

    S: Original story
    F: *Film*
    D: Alan Schneider
    Sc: Samuel Beckett
    P: Grove Press
    R: 1964
    See item 515

BENCHLEY, PETER

    N: *Jaws*
    F: *Jaws*

D: Steven Spielberg
Sc: Peter Benchley, Carl Gottlieb
P: Zanuck-Brown/Universal
R: 1975
See item 939

BERGER, THOMAS

N: *Little Big Man*
F: *Little Big Man*
D: Arthur Penn
Sc: Calder Willingham
P: Hiller-Stockbridge/Cinema Center
R: 1970
See items 602, 1094

BERGMAN, INGMAR

S: Original story
F: *Cries and Whispers*
D: Ingmar Bergman
Sc: Ingmar Bergman
P: Cinematograph/Svenska Filminstitutet
R: 1972
See item 730

BERGMAN, INGMAR

S: Original story
F: *Hour of the Wolf (Vargtimmen)*
D: Ingmar Bergman
Sc: Ingmar Bergman
P: Svensk Filmindustri
R: 1966
See item 547

BERGMAN, INGMAR

S: Original story
F: *The Magician (Ansiktet;* GB title: *The Face)*
D: Ingmar Bergman
Sc: Ingmar Bergman
P: Svensk Filmindustri
R: 1959
See item 828

BERGMAN, INGMAR

    S: Original story
    F: *Persona*
    D: Ingmar Bergman
    Sc: Ingmar Bergman
    P: Svensk Filmindustri
    R: 1966
    See item 871

BERGMAN, INGMAR

    S: Original story
    F: *Through a Glass Darkly*
    D: Ingmar Bergman
    Sc: Ingmar Bergman
    P: Svensk Filmindustri
    R: 1961
    See item 812

BERNANOS, GEORGES

    N: *Diary of a Country Priest*
    F: *Diary of a Country Priest* (*Le Journal d'un Curé de Campagne*)
    D: Robert Bresson
    Sc: Robert Bresson
    P: U.G.C.
    R: 1950
    See item 958

BIERCE, AMBROSE

    SS: "An Occurrence at Owl Creek Bridge"
    F: *An Occurrence at Owl Creek Bridge*
    D: Robert Enrico
    Sc: Robert Enrico
    P: "Filmartic" Marcel Ichac/Films Du Centaure
    R: 1963
    See items 516, 596, 678, 835

BLATTY, WILLIAM PETER

    N: *The Exorcist*
    F: *The Exorcist*
    D: William Friedkin
    Sc: William Peter Blatty
    P: Warner Bros.
    R: 1973
    See items 790, 939

BLOCH, ROBERT

    N: *Psycho*
    F: *Psycho*
    D: Alfred Hitchcock
    Sc: Joseph Stefano
    P: Paramount
    R: 1960
    See item 871

BLOCK, IRVING, and ALLEN ADLER

    N: *Forbidden Planet*
    F: *Forbidden Planet*
    D: Fred McLeod Wilcox
    Sc: Cyril Hume. The story owes much to Shakespeare's
        The Tempest.
    P: MGM
    R: 1956
    See item 364

BOCCACCIO, GIOVANNI

    S: *The Decameron*
    F: *The Decameron*
    D: Pier Paolo Pasolini
    Sc: Pier Paolo Pasolini
    P: Alberto Grimaldi/United Artists
    R: 1971
    See item 1009

BOLT, ROBERT

    Pl: *A Man for All Seasons*
    F: *A Man for All Seasons*

D: Fred Zinnemann
Sc: Robert Bolt
P: Columbia
R: 1966
See items 553, 692

BOULLE, PIERRE

N: *The Bridge over the River Kwai*
F: *The Bridge on the River Kwai*
D: David Lean
Sc: Carl Foreman
P: Columbia
R: 1957
See item 817

BOULLE, PIERRE

N: *Planet of the Apes*
F: *Planet of the Apes*
D: Franklin J. Schaffner
Sc: Michael Wilson, Rod Serling
P: Twentieth Century-Fox
R: 1968
See item 610

BOULLE, PIERRE

N: *Planet of the Apes*
F: *Beneath the Planet of the Apes*
D: Ted Post
Sc: Paul Dehn. Based on the story by Paul Dehn and Mort
    Abrahams which was based on characters in the novel
    by Pierre Boulle
P: Twentieth Century-Fox
R: 1970
See item 610

BRADBURY, RAY

N: *Fahrenheit 451*
F: *Fahrenheit 451*
D: François Truffaut
Sc: François Truffaut, Jean-Louis Richard

P: Vineyard Films
R: 1966
See items 441, 757

BRASHLER, WILLIAM

N: *The Bingo Long Traveling All-Stars and Motor Kings*
F: *The Bingo Long Traveling All-Stars and Motor Kings*
D: Hal Barwood
Sc: Hal Barwood, Matthew Robbins
P: Universal
R: 1976
See item 944

BRECHT, BERTOLT

Pl: *The Business Deals of Mr. Julius Caesar*
F: *History Lessons*
See item 966

BRECHT, BERTOLT

S: Original story
F: *Kuhle Wampe*
D: S.T. Dudow
Sc: Bertolt Brecht
P: George M. Hoellering and Robert Shaarfenberg
R: 1931
See items 781, 792

BRECHT, BERTOLT, and FRITZ LANG

S: Original story
F: *Hangmen Also Die!*
D: Fritz Lang
Sc: John Wexley, Fritz Lang, Bertolt Brecht
P: Arnold Productions/United Artists
R: 1943
See item 940

BRECHT, BERTOLT, and KURT WEILL

Pl: *The Threepenny Opera*
F: *The Threepenny Opera*

D: G.W. Pabst
Sc: Bertolt Brecht, Ladislaus Vajda, Leo Lania, Béla
    Balász. Based on John Gay's *The Beggar's Opera*.
P: Warner Bros./Nero Films/Tobis
R: 1931
See item 940

BRONTË, CHARLOTTE

N: *Jane Eyre*
F: *Jane Eyre*
D: Robert Stevenson
Sc: Aldous Huxley, Robert Stevenson, John Houseman
P: Twentieth Century-Fox
R: 1944
See items 911, 1036

BRONTË, CHARLOTTE

N: *Jane Eyre*
F: *Jane Eyre*
D: Delbert Mann
Sc: Jack Pulman
P: Omnibus (A TV Movie)
R: 1971
See items 911, 988

BRONTË, EMILY

N: *Wuthering Heights*
F: *Wuthering Heights*
D: William Wyler
Sc: Ben Hecht, Charles MacArthur (and John Huston, un-
    credited)
P: Samuel Goldwyn
R: 1939
See items 313, 924

BROWN, HENRY PETER McNAB

N: *A Walk in the Sun*
F: *A Walk in the Sun*
D: Lewis Milestone
Sc: Robert Rossen

    P: Twentieth Century-Fox
    R: 1946
    See item 249

BROWNING, ROBERT

    Pm: "Pippa Passes"
    F: *Pippa Passes*
    D: D.W. Griffith
    Sc: D.W. Griffith
    P: Biograph
    R: 1909
    See items 963, 968

BUCHAN, JOHN

    N: *The Thirty-Nine Steps*
    F: *The Thirty-Nine Steps*
    D: Alfred Hitchcock
    Sc: Charles Bennett, Alma Reville
    P: Gaumont British
    R: 1935
    See item 891

BURGESS, ANTHONY

    N: *A Clockwork Orange*
    F: *A Clockwork Orange*
    D: Stanley Kubrick
    Sc: Stanley Kubrick
    P: Stanley Kubrick
    R: 1971
    See items 585, 633, 655, 697, 720, 733, 738, 924, 984

BURKE, THOMAS

    SS: "The Chink and the Child"
    F: *Broken Blossoms (The Yellow Man and the Girl)*
    D: D.W. Griffith
    Sc: D.W. Griffith
    P: D.W. Griffith Productions
    R: 1919
    See item 644

BURNETT, MURRAY, and JOAN ALISON

    Pl: *Everybody Comes to Rick's* (unproduced)
    F: *Casablanca*
    D: Michael Curtiz
    Sc: Julius J. Epstein, Philip G. Epstein, Howard Koch
    P: Warner Bros.
    R: 1942
    See items 727, 965, 1019

BURNETT, WILLIAM RILEY

    N: *High Sierra*
    F: *High Sierra*
    D: Raoul Walsh
    Sc: William Riley Burnett
    P: Warner Bros.
    R: 1941
    See item 1087

BURNETT, WILLIAM RILEY

    N: *Little Caesar*
    F: *Little Caesar*
    D: Mervyn Le Roy
    Sc: Francis Edwards Faragoh, Robert N. Lee
    P: First National Pictures
    R: 1930
    See item 1072

CAHAN, ABRAHAM

    N: *Yekl, A Tale of the Ghetto*
    F: *Hester Street*
    D: Joan Micklin Silver
    Sc: Joan Micklin Silver
    P: Midwest Films
    R: 1975
    See item 1062

CAIN, JAMES M.

    SS: "Double Indemnity"
    F: *Double Indemnity*

```
D:  Billy Wilder
Sc: Billy Wilder, Raymond Chandler
P:  Paramount
R:  1944
```
See items 814, 1064

CAINE, SIR HALL

```
N:  The Manxman
F:  The Manxman
D:  Alfred Hitchcock
Sc: Eliot Stannard
P:  British International Pictures
R:  1928
```
See item 1099

CAMUS, ALBERT

```
N:  The Stranger
F:  The Stranger (Lo Straniero; The Outsider)
D:  Luchino Visconti
Sc: Luchino Visconti, Suso Cecchi D'Amico, Georges
    Conchon, Emmanuel Robles
P:  Dino De Laurentiis Cinematografica/Master Film/
    Marianne Productions/Casbah Film
R:  1967
```
See items 485, 924

CAPOTE, TRUMAN

```
N:  In Cold Blood
F:  In Cold Blood
D:  Richard Brooks
Sc: Richard Brooks
P:  Richard Brooks
R:  1967
```
See items 485, 747

CAPOTE, TRUMAN

```
SS: "Miriam," "Among the Paths to Eden," "A Christmas
    Memory"
F:  Trilogy (Truman Capote's Trilogy)
D:  Frank Perry
```

Sc: Truman Capote, Eleanor Perry
P: Allied Artists
R: 1969
See item 495

CHAPLIN, CHARLES

S: Original story
F: *Monsieur Verdoux*
D: Charles Chaplin
Sc: Charles Chaplin
P: Chaplin Studios
R: 1947
See item 190

CHANDLER, RAYMOND

N: *The Big Sleep*
F: *The Big Sleep*
D: Howard Hawks
Sc: William Faulkner, Leigh Brackett, Jules Furthman
P: Warner Bros.
R: 1946
See items 815, 897

CHANDLER, RAYMOND

N: *The Long Goodbye*
F: *The Long Goodbye*
D: Robert Altman
Sc: Leigh Brackett
P: Lion's Gate
R: 1973
See item 903

CHAUCER, GEOFFREY

S: *The Canterbury Tales*
F: *The Canterbury Tales* (*I Racconti di Canterbury*)
D: Pier Paolo Pasolini
Sc: Pier Paolo Pasolini
P: PEA/Artistes Associés
R: 1972
See item 962

CHEKHOV, ANTON

    Pl: *Uncle Vanya*
    F: *Uncle Vanya*
    D: John Goetz, Franchot Tone
    Sc: John Goetz, Franchot Tone
    P: Uncle Vanya Co.
    R: 1958
    See item 316

CHRISTIE, AGATHA

    N: *Murder on the Orient Express*
    F: *Murder on the Orient Express*
    D: Sidney Lumet
    Sc: Paul Dehn
    P: Paramount
    R: 1974
    See item 851

CLARK, WALTER VAN TILBURG

    N: *The Ox-Bow Incident*
    F: *The Ox-Bow Incident* (GB title: *Strange Incident*)
    D: William A. Wellman
    Sc: Lamar Trotti
    P: Twentieth Century-Fox
    R: 1943
    See items 313, 946

CLARKE, ARTHUR C.

    SS: "The Sentinel"
    F: *2001: A Space Odyssey*
    D: Stanley Kubrick
    Sc: Stanley Kubrick, Arthur C. Clarke
    P: Stanley Kubrick/MGM
    R: 1968
    See items 481, 504, 509, 519, 622, 653, 686, 695, 708,
    922, 984

COCTEAU, JEAN

    S: Original story
    F: *The Blood of the Poet* (*Le Sang d'un Poète*)
    D: Jean Cocteau
    Sc: Jean Cocteau
    P: Vicomte de Noailles
    R: 1930
    See items 472, 1026

COCTEAU, JEAN

    S: Original story
    F: *Orpheus* (*Orphée*)
    D: Jean Cocteau
    Sc: Jean Cocteau
    P: Andre Paulve
    R: 1946
    See items 379, 1026

COCTEAU, JEAN

    S: Original story
    F: *The Testament of Orpheus* (*Le Testament d'Orphée*)
    D: Jean Cocteau
    Sc: Jean Cocteau
    P: Jean Thulliter
    R: 1959
    See items 472, 1026

CONDON, RICHARD

    N: *The Manchurian Candidate*
    F: *The Manchurian Candidate*
    D: John Frankenheimer
    Sc: George Axelrod
    P: MC Productions
    R: 1962
    See item 534

CONRAD, JOSEPH

    N: *Lord Jim*
    F: *Lord Jim*

D: Richard Brooks
Sc: Richard Brooks
P: Columbia
R: 1965
See item 924

CONRAD, JOSEPH

N: *Secret Agent*
F: *Sabotage* (US titles: *A Woman Alone* and *Hidden Power*)
D: Alfred Hitchcock
Sc: Charles Bennett, Ian Hay, Helen Simpson, E.V.H Emmett
P: Gaumont British Pictures
R: 1936
See item 850

CONRAD, JOSEPH

N: *The Secret Sharer*
F: *Face to Face*. A composite film made of two films
   spliced together. See Crane, Stephen, for reference
   to the second film
D: John Brahm
Sc: Aeneas MacKenzie
P: RKO
R: 1952
See item 924

CONROY, PAT

N: *The Water Is Wide*
F: *Conrack*
D: Martin Ritt
Sc: Irving Ravetch, Harriet Frank, Jr.
P: Twentieth Century-Fox
R: 1974
See item 801

COOPER, JAMES FENIMORE

N: *The Last of the Mohicans*
F: *The Last of the Mohicans*
D: Maurice Tourneur, Clarence L. Brown
Sc: Robert Dillon

P: Maurice Tourneur
R: 1920
See item 1040

CORTÁZAR, JULIO

SS: "Las babas del diablo"
F: *Blow-Up*
D: Michelangelo Antonioni
Sc: Michelangelo Antonioni, Tonino Guerra
P: Bridge Films/MGM
R: 1966
See items 478, 484, 865, 956

CRANE, STEPHEN

SS: "The Bride Comes to Yellow Sky"
F: *Face to Face*. A composite film made of two films
     spliced together. See Conrad, Joseph, for reference
     to the first film
D: Bretaigne Windust
Sc: James Agee
P: RKO
R: 1952
See item 924

CRANE, STEPHEN

N: *The Red Badge of Courage*
F: *The Red Badge of Courage*
D: John Huston
Sc: John Huston, Albert Band
P: MGM
R: 1951
See items 250, 267, 1085

de BEAUMONT, MME. LEPRINCE

SS: "Beauty and the Beast"
F: *Beauty and the Beast (La Belle et la Bête)*
D: Jean Cocteau
Sc: Jean Cocteau
P: Andre Paulve/Films du Palais Royal
R: 1950
See items 211, 533, 877

de MUSSET, ALFRED

    SS: "Les Caprices de Marianne"
    F: *The Rules of the Game (La Règle du Jeu)*
    D: Jean Renoir
    Sc: Jean Renoir, Camille François, Carl Koch
    P: N.E.F. (La Nouvelle Édition Française)
    R: 1939
    See items 522, 1083

de SADE, MARQUIS

    N: *The 120 Days of Sodom*
    F: *The 120 Days of Sodom*
    D: Pier Paolo Pasolini
    Sc: Pier Paolo Pasolini
    P: PEA/Artistes Associés
    R: 1975
    See item 936

DICKENS, CHARLES

    N: *Barnaby Rudge*
    F: *Barnaby Rudge*
    D: Thomas Bentley
    Sc: Cecil Hepworth
    P: Cecil Hepworth
    R: 1915
    See item 15

DICKENS, CHARLES

    N: *A Christmas Carol*
    F: *Scrooge*
    D: Henry Edwards
    Sc: Henry Edwards
    P: Twickenham
    R: 1935
    See items 134, 332

DICKENS, CHARLES

    N: *A Christmas Carol*
    F: *A Christmas Carol*

    D: Edwin L. Marin
    Sc: Hugo Butler
    P: MGM
    R: 1938
    See item 332

DICKENS, CHARLES

    N: *David Copperfield*
    F: *David Copperfield*
    D: Thomas Bentley
    Sc: Cecil Hepworth, Thomas Bentley
    P: Cecil Hepworth
    R: 1913
    See item 1

DICKENS, CHARLES

    N: *David Copperfield*
    F: *David Copperfield*
    D: George Cukor
    Sc: Hugh Walpole, Howard Estabrook
    P: MGM
    R: 1935
    See items 125, 130, 554, 739, 908, 1101

DICKENS, CHARLES

    N: *David Copperfield*
    F: *David Copperfield*
    D: Delbert Mann
    Sc: Jack Pulman
    P: Omnibus (A TV Movie)
    R: 1970
    See items 554, 1101

DICKENS, CHARLES

    N: *Dombey and Son*
    F: *Dombey and Son*
    D: Maurice Elvey
    Sc: Eliot Stannard
    P: Ideal
    R: 1918
    See item 29

DICKENS, CHARLES

    N: *Great Expectations*
    F: *Great Expectations*
    D: Stuart Walker
    Sc: Gladys Unger
    P: Universal
    R: 1934
    See item 127

DICKENS, CHARLES

    N: *Great Expectations*
    F: *Great Expectations*
    D: David Lean
    Sc: David Lean, Ronald Neame
    P: Cineguild
    R: 1946
    See items 187, 244, 393, 491, 739, 833, 334, 846

DICKENS, CHARLES

    N: *Little Dorrit*
    F: *Little Dorrit*
    D: Stanley Morgan
    Sc: Stanley Morgan
    P: Progress
    R: 1920
    See item 35

DICKENS, CHARLES

    N: *The Mystery of Edwin Drood*
    F: *The Mystery of Edwin Drood* (US title: *Vanished into Nowhere*)
    D: Stuart Walker
    Sc: Leopold Atlas, Bradley King, John L. Balderstone, Gladys Unger
    P: Universal
    R: 1935
    See item 128

DICKENS, CHARLES

  N: *Nicholas Nickleby*
  F: *Nicholas Nickleby*
  D: Alberto Cavalcanti
  Sc: John Dighton
  P: Ealing
  R: 1947
  See items 178, 188

DICKENS, CHARLES

  N: *The Old Curiosity Shop*
  F: *The Old Curiosity Shop*
  D: Thomas Bentley
  Sc: Cecil Hepworth, Thomas Bentley
  P: Cecil Hepworth
  R: 1914
  See item 11

DICKENS, CHARLES

  N: *The Old Curiosity Shop*
  F: *The Old Curiosity Shop*
  D: Thomas Bentley
  Sc: Margaret Kennedy, Ralph Neale
  P: Wardour/British International Pictures
  R: 1934
  See item 126

DICKENS, CHARLES

  N: *Oliver Twist*
  F: *Oliver Twist*
  D: Frank Lloyd
  Sc: Frank Lloyd, Harry Weil
  P: Sol L. Lesser
  R: 1922
  See item 48

DICKENS, CHARLES

  N: *Oliver Twist*
  F: *Oliver Twist*

D: David Lean
Sc: David Lean, Stanley Haynes
P: Cineguild
R: 1948
See items 193, 196, 252, 834

DICKENS, CHARLES

N: *Oliver Twist*
F: *Oliver!*
D: Carol Reed
Sc: Vernon Harris, Lionel Bart
P: Warwick/Romulus
R: 1968
See item 584

DICKENS, CHARLES

N: *The Pickwick Papers*
F: *Pickwick Papers*
D: Thomas Bentley
Sc: Cecil Hepworth, Thomas Bentley
P: Cecil Hepworth
R: 1921
See item 45

DICKENS, CHARLES

N: *The Pickwick Papers*
F: *The Pickwick Papers*
D: Noel Langley
Sc: Noel Langley
P: Langley-Minter/Renown
R: 1952
See item 268

DICKENS, CHARLES

N: *A Tale of Two Cities*
F: *A Tale of Two Cities*
D: Jack Conway
Sc: W.P. Lipscomb, S.N. Behrman
P: MGM
R: 1935
See items 139, 739

DICKENS, CHARLES

    N: *A Tale of Two Cities*
    F: *A Tale of Two Cities*
    D: Ralph Thomas
    Sc: T.E.B. Clarke
    P: Rank
    R: 1958
    See item 335

DICKEY, JAMES

    N: *Deliverance*
    F: *Deliverance*
    D: John Boorman
    Sc: James Dickey
    P: Elmer Enterprises
    R: 1972
    See items 668, 688, 694, 843

DIXON, REVEREND THOMAS, JR.

    N: *The Clansman*
    Pl: *The Clansman*
    N: *The Leopard's Spots*
    F: *The Birth of a Nation* (originally titled *The Clansman*)
    D: D.W. Griffith
    Sc: D.W. Griffith, Frank Woods
    P: Epoch
    R: 1915
    See items 414, 647

DOSTOEVSKY, FEODOR

    N: *The Brothers Karamazov*
    F: *The Crime of Dmitri Karamazov*
    D: Fedor Ozep
    Sc: Leonhard Frank, Erich Engel
    P: Terra
    R: 1931
    See item 113

DOSTOEVSKY, FEODOR

    N: *The Brothers Karamazov*
    F: *The Brothers Karamazov*
    D: Richard Brooks
   Sc: Richard Brooks
    P: Avon Productions
    R: 1957
   See item 325

DOSTOEVSKY, FEODOR

    N: *A Gentle Creature*
    F: *A Gentle Creature* (*Une Femme Douce*)
    D: Robert Bresson
   Sc: Robert Bresson
    P: Parc Film/Marianne Productions
    R: 1969
   See item 545

DOSTOEVSKY, FEODOR

    N: *The Idiot*
    F: *The Idiot*
    D: Akira Kurosawa
   Sc: Akira Kurosawa, Eijiro Hasaita
    P: Shochiku
    R: 1951
   See item 411

DOSTOEVSKY, FEODOR

    N: *White Nights*
    F: *Four Nights of a Dreamer*
    D: Robert Bresson
   Sc: Robert Bresson
    P: Victoria Films
    R: 1971
   See item 943

DREISER, THEODORE

    N: *An American Tragedy*
    F: *An American Tragedy*

D: Josef von Sternberg
Sc: Josef von Sternberg
P: Paramount
R: 1931
See items 99, 103, 117, 433, 498, 1020, 1050, 1123

DREISER, THEODORE

N: *An American Tragedy*
F: *A Place in the Sun*
D: George Stevens
Sc: Maurice Wilson, Harry Brown. Based on the novel and
    the Patrick Kearny play.
P: Paramount
R: 1951
See items 234, 247, 433, 1050, 1123

DREISER, THEODORE

N: *Sister Carrie*
F: *Carrie*
D: William Wyler
Sc: Ruth and Augustus Goetz
P: Paramount
R: 1952
See item 1031

du MAURIER, DAPHNE

SS: "The Birds"
F: *The Birds*
D: Alfred Hitchcock
Sc: Evan Hunter
P: Universal
R: 1963
See item 917

DURAS, MARGUERITE

N: *Destroy, She Said*
F: *Destroy, She Said* (*Détruire, dit-elle*)
D: Marguerite Duras
Sc: Marguerite Duras
P: Ancinex-Madeleine Films

R: 1969
See item 895

DURAS, MARGUERITE

S: Original story
F: *Hiroshima Mon Amour*
D: Alain Robbe-Grillet
Sc: Marguerite Duras
P: Argos-Como-Pathé/Daiei
R: 1959
See item 384

DURAS, MARGUERITE

S: Original story
F: *India Song*
D: Marguerite Duras
Sc: Marguerite Duras
P: Sunchild Productions/Les Films Armorial
R: 1975
See item 981

DURAS, MARGUERITE

S: Original story
F: *Last Year at Marienbad*
D: Alain Resnais
Sc: Marguerite Duras
P: Astor Pictures
R: 1961
See items 828, 924

DÜRRENMATT, FRIEDRICH

Pl: *The Visit*
F: *The Visit*
D: Bernhard Wicki
Sc: Ben Barzman
P: Twentieth Century-Fox
R: 1964
See item 941

ELIOT, T.S.

    P1: *Murder in the Cathedral*
    F: *Murder in the Cathedral*
    D: George Hoellering
    Sc: T.S. Eliot
    P: George Hoellering
    R: 1952
    See items 239, 241

ENNERY, ADOLPH D.

    P1: *The Two Orphans*
    F: *Orphans of the Storm*
    D: D.W. Griffith
    Sc: D.W. Griffith
    P: United Artists
    R: 1921
    See item 847

FARRELL, JAMES T.

    N: *Studs Lonigan; A Trilogy*
    F: *Studs Lonigan*
    D: Irving Lerner
    Sc: Philip Yordan
    P: Longridge Enterprises
    R: 1960
    See item 353

FAULKNER, WILLIAM

    N: *Intruder in the Dust*
    F: *Intruder in the Dust*
    D: Clarence Brown
    Sc: Ben Maddow
    P: MGM
    R: 1949
    See items 249, 262, 691, 1047

FAULKNER, WILLIAM

    N: *Pylon*
    F: *The Tarnished Angels*

D: Douglas Sirk
Sc: George Zuckerman
P: Universal-International
R: 1957
See items 569, 635, 1022

FAULKNER, WILLIAM

N: *Sanctuary*
F: *The Story of Temple Drake*
D: Stephen Roberts
Sc: Oliver H.P. Garrett
P: Paramount
R: 1932
See items 752, 951

FAULKNER, WILLIAM

N: *Sanctuary*
Pl: *Requiem for a Nun*
F: *Sanctuary*
D: Tony Richardson
Sc: James Poe
P: Twentieth Century-Fox
R: 1961
See items 752, 951

FAULKNER, WILLIAM

SS: "Tomorrow"
F: *Tomorrow*
D: Joseph Anthony
Sc: Horton Foote
P: Filmgroup Productions
R: 1972
See item 1047

FEIFFER, JULES

Pl: *Little Murders*
F: *Little Murders*
D: Alan Arkin
Sc: Jules Feiffer
P: Twentieth Century-Fox
R: 1971
See item 525

FIELDING, HENRY

    N: *Tom Jones*
    F: *Tom Jones*
    D: Tony Richardson
    Sc: John Osborne
    P: Woodfall
    R: 1963
    See items 417, 538

FITZGERALD, F. SCOTT

    SS: "Babylon Revisited"
    F: *The Last Time I Saw Paris*
    D: Richard Brooks
    Sc: Julius J. Epstein, Philip G. Epstein, Richard Brooks
    P: MGM
    R: 1954
    See item 614

FITZGERALD, F. SCOTT

    N: *The Great Gatsby*
    F: *The Great Gatsby*
    D: Herbert Brenon
    Sc: Becky Gardiner, Elizabeth Meehan. Based on the novel
        and on the play by Owen Davis
    P: Zukor-Lasky/Paramount
    R: 1926
    See item 786

FITZGERALD, F. SCOTT

    N: *The Great Gatsby*
    F: *The Great Gatsby*
    D: Elliot Nugent
    Sc: Cyril Hume, Richard Maibaum. Based on the novel and a
        play by Owen Davis
    P: Paramount
    R: 1949
    See item 786

FITZGERALD, F. SCOTT

    N: *The Great Gatsby*
    F: *The Great Gatsby*
    D: Jack Clayton
    Sc: Francis Ford Coppola
    P: Paramount

R: 1974
See items 786, 795, 816, 872, 1060

FITZGERALD, F. SCOTT

N: *The Last Tycoon*
F: *The Last Tycoon*
D: Elia Kazan
Sc: Harold Pinter
P: Sam Spiegel/Paramount
R: 1976
See items 1006, 1086

FLAUBERT, GUSTAVE

N: *Madame Bovary*
F: *Madame Bovary*
D: Vincente Minnelli
Sc: Robert Ardrey
P: MGM
R: 1949
See items 313, 924

FORESTER, C.S.

N: *The African Queen*
F: *The African Queen*
D: John Huston
Sc: James Agee, John Huston
P: Horizon-Romulus/United Artists
R: 1951
See item 242

FOWLES, JOHN

N: *The Collector*
F: *The Collector*
D: William Wyler
Sc: Stanley Mann, John Kohn
P: Columbia
R: 1965
See item 473

GARDNER, LEONARD

N: *Fat City*
R: *Fat City*

D: John Huston
Sc: Leonard Gardner
P: Columbia
R: 1972
See item 762

GOLDING, WILLIAM

N: *Lord of the Flies*
F: *Lord of the Flies*
D: Peter Brook
Sc: Peter Brook
P: Allen-Hogden/Two Arts
R: 1963
See item 538

GOLDMAN, JAMES

Pl: *The Lion in Winter*
F: *The Lion in Winter*
D: Anthony Harvey
Sc: James Goldman
P: Avco Embassy
R: 1968
See item 551

GOODIS, DAVID

N: *Down There*
F: *Shoot the Piano Player* (*Tirez sur le pianiste*)
D: François Truffaut
Sc: François Truffaut, Marcel Moussy
P: Films de la Pléiade
R: 1960
See item 660

GORKY, MAXIM

Pl: *The Lower Depths*
F: *The Lower Depths*
D: Akira Kurosawa
Sc: Akira Kurosawa, Hideo Oguni
P: Toho
R: 1957
See item 411

GREEN, F.L.

    N: *Odd Man Out*
    F: *Odd Man Out*
    D: Carol Reed
    Sc: F.L. Green, Robert C. Sherriff
    P: Two Cities
    R: 1947
    See item 860

GREENE, GRAHAM

    SS: "Across the Bridge"
    F: *Across the Bridge*
    D: Ken Annakin
    Sc: Guy Elmes, Denis Freeman
    P: Rank
    R: 1957
    See item 829

GREENE, GRAHAM

    SS: "The Basement Room"
    F: *The Fallen Idol*
    D: Carol Reed
    Sc: Graham Greene
    P: London Films
    R: 1948
    See items 829, 892, 1215

GREENE, GRAHAM

    N: *Brighton Rock*
    F: *Brighton Rock* (US title: *Young Scarface*)
    D: John Boulting
    Sc: Graham Greene, Terence Rattigan
    P: Associated British Pictures
    R: 1947
    See items 731, 829

GREENE, GRAHAM

    N: *The Comedians*
    F: *The Comedians*

```
D:  Peter Glenville
Sc: Graham Greene
P:  MGM
R:  1967
```
See item 829

GREENE, GRAHAM

```
N:  The Confidential Agent
F:  The Confidential Agent
D:  Herman Shumlin
Sc: Robert Buckner
P:  Warner Bros.
R:  1945
```
See item 829

GREENE, GRAHAM

```
N:  The End of the Affair
F:  The End of the Affair
D:  Edward Dmytryk
Sc: Lenore Coffee
P:  Columbia
R:  1955
```
See items 740, 829

GREENE, GRAHAM

```
N:  England Made Me
F:  England Made Me (US title: The Shipwrecked)
D:  Peter Duffell
Sc: Desmond Corey, Peter Duffell
P:  Atlantic Productions
R:  1972
```
See item 725

GREENE, GRAHAM

```
N:  A Gun for Sale
F:  This Gun for Hire
D:  Frank Tuttle
Sc: Albert Maltz, W.R. Burnett
P:  Paramount
R:  1942
```
See item 829

GREENE, GRAHAM

    N: *The Heart of the Matter*
    F: *The Heart of the Matter*
    D: George More O'Ferrall
    Sc: Ian Dalrymple, Lesley Storm
    P: London Film Productions
    R: 1953
    See items 735, 829

GREENE, GRAHAM

    SS: "The Lieutenant Died Last"
    F: *Went the Day Well?* (US title: *Forty-Eight Hours*)
    D: Alberto Cavalcanti
    Sc: John Dighton, Diana Morgan, Angus Macthail
    P: Ealing Studios
    R: 1942
    See item 829

GREENE, GRAHAM

    N: *The Man Within*
    F: *The Man Within* (US title: *The Smugglers*)
    D: Bernard Knowles
    Sc: Muriel and Sydney Box
    P: Rank
    R: 1947
    See item 829

GREENE, GRAHAM

    N: *The Ministry of Fear*
    F: *Ministry of Fear*
    D: Fritz Lang
    Sc: Seton I. Miller
    P: Paramount
    R: 1944
    See items 676, 775, 829

GREENE, GRAHAM

    N: *Our Man in Havana*
    F: *Our Man in Havana*

    D: Carol Reed
    Sc: Graham Greene
    P: Columbia
    R: 1959
    See items 680, 829, 1215

GREENE, GRAHAM

    N: *The Power and the Glory*
    F: *The Fugitive*
    D: John Ford
    Sc: Dudley Nichols
    P: RKO
    R: 1947
    See items 663, 829

GREENE, GRAHAM

    N: *The Quiet American*
    F: *The Quiet American*
    D: Joseph L. Mankiewicz
    Sc: Joseph L. Mankiewicz
    P: United Artists
    R: 1957
    See item 829

GREENE, GRAHAM

    N: *Stamboul Train*
    F: *Orient Express*
    D: Paul Martin
    Sc: Paul Martin, William Conselman, Carl Hovey, Oscar
        Levant
    P: Twentieth Century-Fox
    R: 1953
    See item 829

GREENE, GRAHAM

    SS: "The Stranger's Hand" (unpublished story)
    F: *The Stranger's Hand*
    D: Mario Soldati
    Sc: Guy Elmes, Georgio Bassani

    P: Rank
    R: 1954
    See item 829

GREENE, GRAHAM

    N: *Travels with My Aunt*
    F: *Travels with My Aunt*
    D: George Cukor
    Sc: Jay Presson Allen, Hugh Wheeler
    P: MGM
    R: 1972
    See items 702, 829

GREENE, GRAHAM

    S: Original story
    F: *The Third Man*
    D: Carol Reed
    Sc: Graham Greene
    P: London Film Productions
    R: 1949
    See items 581, 714, 772, 829, 1082, 1089, 1215

HALEVY, JULIAN

    N: *The Young Lovers*
    F: *The Young Lovers*
    D: Samuel Goldwyn, Jr.
    Sc: George Garrett
    P: Tigertail Productions/MGM
    R: 1964
    See item 583

HAMMETT, DASHIELL

    N: *The Maltese Falcon*
    F: *The Maltese Falcon* (*Dangerous Lady*)
    D: Roy del Ruth
    Sc: Maude Fulton, Lucien Hubbard, Brown Holmes
    P: Warner Bros.
    R: 1931
    See items 811, 924

HAMMETT, DASHIELL

    N: *The Maltese Falcon*
    F: *Satan Met a Lady*
    D: William Dieterle
   Sc: Brown Holmes
    P: Warner Bros.
    R: 1936
   See items 811, 924

HAMMETT, DASHIELL

    N: *The Maltese Falcon*
    F: *The Maltese Falcon*
    D: John Huston
   Sc: John Huston
    P: Warner Bros.
    R: 1941
   See items 249, 511, 748, 811, 924

HAMSUN, KNUT

    N: *Hunger*
    F: *Hunger*
    D: Henning Carlsen
   Sc: Henning Carlsen, Peter Seeberg
    P: Denmark-Norway-Sweden Production
    R: 1966
   See item 924

HARRIS, MARK

    N: *Bang the Drum Slowly*
    F: *Bang the Drum Slowly*
    D: John Hancock
   Sc: Mark Harris
    P: Paramount
    R: 1973
   See item 858

HARTLEY, L.P.

    N: *The Go-Between*
    F: *The Go-Between*

    D: Joseph Losey
    Sc: Harold Pinter
    P: World Film Services
    R: 1970
    See items 606, 722, 810

HARTLEY, L.P.

    N: *The Hireling*
    F: *The Hireling*
    D: Alan Bridges
    Sc: Wolf Mankowitz
    P: World Film Services-Champion
    R: 1973
    See item 800

HAWTHORNE, NATHANIEL

    N: *The House of the Seven Gables*
    F: *The House of the Seven Gables*
    D: Joe May
    Sc: Lester Cole
    P: Universal
    R: 1940
    See item 1045

HAWTHORNE, NATHANIEL

    N: *The Scarlet Letter*
    F: *The Scarlet Letter*
    D: Victor Seastrom
    Sc: Frances Marion, Victor Seastrom
    P: MGM
    R: 1926
    See items 77, 806, 837

HAWTHORNE, NATHANIEL

    SS: "Young Goodman Brown"
    F: *Young Goodman Brown*
    D: Donald Fox
    Sc: Donald Fox
    P: Learning Corp.
    R: 1973
    See item 782

HAYCOX, ERNEST

    SS: "Stage to Lordsburg"
    F: *Stagecoach*
    D: John Ford
    Sc: Dudley Nichols
    P: Walter Wanger/United Artists
    R: 1939
    See item 577

HELLER, JOSEPH

    N: *Catch-22*
    F: *Catch-22*
    D: Mike Nichols
    Sc: Buck Henry
    P: Paramount
    R: 1970
    See items 555, 570, 597, 726, 841, 924

HEMINGWAY, ERNEST

    N: *A Farewell to Arms*
    F: *A Farewell to Arms*
    D: Frank Borzage
    Sc: Benjamin Glazer, Oliver H.P. Garrett
    P: Paramount
    R: 1932
    See item 1041

HEMINGWAY, ERNEST

    N: *A Farewell to Arms*
    F: *A Farewell to Arms*
    D: Charles Vidor
    Sc: Ben Hecht
    P: David O. Selznick
    R: 1957
    See item 363

HEMINGWAY, ERNEST

    N: *Islands in the Stream*
    F: *Islands in the Stream*

    D: Franklin J. Schaffner
    Sc: Denne Bart Petitclerc
    P: Paramount
    R: 1977
    See item 1032

HEMINGWAY, ERNEST

    SS: "The Killers"
    F: *The Killers*
    D: Robert Siodmak
    Sc: Anthony Veiller
    P: Mark Hellinger/Universal
    R: 1946
    See item 818

HEMINGWAY, ERNEST

    SS: "The Killers"
    F: *The Killers*
    D: Don Siegel
    Sc: Gene L. Coon
    P: Revue Productions
    R: 1964
    See item 818

HEMINGWAY, ERNEST

    N: *The Old Man and the Sea*
    F: *The Old Man and the Sea*
    D: John Sturges
    Sc: Ernest Hemingway, Peter Viertel
    P: Warner Bros.
    R: 1958
    See item 821

HEMINGWAY, ERNEST

    SS: "The Short Happy Life of Francis Macomber"
    F: *The Macomber Affair*
    D: Zoltan Korda
    Sc: Casey Robinson, Seymour Bennett, Frank Arnold
    P: Award Productions
    R: 1947
    See item 986

HEMINGWAY, ERNEST

    N: *To Have and Have Not*
    F: *To Have and Have Not*
    D: Howard Hawks
    Sc: Jules Furthman, William Faulkner
    P: Warner Bros.
    R: 1944
    See item 249

HERLIHY, JAMES LEO

    N: *Midnight Cowboy*
    F: *Midnight Cowboy*
    D: John Schlesinger
    Sc: Waldo Salt
    P: Jerome Hellman-John Schlesinger
    R: 1969
    See items 565, 869

HIGHSMITH, PATRICIA

    N: *Strangers on a Train*
    F: *Strangers on a Train*
    D: Alfred Hitchcock
    Sc: Raymond Chandler, Czenzi Ormonde, Whitfield Cook
    P: Warner Bros.
    R: 1951
    See item 983

HIMES, CHESTER

    N: *Cotton Comes to Harlem*
    F: *Cotton Comes to Harlem*
    D: Ossie Davis
    Sc: Ossie Davis
    P: United Artists
    R: 1970
    See item 602

HUGO, VICTOR

    N: *The Hunchback of Notre Dame*
    F: *The Hunchback of Notre Dame*

```
D:  Wallace Worsley
Sc: Perley Poore Sheehan
P:  Super Jewel/Universal Pictures
R:  1923
```
See item 48

INGE, WILLIAM

```
Pl: Bus Stop
F:  Bus Stop
D:  Joshua Logan
Sc: George Axelrod
P:  Twentieth Century-Fox
R:  1956
```
See item 425

INGE, WILLIAM

```
Pl: Come Back, Little Sheba
F:  Come Back, Little Sheba
D:  Daniel Mann
Sc: Ketti Frings
P:  Hal B. Wallis/Paramount
R:  1952
```
See item 425

INGE, WILLIAM

```
Pl: Picnic
F:  Picnic
D:  Joshua Logan
Sc: Daniel Taradash
P:  Columbia
R:  1956
```
See item 425

ISHERWOOD, CHRISTOPHER

```
SS: "Berlin Stories"
F:  Cabaret
D:  Bob Fosse
```
Sc: Jay Presson Allen. Based on the musical play *Cabaret* by Joe Masteroff and the play *I Am a Camera* by John Van Druten; both works are based on Isherwood

    P: Allied Artists
    R: 1972
    See items 682, 924

JAMES, HENRY

    SS: "The Aspern Papers"
    F: *The Lost Moment*
    D: Martin Gabel
    Sc: Leonardo Bercovici
    P: Universal
    R: 1947
    See item 590

JAMES, HENRY

    SS: "The Bench of Desolation"
    F: *The Bench of Desolation*
    D: Claude Chabrol
    Sc: Roger Grenier
    P: O.R.T.F. Cosmovision Technisoner Production/Scott Free
         Enterprises of London
    R: 1974
    See items 799, 935

JAMES, HENRY

    N: *Daisy Miller*
    F: *Daisy Miller*
    D: Peter Bogdanovich
    Sc: Frederic Raphael
    P: Paramount/Copa de Oro
    R: 1974
    See items 799, 935

JAMES, HENRY

    N: *The Sense of the Past*
    F: *Berkeley Square*
    D: Frank Lloyd
    Sc: Sonya Levien, John L. Balderstone
    P: Twentieth Century-Fox
    R: 1933
    See item 590

JAMES, HENRY

    N: *The Turn of the Screw*
    F: *The Innocents*
    D: Jack Clayton
    Sc: William Archibald, Truman Capote
    P: Twentieth Century-Fox
    R: 1961
    See items 590, 1003, 1068, 1189, 1193

JAMES, HENRY

    N: *Washington Square*
    F: *The Heiress*
    D: William Wyler
    Sc: Ruth and Augustus Goetz, from the James novel and from their play *The Heiress*
    P: Paramount
    R: 1949
    See items 590, 924, 1018

JOYCE, JAMES

    N: *Ulysses*
    F: *Ulysses*
    D: Joseph Strick
    Sc: Joseph Strick, Fred Haines
    P: Walter Reade
    R: 1967
    See item 665

KAFKA, FRANZ

    N: *The Trial*
    F: *The Trial*
    D: Orson Welles
    Sc: Orson Welles
    P: Paris Europa Productions/Hisa-Films/FI-C-IT
    R: 1962
    See items 422, 561, 924

KAZAN, ELIA

    N: *The Arrangement*
    F: *The Arrangement*

```
D:  Elia Kazan
Sc: Elia Kazan
P:  Athena
R:  1969
```
See item 613

KEOWN, ERIC

```
SS: "The Ghost Goes West"
F:  The Ghost Goes West
D:  René Clair
Sc: Robert E. Sherwood
P:  London Films
R:  1936
```
See item 138

KESEY, KEN

```
N:  One Flew Over the Cuckoo's Nest
F:  One Flew Over the Cuckoo's Nest
D:  Milos Forman
Sc: Lawrence Hauben, Bo Goldman
P:  Fantasy Films/United Artists
R:  1975
```
See items 920, 1058, 1081

KNOWLES, JOHN

```
N:  A Separate Peace
F:  A Separate Peace
D:  Larry Peerce
Sc: Fred Segal
P:  Paramount
R:  1972
```
See item 882

KONINGSBERGER, HANS

```
N:  A Walk with Love and Death
F:  A Walk with Love and Death
D:  John Huston
Sc: Dale Wasserman
P:  Carter De Haven
R:  1968
```
See item 506

KUROSAWA, AKIRA

    S: Original story
    F: *Ikiru (To Live)*
    D: Akira Kurosawa
    Sc: Shinobu Hashimoto, Hideo Oguni, Akira Kurosawa
    P: Toho
    R: 1952
    See items 873, 916

KUROSAWA, AKIRA

    S: Original story
    F: *Seven Samurai (Shichinin no Samurai)*
    D: Akira Kurosawa
    Sc: Shinobu Hashimoto, Hideo Oguni, Akira Kurosawa
    P: Toho
    R: 1954
    See item 873

LABICHE, EUGENE, and MARC MICHEL

    Pl: *The Italian Straw Hat*
    F: *The Italian Straw Hat (Un Chapeau de Paille d'Italie)*
    D: René Clair
    Sc: René Clair
    P: Films Albatros-Kamenka
    R: 1927
    See item 275

LACLOS, CHODERLOS de

    N: *Les Liaisons Dangereuses*
    F: *Les Liaisons Dangereuses*
    D: Roger Vadim
    Sc: Roger Vadim, Claude Brule
    P: Les Films Marceu-Cocinor
    R: 1959
    See item 924

LAWRENCE, D.H.

    N: *The Fox*
    F: *The Fox*

D: Mark Rydell
Sc: Lewis John Carlino, Howard Koch
P: Raymond Stross/Motion Picture International
R: 1967
See items 474, 518, 742

LAWRENCE, D.H.

N: *Lady Chatterley's Lover*
F: *Lady Chatterley's Lover*
D: Marc Allegret
Sc: Marc Allegret. Based on the novel and on a play by
    Gaston Bonheur and Philippe de Rothschild
P: Kingsley International Pictures
R: 1955
See item 763

LAWRENCE, D.H.

SS: "The Rocking-Horse Winner"
F: *The Rocking-Horse Winner*
D: Anthony Pelissier
Sc: Anthony Pelissier
P: Two Cities
R: 1949
See items 679, 789

LAWRENCE, D.H.

N: *Sons and Lovers*
F: *Sons and Lovers*
D: Jack Cardiff
Sc: Gavin Lambert, T.E.B. Clarke
P: Company of Artists/Jerry Wald
R: 1960
See items 670, 1208

LAWRENCE, D.H.

N: *The Virgin and the Gypsy*
F: *The Virgin and the Gypsy*
D: Christopher Miles
Sc: Alan Plater
P: Chevron Pictures

R: 1970
See items 570, 573, 578, 769, 1208

LAWRENCE, D.H.

N: *Women in Love*
F: *Women in Love*
D: Ken Russell
Sc: Larry Kramer
P: United Artists
R: 1969
See items 531, 543, 560, 570, 574, 588, 779, 908, 960, 1208

LEWIS, SINCLAIR

N: *Babbitt*
F: *Babbitt*
D: Harry Beaumont
Sc: Uncredited
P: Warner Bros.
R: 1924
See item 1088

LEWIS, SINCLAIR

N: *Babbitt*
F: *Babbitt*
D: William Keighley
Sc: Tom Reed, Niven Bush, Mary McCall, Jr., Ben Markson
P: First National
R: 1934
See item 1088

LEWIS, SINCLAIR

N: *Dodsworth*
F: *Dodsworth*
D: William Wyler
Sc: Sidney Howard, from the Lewis novel and from Howard's play
P: Samuel Goldwyn
R: 1936
See item 1054

LEWIS, SINCLAIR

    N: *Elmer Gantry*
    F: *Elmer Gantry*
    D: Richard Brooks
    Sc: Richard Brooks
    P: Bernard Smith
    R: 1960
    See items 353, 359

LEWIS, SINCLAIR

    N: *Main Street*
    F: *I Married a Doctor*
    D: Archie L. Mayo
    Sc: Harriet Ford, Harvey O'Higgins, Casey Robinson
    P: Warner Bros.
    R: 1936
    See item 1093

LEWIS, TED

    N: *Jack's Return Home*
    F: *Get Carter*
    D: Mike Hodges
    Sc: Mike Hodges
    P: MGM/EMI
    R: 1971
    See item 602

LIBNEY, SHERIDAN, and PIERRE COLLINGS

    S: Original story
    F: *The Story of Louis Pasteur*
    D: William Dieterle
    Sc: Sheridan Libney, Pierre Collings
    P: Cosmopolitan
    R: 1936
    See item 142

LINDSAY, JOAN

    N: *Picnic at Hanging Rock*
    F: *Picnic at Hanging Rock*

D: Peter Weir
Sc: Cliff Green
P: Picnic Productions/Australia Film Corporation
R: 1975
See item 947

LONDON, JACK

N: *The Sea Wolf*
F: *The Sea Wolf*
D: Michael Curtiz
Sc: Robert Rossen
P: Warner Bros.
R: 1941
See item 1028

LUBITSCH, ERNST, and MELCHIOR LENGYEL

S: Original story
F: *To Be or Not To Be*
D: Ernst Lubitsch
Sc: Edwin Justus Mayer
P: Ernst Lubitsch/Alexander Korda/Romaine Film Corporation
R: 1942
See items 828, 1000

McCOY, HORACE

N: *They Shoot Horses, Don't They?*
F: *They Shoot Horses, Don't They?*
D: Sydney Pollack
Sc: James Poe, Robert E. Thompson
P: Palomar/Chartoff-Winkler-Pollack
R: 1969
See items 521, 527

McCULLERS, CARSON

N: *The Member of the Wedding*
Pl: *The Member of the Wedding*
F: *The Member of the Wedding*
D: Fred Zinnemann
Sc: Edna and Edward Anhalt
P: Stanley Kramer/Columbia

R: 1953
See items 321, 959

McDONNELL, GORDON

S: Original story
F: *Shadow of a Doubt*
D: Alfred Hitchcock
Sc: Thornton Wilder, Alma Reville, Sally Benson
P: Universal
R: 1943
See item 684

McMURTRY, LARRY

N: *Horseman, Pass By*
F: *Hud*
D: Martin Ritt
Sc: Irving Ravetch, Harriet Frank, Jr.
P: Paramount
R: 1963
See items 530, 538, 861

McMURTRY, LARRY

N: *The Last Picture Show*
F: *The Last Picture Show*
D: Peter Bogdanovich
Sc: Larry McMurtry, Peter Bogdanovich
P: Columbia
R: 1971
See items 710, 777, 861

MADDUX, RACHEL

N: *A Walk in the Spring Rain*
F: *A Walk in the Spring Rain*
D: Guy Green
Sc: Stirling Silliphant
P: Columbia
R: 1969
See item 537

MAILER, NORMAN

    S: Norman Mailer
    F: *Maidstone*
    D: Norman Mailer
    Sc: Improvised by the Actors
    P: Supreme Mix
    R: 1971
    See item 594

MALRAUX, ANDRÉ

    N: *Man's Hope*
    F: *Man's Hope (Espoir)*
    D: André Malraux
    Sc: André Malraux, M. Aub, B. Peskine
    P: André Malraux/Lopert Films
    R: 1945
    See item 1152

MANN, HEINRICH

    N: *Professor Unrath*
    F: *The Blue Angel*
    D: Josef von Sternberg
    Sc: Karl Zuckermayer, Karl Vollmöller, Robert Liebmann
    P: UFA
    R: 1930
    See items 662, 924

MANN, THOMAS

    N: *Death in Venice*
    F: *Death in Venice (Morte a Venezia)*
    D: Luchino Visconti
    Sc: Luchino Visconti, Nicola Badalucco
    P: Alfa Cinematografica
    R: 1971
    See items 599, 602, 813, 924, 927

MARSHALL, JAMES VANCE

    N: *Walkabout*
    F: *Walkabout*

D: Nicholas Roeg
Sc: Edward Bond
P: Twentieth Century-Fox
R: 1971
See item 603

MASTERSON, WHIT (pseud. of Bob Wade and Bill Miller)

N: *Badge of Evil*
F: *Touch of Evil*
D: Orson Welles (added scene by Harry Keller)
Sc: Orson Welles, from an earlier script by Paul Monash
P: Universal-International
R: 1958
See items 571, 881, 967, 1001

MAUGHAM, ROBIN

N: *The Servant*
F: *The Servant*
D: Joseph Losey
Sc: Harold Pinter
P: Elstree/Springbok
R: 1963
See item 955

MAUPASSANT, GUY de

SS: "Une Partie de Campagne"
F: *A Day in the Country* (*Une Partie de Campagne*; GB title:
    A Country Excursion)
D: Jean Renoir
Sc: Jean Renoir
P: Panthéon
R: 1936
See items 927, 1083

MELVILLE, HERMAN

SS: "Billy Budd"
F: *Billy Budd*
D: Peter Ustinov
Sc: Peter Ustinov, Robert Rossen. Based on the play *Uniform
    of Flesh* by Louis O. Coxe and Robert Chapman.

    P: Allied Artists
    R: 1962
    See items 480, 957, 1067, 1168

MELVILLE, HERMAN

    N: *Moby Dick*
    F: *The Sea Beast*
    D: Millard Webb
    Sc: Bess Meredyth
    P: Warner Bros.
    R: 1926
    See items 480, 919

MELVILLE, HERMAN

    N: *Moby Dick*
    F: *Moby Dick or The Great White Whale*
    D: Lloyd Bacon
    Sc: J. Grubb Alexander
    P: Warner Bros.
    R: 1930
    See items 480, 919

MELVILLE, HERMAN

    N: *Moby Dick*
    F: *Moby Dick*
    D: John Huston
    Sc: Ray Bradbury, John Huston
    P: Moulin/Warner Bros.
    R: 1956
    See items 308, 317, 480, 1029

MILIUS, JOHN

    S: Original story
    F: *Dillinger*
    D: John Milius
    Sc: John Milius
    P: American International
    R: 1973
    See item 683

MILLER, ARTHUR

    Pl: *Death of a Salesman*
    F: *Death of a Salesman*
    D: Laslo Benedek
    Sc: Stanley Roberts
    P: Stanley Kramer/Columbia
    R: 1952
    See items 235, 236

MILLER, ARTHUR

    SS: "The Misfits"
    F: *The Misfits*
    D: John Huston
    Sc: Arthur Miller
    P: Frank E. Taylor/United Artists
    R: 1960
    See items 362, 381, 604

MILLER, HENRY

    N: *Tropic of Cancer*
    F: *Tropic of Cancer*
    D: Joseph Strick
    Sc: Joseph Strick, Betty Botley
    P: Paramount
    R: 1970
    See item 526

MIRBEAU, OCTAVE

    N: *The Diary of a Chambermaid*
    F: *The Diary of a Chambermaid* (*Le Journal d'une Femme de Chambre*)
    D: Jean Renoir
    Sc: Jean Renoir, Burgess Meredith, based on the novel, and on a play by André Heuse, André de Lorde and Thielly Nores
    P: Associated Artists
    R: 1946
    See item 572

MIRBEAU, OCTAVE

    N: *The Diary of a Chambermaid*
    F: *The Diary of a Chambermaid* (*Le Journal d'une Femme de Chambre*)
    D: Luis Buñuel
    Sc: Luis Buñuel, Jean-Claude Carrière
    P: Speva Films/Cine Alliance/Films Sona/Dear
    R: 1964
    See item 572

MITCHELL, MARGARET

    N: *Gone with the Wind*
    F: *Gone with the Wind*
    D: Victor Fleming (and George Cukor, Sam Wood)
    Sc: Sidney Howard
    P: Selznick-International
    R: 1939
    See items 729, 870

MORAVIA, ALBERTO

    N: *The Conformist*
    F: *The Conformist*
    D: Bernardo Bertolucci
    Sc: Bernardo Bertolucci
    P: Maris Film/Marianne/Maran-Film
    R: 1970
    See item 980

MORAVIA, ALBERTO

    N: *Il Disprezzo*
    F: *Contempt* (*Le Mepris, Il Disprezzo, A Ghost at Noon*)
    D: Jean-Luc Godard
    Sc: Jean-Luc Godard
    P: Rome-Paris Films/Films Concordia/Compagnia Cinematografica Champion
    R: 1963
    See items 634, 820

NABOKOV, VLADIMIR

    N: *Lolita*
    F: *Lolita*
    D: Stanley Kubrick
    Sc: Vladimir Nabokov
    P: MGM
    R: 1962
    See items 371, 783, 922

NICHOLS, JOHN

    N: *The Sterile Cuckoo*
    F: *The Sterile Cuckoo* (GB title: *Pookie*)
    D: Alan J. Pakula
    Sc: Alvin Sargent
    P: Boardwalk
    R: 1969
    See item 1073

NORRIS, FRANK

    N: *McTeague*
    F: *Greed*
    D: Erich von Stroheim
    Sc: Erich von Stroheim, June Mathis
    P: Goldwyn Co.
    R: 1923
    See items 284, 290, 393, 479, 886, 924, 1096

O'CASEY, SEAN

    Pl: *Juno and the Paycock*
    F: *Juno and the Paycock*
    D: Alfred Hitchcock
    Sc: Alfred Hitchcock, Alma Reville
    P: British International Pictures
    R: 1930
    See item 1099

ODETS, CLIFFORD

    Pl: *The Country Girl*
    F: *The Country Girl*

D: George Seaton
Sc: George Seaton
P: Perlberg-Seaton
R: 1954
See item 276

O'FLAHERTY, LIAM

    N: *The Informer*
    F: *The Informer*
    D: John Ford
    Sc: Dudley Nichols
    P: RKO
    R: 1935
    See items 313, 393, 482, 938

O'NEILL, EUGENE

    Pl: *Desire Under the Elms*
    F: *Desire Under the Elms*
    D: Delbert Mann
    Sc: Irwin Shaw
    P: Paramount
    R: 1958
    See item 329

O'NEILL, EUGENE

    Pl: *Long Day's Journey into Night*
    F: *Long Day's Journey into Night*
    D: Sidney Lumet
    Sc: Eugene O'Neill
    P: Ely Landau/Embassy Pictures
    R: 1961
    See items 263, 591

O'NEILL, EUGENE

    Pl: *Moon of the Caribbees, Bound East for Cardiff, In the Zone, The Long Voyage Home*
    F: *The Long Voyage Home*
    D: John Ford
    Sc: Dudley Nichols

P: Walter Wanger/United Artists
R: 1940
See item 263

ORR, MARY

SS: "The Wisdom of Eve" (and the radio play by Mary Orr)
F: *All About Eve*
D: Joseph L. Mankiewicz
Sc: Joseph L. Mankiewicz
P: Twentieth Century-Fox
R: 1950
See item 620

ORWELL, GEORGE

N: *Animal Farm*
F: *Animal Farm* (animated)
D: John Halas, Joy Batchelor
Sc: John Halas, Joy Batchelor, Lothar Wolff, Borden Mace
P: Louis de Rochemont/Halas and Batchelor
R: 1954
See item 276

ORWELL, GEORGE

N: *1984*
F: *1984*
D: Michael Anderson
Sc: William P. Templeton, Ralph Bettinson
P: Holiday/Columbia
R: 1955
See item 924

OSBORNE, JOHN

Pl: *The Entertainer*
F: *The Entertainer*
D: Tony Richardson
Sc: John Osborne, Nigel Kneale
P: Harry Saltzman/Bryanston
R: 1960
See items 358, 713

OSBORNE, JOHN

    Pl: *Look Back in Anger*
    F: *Look Back in Anger*
    D: Tony Richardson
    Sc: Nigel Kneale
    P: Harry Saltzman/Woodfall
    R: 1959
    See items 343, 358

PARKER, LOTTIE BLAIR

    Pl: *Way Down East*
    F: *Way Down East*
    D: D.W. Griffith
    Sc: Anthony Paul Kelly
    P: D.W. Griffith Productions
    R: 1920
    See item 885

PASTERNAK, BORIS

    N: *Doctor Zhivago*
    F: *Doctor Zhivago*
    D: David Lean
    Sc: Robert Bolt
    P: Carlo Ponti/MGM
    R: 1965
    See items 402, 692

PINCHON, EDGCOMB

    N: *Zapata, the Unconquerable*
    F: *Viva Zapata!*
    D: Elia Kazan
    Sc: John Steinbeck
    P: Twentieth Century-Fox
    R: 1952
    See items 243, 899

PINTER, HAROLD

    Pl: *The Homecoming*
    F: *The Homecoming*

D: Peter Hall
Sc: Harold Pinter
P: Ely Landau/Seven Keys Ltd.
R: 1973
See item 791

POE, EDGAR ALLAN

SS: "The Fall of the House of Usher"
F: *The House of Usher* (*La Chute de la Maison Usher*)
D: Jean Epstein
R: 1928
See item 1097

POE, EDGAR ALLAN

SS: "The Fall of the House of Usher"
F: *The House of Usher*
D: James Sibley Watson, Jr.
R: 1929
See item 1097

POE, EDGAR ALLAN

SS: "The Fall of the House of Usher"
F: *The House of Usher* (GB title: *The Fall of the House of Usher*)
D: Roger Corman
Sc: Richard Matheson
P: American-International
R: 1960
See item 924

PUSHKIN, ALEXANDER

N: *The Queen of Spades*
F: *The Queen of Spades*
D: Thorold Dickinson
Sc: Rodney Ackland, Arthur Boys
P: Associated British Pictures
R: 1949
See item 214

RAFELSON, BOB, and ADRIEN JOYCE

    S: Original story
    F: *Five Easy Pieces*
    D: Bob Rafelson
    Sc: Adrien Joyce
    P: Columbia/Bert Schneider
    R: 1970
    See item 793

REMARQUE, ERICH MARIA

    N: *All Quiet on the Western Front*
    F: *All Quiet on the Western Front*
    D: Lewis Milestone
    Sc: Maxwell Anderson, Del Andrews, Lewis Milestone, George
        Abbott
    P: Universal
    R: 1930
    See item 98

RENOIR, JEAN

    S: Original story
    F: *The Golden Coach* (*Le Carrosse d'Or*)
    D: Jean Renoir
    Sc: Jean Renoir
    P: Panaria Film-Hoche Production
    R: 1953
    See item 828

RENOIR, JEAN

    S: Original story
    F: *Grand Illusion* (*La Grande Illusion*)
    D: Jean Renoir
    Sc: Jean Renoir, Charles Spaak
    P: R.C.A. (Les Réalisations d'Art Cinématographique)
    R: 1937
    See items 1074, 1083

ROBBE-GRILLET, ALAIN

    S: Original story
    F: *Trans-Europe Express*

D: Alain Robbe-Grillet
Sc: Alain Robbe-Grillet
P: Como Films
R: 1966
See item 493

ROCHÉ, HENRI-PIERRE

N: *Jules et Jim*
F: *Jules and Jim* (*Jules et Jim*)
D: François Truffaut
Sc: François Truffaut, Jean Gruault
P: Les Films du Carrosse/SEDIF
R: 1961
See item 566

ROTH, PHILIP

N: *Portnoy's Complaint*
F: *Portnoy's Complaint*
D: Ernest Lehman
Sc: Ernest Lehman
P: Warner Bros.
R: 1972
See item 979

RUNYON, DAMON

SS: "Madame La Gimp"
F: *Lady for a Day*
D: Frank Capra
Sc: Robert Riskin
P: Columbia
R: 1933
See item 142

RYAN, CORNELIUS

N: *A Bridge Too Far*
F: *A Bridge Too Far*
D: Richard Attenborough
Sc: William Goldman
P: United Artists
R: 1977
See item 1046

RYAN, PATRICK

    N: *How I Won the War*
    F: *How I Won the War*
    D: Richard Lester
    Sc: Charles Wood
    P: United Artists
    R: 1967
    See item 751

ST. MATTHEW

    S: "Gospel According to St. Matthew"
    Pl: *Godspell*
    F: *Godspell*
    D: David Greene
    Sc: David Greene, John-Michael Tebelak
    P: Columbia
    R: 1973
    See item 693

SCHAEFER, JACK

    N: *Shane*
    F: *Shane*
    D: George Stevens
    Sc: A.B. Guthrie, Jr.
    P: Paramount
    R: 1953
    See item 530

SCHULBERG, BUDD

    N: *Some Faces in the Crowd*
    SS: "Your Arkansas Traveller"
    F: *A Face in the Crowd*
    D: Elia Kazan
    Sc: Budd Schulberg
    P: Newtown Productions
    R: 1957
    See item 322

SHAKESPEARE, WILLIAM

    Pl: *Antony and Cleopatra*
    F: *Antony and Cleopatra*
    D: Charlton Heston
    Sc: Charlton Heston
    P: Transac/Izaro/Folio Films
    R: 1972
    See item 640

SHAKESPEARE, WILLIAM

    Pl: *As You Like It*
    F: *As You Like It*
    D: Paul Czinner
    Sc: R.J. Cullen, Carl Meyer
    P: Inter-Allied-Film
    R: 1936
    See item 595

SHAKESPEARE, WILLIAM

    Pl: *Hamlet*
    F: *Hamlet*
    D: Svend Gade, Heinz Schall
    Sc: Erwin Gepard. Based on a book by Edward P. Vining which
        argues that Hamlet, according to legend, was actually
        female but was passed off as male by his mother for
        reasons of state
    P: Art-Film
    R: 1920
    See item 953

SHAKESPEARE, WILLIAM

    Pl: *Hamlet*
    F: *Hamlet*
    D: Laurence Olivier
    Sc: Alan Dent
    P: Two Cities
    R: 1948
    See items 191, 192, 198, 199, 200, 203, 204, 205, 209, 227,
    248, 274, 337, 391, 595, 626, 717, 908, 953, 1043, 1051

SHAKESPEARE, WILLIAM

    Pl: *Hamlet*
    F: *Hamlet*
    D: (Staged by) John Gielgud
    Sc: William Shakespeare
    P: Alexander H. Cohen/Frenman Productions/Theatrofilm
    R: 1964
    See items 465, 717

SHAKESPEARE, WILLIAM

    Pl: *Hamlet*
    F: *Hamlet*
    D: Grigori Kozintsev
    Sc: Grigori Kozintsev, from a translation by Boris Pasternak
    P: Lenfilm
    R: 1964
    See items 432, 595, 626, 642, 718, 724, 969, 1043

SHAKESPEARE, WILLIAM

    Pl: *Hamlet*
    F: *Hamlet*
    D: Tony Richardson
    Sc: Tony Richardson
    P: Woodfall
    R: 1969
    See items 595, 953, 1024

SHAKESPEARE, WILLIAM

    Pl: *Henry V*
    F: *Henry V*
    D: Laurence Olivier
    Sc: Laurence Olivier, Alan Dent, Dallas Bower
    P: Two Cities
    R: 1944
    *See items 174, 184, 227, 248, 274, 391, 428, 494, 595, 626,
    709, 908, 1043, 1057*

SHAKESPEARE, WILLIAM

    Pl: *Henry IV, Parts 1 and 2*; *Henry V*; *The Merry Wives of
        Windsor*; commentary from Raphael Holinshed's **The Chronicles
        of England**
    F: *Chimes at Midnight* (US title: *Falstaff*)
    D: Orson Welles

Sc: Orson Welles
P: International Films Española/Alpine
R: 1966
See items 421, 422, 467, 508, 595, 1043

SHAKESPEARE, WILLIAM

Pl: *Julius Caesar*
F: *Julius Caesar*
D: Joseph L. Mankiewicz
Sc: Joseph L. Mankiewicz
P: MGM
R: 1953
*See items 256, 258, 259, 260, 261, 265, 266, 271, 274,
595, 1043*

SHAKESPEARE, WILLIAM

Pl: *Julius Caesar*
F: *Julius Caesar*
D: Stuart Burge
Sc: Robert Furnival
P: Commonwealth United
R: 1969
See items 595, 626

SHAKESPEARE, WILLIAM

Pl: *King John*
F: *King John*
D: Herbert Beerbohm Tree
Sc: Herbert Beerbohm Tree
P: Mutoscope & Biograph
R: 1899
See item 673

SHAKESPEARE, WILLIAM

Pl: *King Lear*
F: *King Lear*
D: Peter Brook
Sc: Peter Brook
P: Filmways Inc., in association with the Royal Shake-
    speare Company
R: 1970
See items 595, 640, 685, 755, 998, 1008, 1043

SHAKESPEARE, WILLIAM

    Pl: *King Lear*
    F: *King Lear*
    D: Grigori Kozintsev
    Sc: Grigori Kozintsev, from a translation by Boris Pasternak
    P: Lenfilm
    R: 1970
    See items 595, 616, 642, 718, 901, 996, 1037, 1043, 1053

SHAKESPEARE, WILLIAM

    Pl: *Macbeth*
    F: *Macbeth*
    D: Orson Welles
    Sc: Orson Welles
    P: Mercury Production/Republic
    R: 1948
    *See items 207, 227, 248, 337, 595, 619, 626, 749, 809, 987,
    1043*

SHAKESPEARE, WILLIAM

    Pl: *Macbeth*
    F: *Throne of Blood* (*Kumonosu-Djo*, *The Castle of the Spider's
        Web*, *Cobweb Castle*)
    D: Akira Kurosawa
    Sc: Akira Kurosawa, Shinobu Hashimoto, Ryuzo Kikushima,
        Hideo Oguni
    P: Toho
    R: 1957
    See items 401, 411, 595, 711, 746, 848, 1007, 1043, 1049

SHAKESPEARE, WILLIAM

    Pl: *Macbeth*
    F: *Macbeth*
    D: George Schaefer
    Sc: George Schaefer
    P: Grand Prize Films
    R: 1960
    See items 352, 595

SHAKESPEARE, WILLIAM

    Pl: *Macbeth*
    F: *Macbeth*
    D: Roman Polanski
    Sc: Roman Polanski, Kenneth Tynan

P: Playboy/Caliban
R: 1971
See items 615, 632, 640, 681, 755, 759, 948, 1043

SHAKESPEARE, WILLIAM

Pl: *A Midsummer Night's Dream*
F: *A Midsummer Night's Dream*
D: Max Reinhardt, William Dieterle
Sc: Charles Kenyon, Mary McCall, Jr.
P: Warner Bros.
R: 1935
See items 132, 148, 595, 1043

SHAKESPEARE, WILLIAM

Pl: *A Midsummer Night's Dream*
F: *A Midsummer Night's Dream*
D: Peter Hall
Sc: Peter Hall
P: Royal Shakespeare Company and Alan Clore
R: 1969
See items 502, 595, 1043

SHAKESPEARE, WILLIAM

Pl: *Othello*
F: *Othello*
D: Dimitri Buchowetzki
Sc: Dimitri Buchowetzki
P: Wörner-Film
R: 1922
See item 49

SHAKESPEARE, WILLIAM

Pl: *Othello*
F: *Othello*
D: Orson Welles, Alexander Trauner
Sc: Orson Welles
P: Mercury Productions/Mogador Films
R: 1951
See items 245, 274, 287, 296, 337, 398, 513, 595, 626, 908, 974, 1043

SHAKESPEARE, WILLIAM

    Pl: *Othello*
    F: *Othello*
    D: Sergei Yutkevitch
    Sc: Sergei Yutkevitch
    P: Mosfilm
    R: 1955
    See items 595, 626

SHAKESPEARE, WILLIAM

    Pl: *Othello*
    F: *Othello*
    D: Stuart Burge
    Sc: William Shakespeare. Film version of The National
        Theatre of Great Britain production of the play directed
        by John Dexter.
    P: Anthony Havelock-Allan-John Brabourne/BHE
    R: 1965
    See items 428, 434, 595, 703, 1043

SHAKESPEARE, WILLIAM

    Pl: *Richard III*
    F: *Richard III*
    D: Laurence Olivier
    Sc: Laurence Olivier, Alan Dent
    P: London Films
    R: 1955
    *See items 296, 299, 302, 305, 309, 315, 337, 391, 428,
    448, 595, 626, 972, 1043*

SHAKESPEARE, WILLIAM

    Pl: *Romeo and Juliet*
    F: *Romeo and Juliet*
    D: George Cukor
    Sc: Talbot Jennings
    P: MGM
    R: 1936
    See items 136, 147, 595, 626, 758

SHAKESPEARE, WILLIAM

    Pl: *Romeo and Juliet*
    F: *Romeo and Juliet*
    D: Renato Castellani
    Sc: Renato Castellani
    P: Verona
    R: 1954
    See items 276, 281, 286, 296, 337, 595, 626, 758

SHAKESPEARE, WILLIAM

    Pl: *Romeo and Juliet*
    F: *Romeo and Juliet*
    D: Franco Zeffirelli
    Sc: Franco Zeffirelli, Masolino D'Amico
    P: BHE/Verona/De Laurentiis
    R: 1968
    See items 476, 487, 496, 595, 626, 758, 1024, 1033, 1043, 1080

SHAKESPEARE, WILLIAM

    Pl: *The Taming of the Shrew*
    F: *The Taming of the Shrew*
    D: Sam Taylor
    Sc: Sam Taylor
    P: Pickford/Elton
    R: 1929
    See items 595, 671, 776, 852

SHAKESPEARE, WILLIAM

    Pl: *The Taming of the Shrew*
    F: *The Taming of the Shrew*
    D: Franco Zeffirelli
    Sc: Paul Dehn, Suso Cecchi D'Amico, Franco Zeffirelli
    P: Royal Films International/FAI
    R: 1966
    See items 487, 595, 1043

SHAKESPEARE, WILLIAM

    Pl: *Twelfth Night*
    F: *Twelfth Night* (*Dwenatzataja Notch*)

D: Yakov Fried
Sc: Yakov Fried
P: Lenfilm
R: 1955
See item 626

SHAKESPEARE, WILLIAM

Pl: *The Winter's Tale*
F: *The Winter's Tale*
D: Frank Dunlop
Sc: Frank Dunlop
P: Cressida/Hurst Park
R: 1966
See item 595

SHAW, GEORGE BERNARD

Pl: *Pygmalion*
F: *Pygmalion*
D: Anthony Asquith, Leslie Howard
Sc: George Bernard Shaw, Anatole de Grunwald, W.P. Lipscomb,
    Cecil Lewis, Ian Dalrymple
P: Gabriel Pascal Productions
R: 1938
See items 462, 482

SHAW, GEORGE BERNARD

Pl: *St. Joan*
F: *St. Joan*
D: Otto Preminger
Sc: Graham Greene
P: Preminger
R: 1957
See item 334

SHERWOOD, ROBERT EMMETT

Pl: *The Petrified Forest*
F: *The Petrified Forest*
D: Archie L. Mayo
Sc: Charles Kenyon, Delmer Daves
P: Warner Bros.

R: 1936
See item 938

SIMON, NEIL

Pl: *Prisoner of Second Avenue*
F: *Prisoner of Second Avenue*
D: Melvin Frank
Sc: Neil Simon
P: Warner Bros.
R: 1975
See item 894

SOPHOCLES

Pl: *Oedipus Rex*, *Oedipus at Colonus*
F: *Edipo Re*
D: Pier Paolo Pasolini
Sc: Pier Paolo Pasolini
P: Arco Films
R: 1967
See item 1098

SOUTHERN, TERRY

N: *Candy*
F: *Candy*
D: Christian Marquand
Sc: Buck Henry
P: Selmur/Dear/Corona
R: 1968
See item 915

STARK, RICHARD

N: *The Hunter*
F: *Point Blank*
D: John Boorman
Sc: Alexander Jacobs, David Newhouse, Rafe Newhouse
P: Bernard-Winkler
R: 1967
See item 477

STEINBECK, JOHN

    N: *East of Eden*
    F: *East of Eden*
    D: Elia Kazan
   Sc: Paul Osborn
    P: Warner Bros.
    R: 1955
   See item 449

STEINBECK, JOHN

   SS: "The Forgotten Village"
    F: *The Forgotten Village*
    D: Herbert Kline
   Sc: John Steinbeck
    P: Herbert Kline
    R: 1941
   See item 587

STEINBECK, JOHN

    N: *The Grapes of Wrath*
    F: *The Grapes of Wrath*
    D: John Ford
   Sc: Nunnally Johnson
    P: Twentieth Century-Fox
    R: 1940
   See items 164, 313, 393, 412, 706

STEINBECK, JOHN

    N: *Lifeboat* (an unpublished, unfinished short novel)
    F: *Lifeboat*
    D: Alfred Hitchcock
   Sc: John Steinbeck, Jo Swerling
    P: Twentieth Century-Fox
    R: 1944
   See item 985

STEINBECK, JOHN

    N: *The Pearl*
    F: *The Pearl*

D: Emilio Fernandez
Sc: John Steinbeck, Emilio Fernandez, Jack Wagner
P: RKO
R: 1948
See item 600

STENDHAL (MARIE HENRI BEYLE)

N: *The Charterhouse of Parma*
F: *Before the Revolution (Prima della Rivoluzione)*
D: Bernardo Bertolucci
Sc: Bernardo Bertolucci
P: Iride Cinematografica
R: 1964
See item 999

STEVENSON, ROBERT LOUIS

N: *The Strange Case of Dr. Jekyll and Mr. Hyde*
F: *Dr. Jekyll and Mr. Hyde*
D: John S. Robertson
Sc: Clara S. Beranger
P: Famous Players-Lasky
R: 1920
See item 1056

STEVENSON, ROBERT LOUIS

N: *The Strange Case of Dr. Jekyll and Mr. Hyde*
F: *Dr. Jekyll and Mr. Hyde*
D: Rouben Mamoulian
Sc: Samuel Hoffenstein, Percy Heath
P: Paramount
R: 1932
See item 1056

STEVENSON, ROBERT LOUIS

N: *The Strange Case of Dr. Jekyll and Mr. Hyde*
F: *Dr. Jekyll and Mr. Hyde*
D: Victor Fleming
Sc: John Lee Mahin
P: MGM
R: 1941
See item 1056

STONE, ROBERT

    N: *Dog Soldiers*
    F: *Who'll Stop the Rain?*
    D: Karel Reisz
    Sc: Judith Rascoe, Robert Stone
    P: United Artists
    R: 1978
    See item 1102

SUDERMANN, HERMANN

    SS: "A Trip to Tilsit"
    F: *Sunrise*
    D: F.W. Murnau
    Sc: Carl Mayer
    P: Fox
    R: 1927
    See item 75

TARKINGTON, BOOTH

    N: *Alice Adams*
    F: *Alice Adams*
    D: George Stevens
    Sc: Dorothy Yost, Mortimer Offner
    P: RKO
    R: 1935
    See item 1084

TARKINGTON, BOOTH

    N: *The Magnificent Ambersons*
    F: *Pampered Youth*
    D: David Smith
    Sc: Jay Pilcher
    P: Vitagraph
    R: 1925
    See item 535

TARKINGTON, BOOTH

    N: *The Magnificent Ambersons*
    F: *The Magnificent Ambersons*

D: Orson Welles (added scenes by Freddie Fleck and
    Robert Wise)
Sc: Orson Welles
P: Mercury Production/RKO
R: 1942
See items 535, 576, 838

TEVIS, WALTER S.

N: *The Man Who Fell to Earth*
F: *The Man Who Fell to Earth*
D: Nicholas Roeg
Sc: Paul Mayersberg
P: British Lion International
R: 1976
See item 896

THACKERAY, WILLIAM M.

N: *Barry Lyndon*
F: *Barry Lyndon*
D: Stanley Kubrick
Sc: Stanley Kubrick
P: Hawk/Peregrine
R: 1975
See item 984

THOMAS, DYLAN

Pl: *Under Milk Wood*
F: *Under Milk Wood*
D: Andrew Sinclair
Sc: Andrew Sinclair
P: Timon Films
R: 1971
See items 704, 766

TOLSTOY, LEO

N: *War and Peace*
F: *War and Peace*
D: King Vidor (battle scenes by Mario Soldati)
Sc: Bridget Boland, Robert Westerby, King Vidor, Mario
    Camerini, Ennio de Concini, Ivo Perelli

P: Ponti-De Laurentiis
R: 1956
See item 307

TOWNE, ROBERT

S: Original story
F: *Chinatown*
D: Roman Polanski
Sc: Robert Towne
P: Paramount
R: 1974
See items 893, 903, 1069

TWAIN, MARK

N: *The Adventures of Tom Sawyer*
F: *Tom Sawyer*
D: John Cromwell
Sc: Sam Mintz, Grover Jones, William Slavens McNutt
P: Paramount
R: 1930
See item 1030

TWAIN, MARK

N: *The Prince and the Pauper*
F: *The Prince and the Pauper*
D: William Keighley
Sc: Laird Doyle
P: Warner Bros.
R: 1937
See item 1017

VOLTAIRE

N: *Candide*
F: *Candide*
D: Norbert Carbonnaux
Sc: Norbert Carbonnaux, Albert Simonon
P: Pathé Cinema
R: 1960
See item 924

VONNEGUT, KURT

    N: *Slaughterhouse-Five*
    F: *Slaughterhouse-Five*
    D: George Roy Hill
    Sc: Stephen Geller
    P: Universal
    R: 1972
    See items 657, 669, 696, 720, 750

WELLES, ORSON and HERMAN J. MANKIEWICZ

    S: Original screenplay
    F: *Citizen Kane*
    D: Orson Welles
    Sc: Orson Welles, Herman J. Mankiewicz
    P: RKO
    R: 1941
    See items 856, 924, 1027

WEST, JESSAMYN

    N: *The Friendly Persuasion*
    F: *Friendly Persuasion*
    D: William Wyler
    Sc: Michael Wilson, Jessamyn West, Robert Wyler (all
        uncredited)
    P: Allied Artists
    R: 1956
    See item 310

WEST, NATHANAEL

    N: *The Day of the Locust*
    F: *The Day of the Locust*
    D: John Schlesinger
    Sc: Waldo Salt
    P: Robert Sheldo/Paramount
    R: 1975
    See items 780, 853

WIERS-JENSSEN, HANS

    Pl: *Anne Pedersdotter*
    F: *The Day of Wrath (Vredens Dag)*
    D: Carl Theodor Dreyer
    Sc: Carl Theodor Dreyer, Poul Knudsen, Mogens Skot-Hansen
    P: Palladium Copenhagen-Tage Nielsen
    R: 1943
    See item 541

WILDE, OSCAR

    Pl: *The Importance of Being Earnest*
    F: *The Importance of Being Earnest*
    D: Anthony Asquith
    Sc: Anthony Asquith
    P: Javelin/Two Cities
    R: 1952
    See item 270

WILDER, THORNTON

    Pl: *Our Town*
    F: *Our Town*
    D: Sam Wood
    Sc: Thornton Wilder, Frank Craven, Harry Chantlee
    P: Sol Lesser/United Artists
    R: 1940
    See item 165

WILLIAMS, TENNESSEE

    Pl: *Battle of Angels* (rewritten as *Orpheus Descending*)
    F: *The Fugitive Kind*
    D: Sidney Lumet
    Sc: Tennessee Williams, Meade Roberts
    P: Jurow-Shepherd-Pennebaker/United Artists
    R: 1960
    See item 1100

WILLIAMS, TENNESSEE

    Pl: *Cat on a Hot Tin Roof*
    F: *Cat on a Hot Tin Roof*

    D: Richard Brooks
    Sc: Richard Brooks, James Poe
    P: Avon/MGM
    R: 1958
    See item 1100

WILLIAMS, TENNESSEE

    Pl: *The Glass Menagerie*
    F: *The Glass Menagerie*
    D: Irving Rapper
    Sc: Tennessee Williams, Peter Berneis
    P: Jerry Wald, Charles K. Feldman/Warner Bros.
    R: 1950
    See item 1100

WILLIAMS, TENNESSEE

    Pl: *Kingdom of Earth* (also titled *The Seven Descents of Myrtle*)
    F: *Last of the Mobile Hot-shots*
    D: Sidney Lumet
    Sc: Gore Vidal
    P: Sidney Lumet/Warner Bros./Seven Arts
    R: 1969
    See item 1100

WILLIAMS, TENNESSEE

    SS: "Man Bring This Up Road" (Rewritten as the play *The Milk Train Doesn't Stop Here Anymore*)
    F: *Boom*
    D: Joseph Losey
    Sc: Tennessee Williams
    P: Limites/World Film Service Limited
    R: 1968
    See item 1100

WILLIAMS, TENNESSEE

    Pl: *The Night of the Iguana*
    F: *The Night of the Iguana*
    D: John Huston
    Sc: Anthony Veiller, John Huston

P: John Huston-Ray Stark
R: 1964
See item 1100

WILLIAMS, TENNESSEE

Pl: *Period of Adjustment*
F: *Period of Adjustment*
D: George Roy Hill
Sc: Isobel Lennart
P: Lawrence Weingarten/MGM
R: 1962
See item 1100

WILLIAMS, TENNESSEE

N: *The Roman Spring of Mrs. Stone*
F: *The Roman Spring of Mrs. Stone*
D: José Quintero
Sc: Gavin Lambert
P: Seven Arts/Warner Bros.
R: 1961
See item 1100

WILLIAMS, TENNESSEE

Pl: *The Rose Tattoo*
F: *The Rose Tattoo*
D: Daniel Mann
Sc: Tennessee Williams, Hal Kanter
P: Hal Wallis/Paramount
R: 1955
See item 1100

WILLIAMS, TENNESSEE

Pl: *A Streetcar Named Desire*
F: *A Streetcar Named Desire*
D: Elia Kazan
Sc: Elia Kazan, Oscar Saul
P: Charles K. Feldman/Warner Bros.
R: 1951
See items 251, 449, 794, 1100, 1187

WILLIAMS, TENNESSEE

    Pl: *Suddenly Last Summer*
    F: *Suddenly Last Summer*
    D: Joseph L. Mankiewicz
    Sc: Gore Vidal, Tennessee Williams
    P: Sam Spiegel/Columbia
    R: 1959
    See item 1100

WILLIAMS, TENNESSEE

    Pl: *Summer and Smoke*
    F: *Summer and Smoke*
    D: Peter Glenville
    Sc: James Poe, Meade Roberts
    P: Hal Wallis
    R: 1961
    See item 1100

WILLIAMS, TENNESSEE

    Pl: *Sweet Bird of Youth*
    F: *Sweet Bird of Youth*
    D: Richard Brooks
    Sc: Richard Brooks
    P: Pandro S. Berman/MGM
    R: 1962
    See item 1100

WILLIAMS, TENNESSEE

    Pl: *This Property Is Condemned*
    F: *This Property Is Condemned*
    D: Sidney Pollack
    Sc: Francis Ford Coppola, Fred Coe, Edith Sommer
    P: Ray Stark/Seven Arts
    R: 1966
    See item 1100

WILLIAMS, TENNESSEE

    Pl: *27 Wagons Full of Cotton* and *The Unsatisfactory Supper;
    or, The Long Stay Cut Short*

```
F:  Baby Doll
D:  Elia Kazan
Sc: Tennessee Williams
P:  Newtown Productions/Warner Bros.
R:  1956
```
See items 291, 449, 794, 1100

WISTER, OWEN

```
N:  The Virginian
F:  The Virginian
D:  Victor Fleming
Sc: Victor Fleming, Howard Estabrook, Edward E. Paramore,
    Jr.
P:  Paramount/Famous Players-Lasky
R:  1929
```
See item 659

WISTER, OWEN

```
N:  The Virginian
F:  The Virginian
D:  Stuart Gilbert
Sc: Frances Goodrich, Albert Hackett, Edward E. Paramore,
    Jr., Howard Estabrook. Based on the novel and on the
    play by Kirk La Shelle and Owen Wister
P:  Paramount
R:  1946
```
See item 659

WOOLRICH, CORNELL (pseud. of William Irish)

```
N:  The Bride Wore Black
F:  The Bride Wore Black (La Mariée Était en Noir)
D:  François Truffaut
Sc: François Truffaut, Jean-Louis Richard
P:  Les Films du Carrosse/Artistes Associés/Dino De
    Laurentiis Cinematografica
R:  1968
```
See item 757

INDEX

Abel, Richard, 849
Abele, Rudolph Von, 665
Across the Bridge (1957), 829
Act Without Words II, 952
Acting in Film, 102, 166, 213, 277, 428, 630, 1091, 1111
Adams, Dale Talmadge, 1192
Adams, Robert H., 563
Adams, Samuel Hopkins, 142
Adamson, Judith Emily, 1223
Adler, Mortimer, 149
Aeneid, The, 510
African Queen, The (1951), 242
Agee, James, 159, 242, 458, 460, 728, 949, 950, 1131, 1140
Agel, James, 519
Aiken, Conrad, 618
Aird, Forbes, 637
Akutagawa, Ryunosuke, 273, 652
Alain-Fournier (pseud. of Henri Alain Fournier), 602
Albee, Edward, 979, 1132
Albert, Richard N., 399
Albicocco, Jean Gabriel, 602
Alcott, Louisa May, 142, 1025
Alexandrov, G.V., 103, 498
Alice Adams (1935), 1084
Alison, Joan, 965
All About Eve (1950), 620
All Quiet on the Western Front (1930), 98
Allen, Dede, 657
Allen, Jeanne Thomas, 1003, 1193
Allen, Robert Clyde, 1224

Allyn, John, 782
Alpert, Hollis, 283, 368, 416, 1095
Altman, Charles F., 1004
Altman, Robert, 819, 903
Altschuler, Thelma, 444
Ambler, Eric, 226
American Adam, The, 668
American Tragedy, An, 247, 433, 1020, 1050, 1123, 1167
American Tragedy, An (1931), 99, 103, 117, 433, 498, 1050
"Among the Paths of Eden," 495
Anderegg, Michael A., 850, 933
Anderson, Edward, 819
Anderson, John, 83
Anderson, Lindsay, 427, 798
Anderson, Maxwell, 553
Andrew, James Dudley, 1144
Andrews, Joseph L., 331
Anhalt, Edna, 959
Anhalt, Edward, 959
Animal Farm (1954), 276
Animated Film, 276
"Anna Livia Plurabelle," 225
Anne of a Thousand Days, 553
Anouilh, Jean, 551
"Ant and the Grasshopper, The," 226
Antonioni, Michelangelo, 377, 413, 478, 865, 956, 1023
Antony and Cleopatra (1972), 640
Appel, Alfred, Jr., 666, 667, 783, 784
Aristotle, 149, 796, 1182
Arkin, Alan, 525

Dozier, William, 173
Dracula, 753
Dreiser, Theodore, 99, 103,
    117, 234, 247, 433, 498,
    649, 1020, 1031, 1050, 1123
Dreyer, Carl Theodor, 541,
    698
Duffell, Peter, 725
Duffy, Robert A., 953
Dukes, Ashley, 97
Dumont, Lillian, 954
Duras, Marguerite, 895, 934,
    981
Durgnat, Raymond, 379, 388,
    451
Durrell, Lawrence, 532
Dürrenmatt, Friedrich, 941
Dwan, Allan, 30, 64, 976
Dworkin, Martin S., 802,
    1024

Earle, William, 452
East of Eden (1955), 449
Easter, 812
Eaton, Walter Prichard, 1,
    9, 19, 23, 36, 65
Ecclestone, J., 50
Eckert, Charles W., 132, 281,
    390, 436, 619, 643
Edel, Leon, 803
Edipo Re (1967), 1098
Editing Film, 81, 90, 170,
    288, 657, 930
Eidsvik, Charles, 699, 804,
    866, 1133
Eikenbaum, Boris, 700
Eisenschitz, Bernard, 781
Eisenstein, Sergei M., 103,
    117, 135, 170, 201, 372,
    498, 528, 773, 904, 930,
    961, 1020, 1053, 1158
Elder, Lonne, III, 761
Eliot, T.S., 239, 241, 413
Ellis, Kate, 1025
Elmer Gantry (1960), 353,
    359
Embler, Jeffrey Brown, 1139

End of the Affair, The (1955),
    740, 829
End of the Road, 552
England Made Me, 725
Enrico, Robert, 596, 835
Enser, A.G.S., 575
Entertainer, The (1960), 358,
    713
Epic Theater, 386, 627
Erickson, James, 624
Erskine, John, 74
Erskine, Thomas L., 618, 678,
    789
Eskin, Stanley G., 701
Esselman, Kathryn C., 805
Estrin, Mark Walter, 806, 1128
Euripides, 1066
Evans, Arthur B., 1026
Everybody Comes to Rick's,
    964
Existentialism, 594
Exorcist, The, 790
Exorcist, The (1973), 939
Expressionism in Literature
    and Film, 1221

Fabun, Don, 254
Face in the Crowd, A (1957),
    322
Face to Face (1953), 924
Fadiman, William, 405
Fagin, Steven, 702
Fahrenheit 451 (1966), 441, 757
"Fall of the House of Usher,
    The," 1097
Fallen Idol, The (1948), 778,
    829, 892, 1215
Falstaff. See Chimes at Mid-
    night (1966)
Famous Players Film Company,
    9
Farber, Stephen, 477, 576
Farewell to Arms, A, 363
Farewell to Arms, A (1932),
    1041
Farrell, James T., 353
Fassbinder, Rainer Werner,
    1042

Kauffmann, Stanley, 484, 638, 885
Kawin, Bruce F., 639, 1047, 1048
Kazan, Elia, 243, 291, 318, 322, 449, 568, 613, 794, 899, 1086, 1173, 1187, 1209
Keenan, Richard C., 963
Kelman, Ken, 382, 886
Kennedy, Margaret, 167
Keown, Eric, 138
Kermode, Frank, 640
Kesey, Ken, 920, 1058, 1081
Kestner, Joseph A., III, 641
Keyser, Les, 725
Khatchadourian, Haig, 887
Kiesling, Barrett C., 152
Kiley, Frederick T., 726
"Killers, The," 818
Killers, The (1946), 818
Killers, The (1964), 818
Kinder, Marsha, 975, 1049
King, Katherine Viola, 1124
King John (1899), 673
King Lear (Brook) (1970), 595, 640, 685, 755, 998, 1008
King Lear (Kozintsev) (1970), 595, 616, 642, 718, 901, 996, 1037, 1043, 1053
King Who Was a King, The, 93
Kirby, Michael, 431
Kirschner, Paul, 319
Kitchin, Laurence, 391, 407
Kittredge, George Lyman, 209
Klein, Michael, 392
Kliman, Bernice, 1050, 1051
Kline, Herbert, 587
Klingler, Werner, 98, 113
Knight, Arthur, 276
Knight, Damon, 686
Knoll, John Francis, 1149
Knoll, Robert F., 588
Koch, Howard, 212, 727
Koch, Stephen, 505
Kolker, Robert, 819
Koningsberger, Hans, 506
Korda, Zoltan, 986

Korte, Walter, 820
Koszarski, Richard, 976, 1052
Kott, Jan, 948
Kovács, Katherine Singer, 977
Kozelka, Paul, 287, 299
Kozintsev, Grigori, 432, 595, 616, 642, 718, 724, 901, 969, 996, 1037, 1043, 1053
Kozloff, Max, 485
Kracauer, Siegfried, 354, 1021
Kramer, Karen, 1230
Kramer, Stanley, 574
Kramer, Victor A., 728
Krows, Arthur Edwin, 67
Kubrick, Stanley, 371, 481, 504, 509, 519, 585, 633, 653, 655, 661, 686, 695, 697, 720, 733, 738, 922, 984
Kuhle Wampe (1931), 781, 792
Kuhns, William, 486
Kurosawa, Akira, 374, 401, 411, 595, 652, 711, 848, 873, 916, 1007, 1043, 1049
Kurtz, Mr., 623
Kuttner, Alfred, 17
Kwapy, William, 507

Labiche, Eugene, 275
Lady Chatterley's Lover (1955), 763
Lady for a Day (1933), 142
Lambert, Gavin, 355, 729
Lane, Tamar, 137
Lang, Fritz, 676, 775
Langer, Suzanne K., 264
Lansbury, Coral, 730
Last of the Mobile Hot-shots (1969), 1100
Last of the Mohicans, The (1920), 1040
Last Picture Show, The (1971), 710, 777, 861
Last Tycoon, The (1976), 1006, 1086
Last Year at Marienbad (1961), 828, 924, 1127
Latham, John Aaron, 1134